Writing Immigration

Writing Immigration

Scholars and Journalists in Dialogue

EDITED BY

Marcelo M. Suárez-Orozco
Vivian Louie
Roberto Suro

UNIVERSITY OF CALIFORNIA PRESS
Berkeley · Los Angeles · London

University of California Press, one of the most distinguished university presses in the United States, enriches lives around the world by advancing scholarship in the humanities, social sciences, and natural sciences. Its activities are supported by the UC Press Foundation and by philanthropic contributions from individuals and institutions. For more information, visit www.ucpress.edu.

University of California Press
Berkeley and Los Angeles, California

University of California Press, Ltd.
London, England

Library of Congress Cataloging-in-Publication Data

Writing immigration : scholars and journalists in dialogue / edited by Marcelo M. Suárez-Orozco, Vivian Louie, and Roberto Suro.

    p. cm.
  Includes index.
  ISBN 978-0-520-26717-6 (cloth : alk. paper)
  ISBN 978-0-520-26718-3 (pbk. : alk. paper)
   1. United States—Emigration and immigration.
2. Emigration and immigration—Press coverage—United States.   I. Suárez-Orozco, Marcelo M., 1956–
II. Louie, Vivian S.   III. Suro, Roberto.
  JV6465.W75 2011
  304.8'73—dc22   2011006615

Manufactured in the United States of America

20 19 18 17 16 15 14 13 12 11
10 9 8 7 6 5 4 3 2 1

In keeping with a commitment to support environmentally responsible and sustainable printing practices, UC Press has printed this book on Rolland Enviro100, a 100% post-consumer fiber paper that is FSC certified, deinked, processed chlorine-free, and manufactured with renewable biogas energy. It is acid-free and EcoLogo certified.

For Howard Gardner

Contents

Preface

**MARCELO M. SUÁREZ-OROZCO,
VIVIAN LOUIE,
AND ROBERTO SURO**

The world is on the move. As we enter the second decade of the twenty-first century, the lives of millions of people are shaped by the experience of migration. Arguably, for the first time in human history, all continents are involved in the massive movement of people: as areas of immigration, emigration, or transit—and often as all three at once. Immigration is the human face of globalization—the sounds, colors, and smells of a miniaturized, interconnected, and fragile world. With approximately 214 million transnational immigrants, 15 million refugees, over 740 million internal migrants, and millions more as immediate relatives left behind, immigration defines our era.[1] Leicester, England, will be the first European city with a nonwhite majority.[2] Frankfurt is about 30 percent immigrant today; Rotterdam 45 percent immigrant. By the year 2015, Amsterdam will be 50 percent immigrant. Sweden has more than a million immigrants. But the epicenter of global migration is now Asia. The insertion of China and India into global capitalism has led to the greatest movement of people ever recorded. China has well over two hundred million internal immigrants—rural to urban folk on the move, many as unauthorized migrants in their own country. In India the World Bank estimates that perhaps a third of the entire population, more than 320 million folk, are now rural-to-urban migrants.[3]

Immigration's magnitude—its deep demographic, economic, and social implications—calls for reasoned and disinterested debate grounded on quality data, coherent principles, and ethical values. Yet throughout the postindustrial world few topics are as unsettling as the economic consequences of immigration, the ubiquitous presence of undocumented immigrants, and the adaptation problems of the children of immigrants. The story of immigration during the first decades of the twenty-first century is one of paradoxes. More people are now on the move than ever before, a lot more, and the number is on the rise, with 214 million people classified as international migrants by the United Nations in 2010 compared with 178 million just a decade earlier and 156 million in 1990 (see figure 1).

However, an equally important measure is the *share* of the world's population that is on the move rather than simply the absolute number of migrants. From that perspective, international migration has remained remarkably stable over the last generation, with roughly 2.5 to 3 percent of the world's population living beyond their country of birth. This is the case after two generations of near-apocalyptic predictions forecasting the imminent uncontainable movement of people emanating from multiple sources—growing inequality and deep poverty, environmental catastrophes, and unchecked population growth. Despite the very significant pressures for international migration, the architectures of the nation-state remain a force placing powerful constraints on the movement of people.[4]

While the *potential* for immigration continues to gather momentum, the reality of international immigration remains quite stable when viewed as a global phenomenon in a world with a growing population. Although migration is at once a local and global phenomenon in its causes and impacts, it is not occurring everywhere at the same pace. Consider Europe, for example. The continent that shed over fifty million souls in the great mass migration of 1890 to 1910 has seen a rapid growth in new migration. With approximately seventy million immigrants, the rate of international migration into Europe today is greater than that of any other region of the world. In some countries, such as Spain, Italy, and Ireland, this is new and without precedent in the modern era. Overall the rate of immigration is now ten times greater in the higher-income countries than in the developing world. In the United States the foreign-born share of the population—approximately thirty-eight million (12 percent)—is lower than at the peak of the transatlantic migration in 1890 (14.8 percent), but it is much higher than it was just thirty years ago, when the current era of migration was getting under way (6.2 percent).

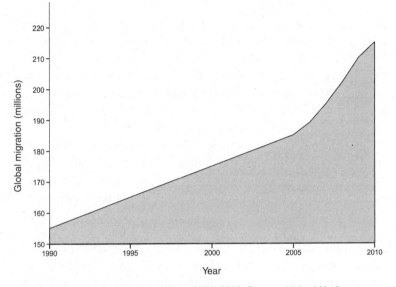

FIGURE 1. Growth of global migration, 1990–2010. Source: United Nations Department of Economic and Social Affairs.

Why the sudden globalization of migration? The integration and disintegration of markets, new information and communication technologies, the ease and declining costs of mass transportation, the brisk growth of inequality across the world, changing social practices and cultural models, and new demographic factors have combined into the rocket fuel of globalization's migratory vertigo. The alignment of these factors unleashed a huge migration wave, which we can now precisely date as beginning on November 9, 1989 (the day the Berlin Wall fell) and crashing—above all unauthorized immigration—on September 15, 2008, the day Lehman Brothers filed for bankruptcy. During that generation, spanning the heady days of "The End of History" and the triumphalism of the "Washington Consensus," well over a million immigrants entered the United States every year for more than twenty years—on average gaining one international migrant (net) every thirty-seven seconds. Today over thirty-eight million immigrants live in the United States. We know now that this surge was not permanent. Flows to the United States and most other industrial countries have fallen off sharply since the onset of the Great Recession.[5]

International migration may be ubiquitous and deeply rooted in historical relationships between well-traveled sending and receiving corridors, but sometimes the context is dystopic.[6] The United States is a case in point. It is contending with the largest number and proportion of unauthorized immigrants in recent history, even as it is facing a bevy of unrelated but relevant woes: the deepest economic crisis since the Great Depression, war, terrorism on a global scale, and a neighbor to the south convulsed by a drug war. A political ethos of divisiveness and the resulting gridlock add their own alchemy to the increasingly combustive problem of unauthorized immigration.

This new master context bedevils serious efforts to manage migration. Furthermore, in the United States, current difficulties have been building because the country has never adequately adjusted its policies and bureaucracies to the new realities of global migration. We have an early-twentieth-century system in place to manage a twenty-first-century problem. As a result, all immigration lines seem broken: the line at the border (where more people are dying trying to enter the United States than ever), the queues in U.S. consulates, and in U.S. Citizenship and Immigration Services offices all over the homeland. All factions in the multisided debate over migration agree on one point: the system is broken. The size of the unauthorized population, an estimated eleven million or so, is only one symptom. There are over three million people waiting between four to twenty years *to join relatives who are U.S. citizens and permanent migrants.* If you are a U.S. citizen and your sister is in the Philippines, you will have to wait on average twenty years before she can join you. If you are a U.S. citizen and would like to sponsor your unmarried adult child in Mexico, you will wait sixteen years. And if you are a start-up in Massachusetts and set out to hire a skilled Indian worker with college education and proven experience in her field, you will pay thirteen thousand dollars in fees and wait twenty years.

But for all the dystopia playing out in the media, in politics, and in the public sphere, much of what is going on in American immigration—albeit below the radar screen—is a story of successful adaptations, cultural invigoration, and mutual accommodations, especially when compared with Europe. The vast majority of immigrants in the United States are legal, they have very high levels of engagement in the labor market, they tend to be optimistic about the future, they tend to trust key U.S. institutions, their children are learning English faster and better than before, and the children of immigrants are outperforming their parents in terms of their experiences in the labor market (see Mary C. Waters's chapter in this volume). While Europe has a lower rate of clandestine immigration than the United States (in part because of the multiple periodic amnesties granted to their illegal immigrants), in nearly every other measure of social and economic integration many European democracies with large numbers of immigrants are found wanting.[7]

Three features characterize recent immigration to the United States and many other high-income countries:

1. Unauthorized migration has become persistent and widespread. The population of unauthorized migrants is larger both in number and as a share of the total than at any time since the United States began trying to regulate immigration in the early twentieth century. While they account for less than a third of the overall immigrant population, the unauthorized dominate public perceptions and nearly all policy debates and interventions.

2. Despite the economic crisis, there are demographic and structural factors embedding immigrant-origin workers in many sectors of the segmented U.S. labor market and economy, and in ever more diverse destinations.[8]

3. The mass migration wave of the past generation has had a lasting demographic echo. The children of immigrants, estimated at over seventeen million, are a fast-growing sector of the child population in the United States. This is especially significant during an era of low and declining birthrates in the native-born population. In the United States more than three-fourths of the population growth over the past decade is accounted for by immigrants and their children.

These features of the new immigration constitute discrete scholarly domains and also have come to dominate the work of journalists working to inform our national debate. In this book we bring perspective to the contentious subject of immigration by gathering the experiences of a group of leading academics and journalists who make it their vocation to grasp and explain a phenomenon that is at once local and global, familiar and uncanny, concrete and abstract, timely and eternal. We examine how scholars and journalists enter, shape, and reshape the national conversation on immigration. While the ethos and eidos of writing immigration differ in the cultures of journalism and academia, the two domains live in a state of synergy, tension, and sometimes misunderstanding. The chapters in this book detail how scholars and journalists manage the complexities of immigration—and of working with each other—as they inform and sometimes transform the national debate, each with distinct sets of incentives, sensibilities, and values.

The habitus animating the world of journalism is profoundly different and in some ways incommensurable to that of academia, yet the two domains live in a state of mutual interdependence. Journalists are consumers of scholarship—materials that are typically gathered in a tempo and style that is antithetical to the I-need-it-now world of the twenty-four-hour news cycle. The culture of the footnote—exhausting, full of qualifiers, exceptions, and caveats—and the culture of the sound bite or of the 750-word newspaper article are like oil and vinegar. Scholars work with the long view in mind and are always mindful of the peer-review process and the vicissitudes of grant making. Journalists live under the tyranny of the next deadline, the gaze of the editor, and, as the business model for print news continues to face difficult odds, the bottom line.

If it is obvious why journalists need academics, scholars are willing partners. The mass media is a vehicle to convey the lessons learned to broader audiences (and, albeit momentarily, see scholarly contributions move out of the splendid isolation in which perhaps most academic research dwells). The officers at the granting foundations—the lifeline of new research—value references to work they have supported in the major media because they hope to influence public opinion and policymaking. Deans and development officers scan the prestige outlets every morning for references to work by their faculty members to earn bragging rights for their institutions.

In his introduction, Roberto Suro, a veteran newspaper journalist, senior researcher, and now a professor of journalism and public policy at the University of Southern California, frames the representation of immigration in the two domains. Both the news media and the social sciences, he claims, have contributed to misperceptions about contemporary immigration in ways that have raised the public's anxieties and hindered effective policymaking. For different reasons, journalists and academic researchers have tended to focus on individual narratives or group characteristics in rendering portrayals of immigration. The cumulative effect is to depict the immigrant as the protagonist who drives all of the action. Meanwhile, little attention is given to the many ways that the host society is structuring the trajectories of immigrant flows. The immigration story is thus robbed of context, and the results are evident in public policies that focus almost exclusively on trying to affect the migrants' behavior—for example, physically preventing them from crossing the border, apprehending and deporting those without authorization, and the like—rather than acting on causal factors in American society.

Furthermore, Suro argues that changes in the U.S. news media are exacerbating long-standing characteristics of immigration coverage, including highly episodic attention to the subject and a disproportionate focus on illegality. Meanwhile, a variety of recent developments have challenged both journalists and social scientists to find new ways to frame their accounts of immigration. Chief among them is the need to understand the factors that produced an extraordinary, and perhaps anomalous, surge in the number of low-skilled migrants coming to the United States from 1995 to 2005. While much work has been done on the long-term structural underpinnings of migration flows, we have a much weaker grasp on the effects of business cycles and other short-term factors despite their importance to public perceptions and policy formation.

The prolonged controversy over mass immigration is embodied in the lives of the eleven million U.S. immigrants without papers. Part One of the book explores immigration and the law. In chapter 1, "The Making of an Outlaw Generation," Nina Bernstein reflects on her five years of immigration coverage for the *New York Times*. She examines the impact of escalating immigration enforcement on a generation of children in unauthorized or mixed-status immigrant families. More than a million are coming of age without proper papers; at least four million others are at risk of deportation or family separation because a parent is in the country illegally. Bernstein asks, "Are these children and young adults forming a new kind of American caste system, one that challenges the nation's concepts of civil rights? At a time when a culture of fear permeates many immigrant communities, and demands for more stringent enforcement come from both political parties, how do journalists and academics researching questions of assimilation deal honestly with the issue of legal status without putting vulnerable subjects at risk?" Using examples from her work, Bernstein discusses this growing challenge and how it affects both news coverage and social science research.

In chapter 2, "The Integrated Regime of Immigration Regulation," Cristina M. Rodríguez of New York University School of Law turns to the matter of state and federal mechanisms for regulating migration. The case of Arizona's controversial law requiring that "the police check the documents of anyone they stop or detain whom they suspect of being in the country illegally" is a case in hand.[9] It is also the tip of the iceberg. During the first three months of 2010, "legislators in 45 states introduced 1,180 bills and resolutions relating to immigration; 102 laws have passed compared with 222 in all of 2009, according to the national Conference of State Legislators."[10] Rodríguez argues that while the involvement of states and localities in immigration regulation has long been considered legally aberrant, in practice, subfederal activity represents a crucial component of a comprehensive regulatory regime. She explores how the overemphasis on conceptual and regulatory uniformity obscures the potential of policy diversity and federal-state cooperation to address the social and political challenges immigration presents. Rodríguez suggests that federal-state relations should not be understood as a zero-sum game in the immigration context. In developing this claim, she considers the obligations each level of government owes to the other, as well as how mechanisms of oversight and accountability can be implemented to ensure that the federal-state balance of power remains stable and functional.

In chapter 3, "What Part of 'Illegal' Don't You Understand?" Dianne Solís of the *Dallas Morning News* suggests that answering that question is not easy. Immigration law is increasingly intertwined with criminal law to the point of creating a new "crimmigration" regime. Due process questions come up frequently as the toughest crackdown in decades touches the lives of illegal immigrants, legal permanent residents, and U.S. citizens. Moreover, in her reporting, Solís found the law is full of contradiction. Unauthorized children have a right to a free public education under the Supreme Court decision of *Plyer v. Doe* (see Cristina M. Rodríguez's chapter in this volume) but cannot take a job legally when they graduate from high school. "Mixed-status families," Solís writes, "live with both the fruits of citizenship and the risk of deportation." From her years of reporting in Texas, Solís argues for the importance of calibrating the legal lens while recognizing the essence of the writer's craft is finding the humanity in the story. That can mean changing the camera angle frequently through story selection that takes readers inside the lives of police officers, and clinic directors, as well as children with a parent who has been deported.

In chapter 4, "Some Observations about Immigration Journalism," Peter H. Schuck of Yale Law School argues that "immigration journalists are congenitally and perhaps professionally and ideologically drawn to individual stories, usually stories of incompetence or illegality by the immigration agency." By exposing the injustices "the little guy" suffers at the hand of a cold-hearted bureaucracy, journalists perform a tried-and-true public service. Echoing a theme developed by Roberto Suro in the introduction, Schuck suggests that journalists should also strive to inform readers about the more systemic, less individualized effects of immigration and the challenges and trade-offs encompassed in immigration policy and control in a modern democracy.

In Interlude I, "Covering Immigration: From Stepchild Beat to Newsroom Mainstream," the veteran *Los Angeles Times* writer Patrick J. McDonnell takes us to ground zero of the new immigration debate: Southern California in the 1990s. He reflects on the two distinct challenges he faced day in and day out: the first was "how to get attention for stories about immigrants and refugees, a population little known to most editors, and reporters." The second challenge was "how to write such articles without being perceived as an advocate." He reminds us of the principle of "fairness" to all sides in the debate, even if he acknowledges that absolute objectivity is an illusory goal. Most reporters, McDonnell suggests, are sympathetic with the plight of immigrants. "Standing up for the underdog," he notes, is a hallowed journalistic tradition. Behind the immigration story is a fundamental human drama of searching for a better life in a new country. It is a narrative that most journalists find irresistible. But what to do with the "backlash" that mass migration generates in times of crisis? McDonnell revisits his own struggles throughout his career "to help explain what was going on, and how California was pushed to this nasty precipice." He returns to the time-honored journalistic values of "fairness and listening to all sides" of the story as the safest path to documenting the multiplicity of voices in the immigration debate.

In Part Two of the book we turn to immigration and the economy in a time of crisis. In chapter 5, "Consensus, Debate, and Wishful Thinking: The Economic Impact of Immigration," Edward Schumacher-Matos, formerly of the *New York Times* and the *Wall Street Journal* and currently the director of the Harvard Migration and Integration Studies Project and a columnist for the *Washington Post,* asks what is the economic impact of immigration—including illegal immigration—at a time of economic crisis? The answer, Schumacher-Matos suggests, is crucial for Americans and immigrants alike. He reviews in careful detail the nature of the debates in the field of economics. The consensus among economists is that on balance immigration's impact on the economy is positive. However, it is a complex story defying easy generations, never mind sound bites. Schumacher-Matos presents the state-of-the-art research and prudently paints a nuanced picture of what is known and not known in this ever-contentious debate. Immigration's negative effects, he notes, have been on the wages of unskilled workers, many of whom are poor African Americans and United States–born Latinos, and on local taxes in communities that have to deal with the services required with the sudden influx of young families with education and medical needs. But at the macroeconomic level, immigrant workers benefit the economy. "The expanded supply of cheaper labor stimulates the economy," he writes. "Some immigrants, particularly high-skilled ones, stimulate it even further by contributing to innovation. All workers thus benefit; complementary workers benefit the most." But perhaps what is most important eludes neat measures. Think of how the inventions of immigrants from diverse regions of the world—such as Hungarian mathematician John Von Neumman (computer), Argentinean physician René Favarolo (cardiac bypass surgery), and Russian computer scientist Sergey Brin (Google)—have completely transformed entire sectors of the U.S. economy and society, from defense to health to information technology.

In chapter 6, Barry R. Chiswick, chair of the Department of Economics at George Washington University, reviews his "Ten Top Myths and Fallacies Regarding Immigration" to the United States. According to Chiswick, these "myths and fallacies have impeded the development of a national consensus regarding the reform of immigration law and policy so as to better serve the economic, humanitarian, and international interests of the United States." The chapter closes with Chiswick's response to the least favorite question he is frequently asked: "Are you for or against immigration?"

In Interlude II, "A Son of Immigrants on Covering Immigration," George de Lama, the former managing editor for news at the *Chicago Tribune* and currently head of communications at the Inter-American Development Bank, offers an instructive personal reflection on three decades of journalism starting as a cub reporter in Chicago. Back then, writing immigration in the Windy City was an exotic "cross-cultural experience" akin to writing about the Bororo or the Arunta in faraway places. Immigrants were the Other next door. De Lama is not only a witness to the changing practice of journalism qua immigration; his career embodies the very transformations that define how journalism continues to struggle with writing immigration. Yet reading his personal narrative today, we are also reminded of the old French adage: "The more things change, the more they remain the same."

The fundamental unit of migration is the family—variously conceived and structured in different regions throughout the world. While at the manifest level immigration is driven by labor, demographic, and economic variables (among other things, segmented labor markets and wage differentials), at the latent level immigration's enduring root is the family. Immigration is an ethical act of, and for, the family. Immigration typically starts with the family, and family bonds sustain it. Immigration will profoundly change families as well as the societies in which immigrants settle.

The children of immigrants are the fruit borne of immigration. They are a fast-growing sector of the youth population in nearly every immigration-dependent country today, including Australia, Canada, Germany, Italy, the Netherlands, Spain, and Sweden. In the United States, approximately one quarter of all youth are of immigrant origin, and it is projected that by 2050 over a third of all children will be growing up in immigrant households. The transition of immigrant-origin children to their new societies is a topic of scholarly concern and journalistic relevance. But the long-term consequences of mass migration, embodied in the lives of the children of immigrants, are a neglected *problematique* in the field of migration studies.

In Part Three of the book, we turn to some of the most urgent issues defining the second generation of immigrants. In chapter 7, "The Education Transformation: Why the Media Missed One of the Biggest Stories in America," Ginger Thompson of the *New York Times* deconstructs her rich experiences writing about the littlest, newest Americans. She argues that in the past decade immigration "has fueled the most robust growth in public schools since the baby boom, severely straining the capacity of districts already short on resources needed to serve students with special needs, and putting classrooms on the front lines of this nation's fights over how to assimilate immigrants and their children." Making matters more complex yet, the mass influx of English-language learners coincided with the federal No Child Left Behind law, arguably the most sweeping education reform in modern American history. "Then, as if their obligations to provide equal opportunities were not impossible enough," she writes, "schools across the country were thrust into the crosscurrents of a severe economic crisis and an anti-immigrant firestorm that not only slowed the pace of immigration, but also shifted the terms of the national debate from how to best educate immigrant children to whether those living here illegally should be educated at all." Based on her work with education reporters, researchers, and school officials across the country, Thomson shares the challenges trying to cover education in a time of deep demographic change, educational crisis, and political malaise.

In chapter 8, "Moving Stories: Academic Trajectories of Newcomer Immigrant Students," Carola Suárez-Orozco of New York University, Steinhardt School of Culture, Education, and Human Development, reviews some findings from one of the signature social science studies of immigrant children in American society. According to C. Suárez-Orozco, immigration to the United States presents both challenges and opportunities that shape students' academic achievement. She identifies varying academic pathways of newcomer adolescent immigrant students over the course of a five-year longitudinal study. Her findings are multifaceted and defy sound bites about the nexus between immigration and education, "although some newcomer students performed at high or improving levels over time, others showed diminishing performance." It is a complex tale involving school characteristics (including school segregation, school poverty rate, and student perceptions of school violence), family characteristics (including maternal education, paternal employment, household structure, country of origin, and undocumented status), and individual characteristics (including academic English proficiency, academic engagement, psychological symptoms, gender, family separations, and number of school transitions). These constellations of factors were associated with different trajectories of academic performance over time. C. Suárez-Orozco draws on a series of case studies to illustrate the ways in which multiple variables work together to shape the experiences and trajectories of newcomer immigrant students.

Tyche Hendricks, formerly of the *San Francisco Chronicle* and now at the University of California–Berkeley's Graduate School of Journalism and KQED Public Radio in San Francisco, writes about California's struggle with deep demographic changes at a time of economic crisis and cultural concerns. In chapter 9, "Who Will Report the Next Chapter of America's Immigration Story?" she focuses on how California is integrating newcomers and in turn how they reshape the state. Hendricks draws on seven years of reporting, trying to provide readers with "an understanding of the history, causes, and context for immigration as well as its consequences." She argues that journalists are supposed to raise questions about the "social impacts of immigration and the nation's struggle to integrate immigrant families and, at the same time, to examine the way immigrants and their children assert themselves and transform their new environs. One way to do that is through telling the human stories that help readers understand other people in their communities as individuals." She draws on examples of her reporting for the *San Francisco Chronicle* at a time of industry-wide changes within journalism.

In chapter 10, "Complicating the Story of Immigrant Integration," Vivian Louie of the Harvard Graduate School of Education deconstructs the matter of immigrant parental involvement in education. Based on a sociological study of second-generation Dominican and Colombian young adults and their parents, Louie reframes parental involvement by examining the world of parents *as immigrants*. The immigrant family experience, Louie reports, is shaped by the social isolation of parents and an emerging immigrant cultural identity of marginalization. This identity persists long after arrival and cuts across social mobility paths, although it is experienced in different ways according to social class. Louie describes a poignant "sense of being alone in America among the immigrant parents" that bears upon their children's sense of being on their own in American schools. Louie argues that policymakers need to consider how best to incorporate newly arrived immigrants and their children, particularly strategies for immigrants to develop strong affiliations in the multiple domains of their lives in the United States.

Mary C. Waters of Harvard University concludes on a more optimistic note in chapter 11, "Debating Immigration: Are We Addressing the Right Issues?" This chapter reminds us of Sherlock Holmes's marvelous story of a crime solved because the dog in the barn did not bark. Sometimes what is most important is what is not heard. She comes back to Suro's dictum that immigration coverage tends to be crisis-driven. Waters overviews research on patterns of socioeconomic mobility and integration among the adult children of immigrants to the United States. The story is that "these young people are showing patterns of upward generational mobility, [and are] doing better than their parents and better than comparable native-born Americans of the same racial backgrounds." Waters contrasts the American experience with "more difficult and troubling patterns of integration of the second generation in Western Europe." She concludes with a reflection of why the media finds more space for stories of downward mobility and blocked incorporation "and the policy implications of not publicizing and recognizing the generally good news about immigrant incorporation that social science has documented."

. . .

This book addresses many of the central themes in early-twenty-first-century U.S. immigration and the various approaches that prominent journalists and scholars have taken to understanding it. Their accounts cover many domains but all point to the challenges and rewards of writing the story of immigration. These are dispatches from the frontlines of an intellectual endeavor of global scope and importance. Each chapter reflects a work in progress, an individual's effort to set down a story that is as old as humanity itself but is again rapidly evolving in the modern era. There is both convergence and contrast throughout these pages as authors apply different data, methodologies, experiences, and biases to the same broad subject. The editors have not sought consensus or harmony. Instead, by bringing together diverse voices from both journalism and academia and from several disciplines within those professions, this book intends to offer readers multiple perspectives on a phenomenon too rich to be captured by any one point of view.[11]

NOTES

1. United Nations Development Programme, *Human Development Report 2009—Overcoming Barriers: Human Mobility and Development* (New York: United Nations Development Programme, 2009).

2. In the United States, California, Hawaii, New Mexico, and Texas are majority-minority states.

3. See Sanket Mohapatra, "Almost a Third of Indians, or over 300 Million People, Are Migrants," at *People Move: A Blog about Migration, Remittances, and Development,* online at http://blogs.worldbank.org/peoplemove/almost-a-third-of-indians-or-over-300-million-people-are-migrants.

4. See Aristede Zolberg, "Beyond the Crisis," in *Global Migrants, Global Refugees: Problems and Solutions,* edited by Aristede Zolberg and P. Benda (London: Berghahn Books, 2001), 1–16.

5. The U.S. Department of Homeland Security estimates that the unauthorized immigrant population living in the United States decreased to 10.8 million in January 2009 from 11.6 million a year earlier, and the estimated annual inflow of unauthorized immigrants to the United States was nearly two-thirds smaller in the March 2007 to March 2009 period than it had been from March 2000 to March 2005, according to new estimates by the Pew Hispanic Center. This reverses a pattern of nearly three decades of unauthorized immigration to the United States. The collapse of Lehmann Brothers and the deep recession it ignited did what 9/11 failed to do: it froze illegal immigration to the United States for the first time in thirty years. The "new normal" in immigration today, at least in the United States, seems to be inertia. Would-be returnees are staying

put as are those who under the previous regime might have considered migrating without authorization. Any expectation that the economic debacle would result in massive self-deportations has not materialized. Likewise, there have been no changes in the patterns of legal—read: family reunification—migration to the United States.

6. "The gap between the *goals* of national immigration policy . . . and the actual results of policies in this area . . . is wide and growing in all major industrialized democracies, thus provoking greater hostility toward immigrants in general (regardless of legal status) and putting intense pressure on political parties and government officials to adopt more restrictive policies." From "Introduction: The Ambivalent Quest for Immigration Control," in *Controlling Immigration: A Global Perspective,* edited by Wayne Cornelius, Philip Martin, and James Hollifield (Stanford, Calif.: Stanford University Press, 1994), 3.

7. In the past decade, between five million and six million unauthorized migrants in the European Union have been regularized through various programs. Among the twenty-seven EU countries, twenty-two have adopted some measures of regularization in the past decade. See Maurizio Ambrozini, *Undocumented Migrants and Invisible Welfare: Beyond the Rhetoric* (Milan: Department of Sociology, Università degli studi di Milano, 2010).

8. This is happening in the context of a fundamental shift: below-replacement fertility rates at a time rapidly aging native populations are entering the demographic winter of their lives in huge numbers. This is the case Germany, Greece, Italy, Japan, Russia, Spain, and elsewhere. In the United States some eighty million baby boomers, the vast majority of them of white-European non-immigrant origin, will retire shortly, generating a void in various sectors of the economy and society.

9. Jennifer Steinhauer, "Arizona Law Reveals Split within G.O.P.," *New York Times,* May 22, 2010, 1–11 (quotation on page 1).

10. Ibid.

11. The chapters in this book are original and were developed for a conference in 2008, the first of its kind, of the Nieman Foundation for Journalism at Harvard University on "Covering Immigration: Journalist and Academic Perspectives."

Acknowledgments

In 2008, Immigration Studies at New York University and the Nieman Foundation for Journalism at Harvard University convened a seminar of scholars and journalists who work in the area of migration. All of the chapters in this book were first commissioned for that gathering during a golden Massachusetts autumn day at the Walter Lippmann House on Francis Avenue in Cambridge. We are grateful to Bob Giles, curator of the Nieman Foundation, for his warm hospitality, generous support, and vigorous engagement during our sojourn to the foundation. We are happy to acknowledge generous grants from the Western Union Foundation, the David Rockefeller Center for Latin American Studies at Harvard University, the Harvard Graduate School of Education, the University of Southern California Annenberg School for Communication and Journalism, the Ford Foundation, and Immigration Studies at New York University. Carola and Marcelo Suárez-Orozco's work was supported by generous fellowships at the Institute for Advanced Study in Princeton, New Jersey. The institute's idyllic setting and extraordinary support systems provided the Suárez-Orozcos much needed time free of the usual academic disturbances to complete work for this book.

We are thankful for the participation, lively contributions, insights, and wise counsel of Jess Benhabib, New York University; Nina Bernstein, *New York Times;* Barry R. Chiswick, George Washington University; Tyche Hendricks, KQED Public Radio and the University of California–

Berkeley; Miriam Jordan, *Wall Street Journal;* Patrick J. McDonnell, *Los Angeles Times;* Martha Mendoza, the Associated Press; Eduardo Porter, *New York Times;* Cristina Rodríguez, New York University School of Law; Peter Schuck, Yale Law School; Edward Schumacher-Matos, Harvard University; Andrea Simakis, *The Plain Dealer;* Dianne Solís, *Dallas Morning News;* Carola Suárez-Orozco, New York University; Ginger Thompson, *New York Times;* and Mary C. Waters, Harvard University. We would like to acknowledge Professor Kathleen McCartney, dean of the Harvard Graduate School of Education, and Professor Merilee Grindle, director of the David Rockefeller Center for Latin American Studies at Harvard for their support and gracious remarks at the Harvard Faculty Club as we all gathered to hear a marvelous, moving after-dinner address by George de Lama.

Naomi Schneider, our editor at the University of California Press, nurtured this project from before it was a fully formed book with her magisterial tact, kind humor, and infinite publication wisdom.

Introduction

ROBERTO SURO

Over three decades ago a congressionally mandated commission on immigration proposed a sweeping overhaul of laws, policies, and procedures. The core recommendation, as summarized by the chairman, the Reverend Theodore M. Hesburgh, then president of the University of Notre Dame, was to close the "back door" of illegal migration so as to keep the "front door" open to a reasonable number of legal arrivals.[1] If that sounds familiar, even hauntingly contemporary, it should. Hesburgh's seemingly simple formulation has enjoyed an exceptional shelf life. Repeated time and again by politicians, advocates, and commentators, including a number of the authors in this book, this prescription has been at the heart of immigration policy debates for three decades. Nonetheless, the objective of a back door shut tight and a well-regulated front door seems as unattainable today as when Hesburgh offered it up.

Even by contemporary Washington, D.C., standards of gridlock, immigration has a remarkable track record of failure in policy creation. We have had lengthy, full-blown, multiyear congressional debates in the 1980s, 1990s, and 2000s, and the jockeying has begun for another round in this decade, although much of the action is spreading to state capitals and the courts. All the while we have been kicking around many of the same policy mechanisms suggested by the Hesburgh commission. These include tougher enforcement at the border and worksites, a legalization program for the current population of unauthorized migrants, and better mechanisms to ensure that legal flows satisfy the nation's economic, social, and foreign policy needs.

Given how much American politics has changed and how much the phenomenon of immigration has changed over the past thirty years, it seems reasonable to look broadly for the causes of stalemate and stasis. Rereading the Hesburgh commission report offers a clue, pointing to another unaccomplished agenda. Back in the late 1970s, the commission conducted an extensive review of the existing research, heard testimony from leading scholars, and ordered its own studies. Despite this considerable effort—arguably more systematic and extensive than any conducted since—the commission found worrisome knowledge gaps. Regardless of some accepted findings on the characteristics of unauthorized migration, the commission stated that "the literature on this subject is inconclusive" and concluded that "there is almost no consensus regarding the impact of illegal immigration on U.S. society."[2]

The commission found uncertainty or unresolved contention on such key matters as the impact on social services, job displacement, and wage depression. Would a similar effort today find greater certainty, given that the literature is now vastly larger and more sophisticated? Disturbingly, the commission came to an assessment of public opinion that seems also depressingly familiar: on the "most pressing" issue, that of unauthorized migration, "current policy and law enforcement efforts have been criticized from all sides."[3] Hesburgh worried that Americans would lose sight of the advantages of a well-regulated immigration system because they felt the system itself was "out of control."[4] He was reflecting on the aftermath of the Mariel boatlift of 1980, when more than 125,000 Cubans arrived in southern Florida from Port of Mariel, Cuba, but the sentiment is often heard today even in the absence of a big attention-grabbing event.

Over the course of the past thirty years, a great deal has changed of course. Most notably, immigration has become a much more important factor in the life of the nation. In 1980 the foreign-born population comprised about 6 percent of the U.S. population, which was close to a historical low, and its share has more than doubled, to nearly 13 percent, which is approaching a historical high (see figure 2). In retrospect, we now know that the Hesburgh commission was witnessing the early stages of a vast, and in some ways unprecedented, era of immigration. Yet, I would argue, our policy structures have never adapted, key aspects of the intellectual agenda remain unfulfilled, and the issue of immigration repeatedly emerges as a source of

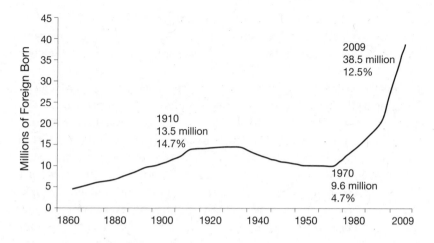

FIGURE 2. Foreign-born population, 1860–2009, number and share of total U.S. population. Source: United States Census.

contention, dissatisfaction, and anxiety for many Americans, sometimes a majority.

On the one hand, we have an epochal social, economic, and demographic event, an event that is transforming the nation. On the other hand, we have a long, unhappy stalemate over how American government and society should address this event, a stalemate that has grown more pronounced and more bitter as time has passed. Scholars and journalists cannot avoid some responsibility for the unhappy outcome. Because they are important interlocutors in the national immigration debate, it is important to ask how they may have contributed to both the policy failure and the popular malaise that ensues. To engage in this exercise, one need not argue that these professions should act as advocates for specific policy outcomes nor even that they are obliged to promote consensus. However, both the press and the academy have missions in this democracy—among other things, to improve self-governance by informing and educating the public.

Both the scholarly and journalistic domains receive benefits from the public for performing those missions, whether in the form of material support or intellectual license. Stalemate is a form of failure in self-governance. There have been many costs to this stalemate, starting with the lost opportunities to have thought more deliberately about the size and character of immigration flows, to have planned better for the successful integration of immigrants and their children, and most of all to have avoided, or at least minimized, the presence of a large, semi-permanent but subordinate class of residents living outside our civic sphere.

Just as there have been many costs, there have been many causes leading to the current state. We are not claiming that either the press or the academy exercises a controlling influence over government or society. We are not trying to draw lines of causality here; we don't need to set the bar so high. Other actors have surely exercised much greater sway over the outcomes. But both the news media and the academy help to shape perceptions among both the public and the policy makers. They present chronicles and analyses. They pose conceptual frameworks and present cues about the relative importance of contemporary events. Even if that is all they do—help to shape perceptions—then they have helped produce the immigration stalemate. Understanding the roles played by journalism and scholarship will help us understand how the stalemate developed.

This inquiry can also help us understand the professions themselves. The depictions of immigration by the academy and the news media reflect deeply entrenched intellectual mind-sets, well-established methods of inquiry, and old professional norms. Immigration is a particularly useful topic in the study of journalism because the current wave of immigration and accompanying policy debate coincide with a period of profound change in both the technology and business of communications. Finally, this kind of inquiry can help set the stage for an understanding of how journalism and scholarship relate to each other, reflecting initially on how their depictions of immigration compare and eventually moving toward an examination of how they relate to each other. That understanding might prompt new agendas in both fields that aim for a more mutually beneficial interaction between them. This book and the discussions among the authors that it reflects are important first steps in that direction.

My own exploration of this topic has focused far more on journalism than on the academy. In 2008, just weeks before the authors convened in Cambridge, Massachusetts, my monograph *The Triumph of No: How the Media Influence the Immigration Debate* was published by the Brookings Institution and the Norman Lear Center at the University of Southern California. That effort was based on various forms of content analysis conducted by several researchers examining more than eighty thousand news stories or commentaries from print, broadcast, and digital media dating back to 1980, and I have subsequently returned to and updated the research.⁵ This quantitative work assessed both the pace of coverage by a variety of news organizations and the primary focus of that coverage across long periods of time. In addition, coverage of specific episodes by individual news organizations was analyzed in detail. The project also involved a separate analysis by the Project for Excellence in Journalism that focused on coverage across all news platforms in 2007, the year of the last major congressional debate on immigration policy. I readily confess that my views on academic depictions of immigration are more impressionistic and are not based on a systematic effort to collect and analyze data. And, while I am making confessions, I'll also readily admit that I am guilty of every practice cited here, having written about immigration for some thirty-five years first as a journalist and more recently as a policy analyst and academic researcher.

. . .

If I had to pick one episode that epitomizes the way immigration has been portrayed by the American news media, I would have to say it is the saga of little Elian Gonzalez. Rescued off the coast of Florida in November 1999, the six-year-old Cuban boy who had lost his mother at sea, became the object of a seven-month-long soap opera as his Miami relatives and his Cuban father contested his custody. Throughout 2000 the Elian saga accounted for more than half of all immigration coverage in the *New York Times,* nearly two-thirds of the coverage on the *CBS Evening News,* and similarly astounding shares in the reports of many other news organizations. That year also happened to mark the largest single influx of immigrants to the United States in the current era of migration and perhaps the largest in American history: about 1.5 million people born abroad joined the U.S. population in 2000, according to the best available estimates.⁶

For more than four decades now, the great migration of the contemporary era has proceeded overwhelmingly through legal and orderly channels. That fact has often been overlooked in the news coverage while the attention has focused on the outliers like Elian and illegal crossers on the Rio Grande. Moreover, that great migration responded very directly to the needs of the U.S. labor market and was a component of an exceptional period of economic growth, increasing productivity, and generally rising incomes. This story too has been largely ignored by the news media. Finally, the great migration changed the nation's demographic destiny, but that fact only drew recognition in the media after the transformation was largely set in place.

By contrast, the Elian saga had no lasting impact on the nation, at least directly.[7] The stories about Elian were accurate enough individually; that is not the issue here. It is easy to understand why the saga was so compelling to journalists and audiences alike, loaded as it was with drama, suspense, wacky characters, and colorful locales. But while the media and the public obsessed over an irresistible family drama, they were missing the much larger, much less dramatic story that made history and whose consequences are still playing out. Even more is at stake, though. In the larger story of immigration, the Elian saga was exemplary of neither specific significant events nor public policy issues; it was far more an exception than the rule. So the extraordinary attention focused on the Elian story created not only a distraction but also a distortion. Consumed by coverage of this uniquely weird little story, audiences could come away with very mistaken impressions about the enormous migration that was reaching a historic peak.

Although there has never been another story quite like Elian's, it is a narrative that has been told and retold for decades. It is a narrative that emerges out of crisis and confrontation rather than everyday life. It is a narrative haunted by failures to obey and enforce laws. It is the narrative that has dominated the news media's coverage of immigration over the course of three decades, which has conditioned the American public to associate immigration with chaos, controversy, and criminality. This narrative was authored originally by America's mainstream media decades ago—not the shrill voices of advocacy that have taken up the storyline in recent years. My content analysis of coverage from 1980 to 2010 examined the work of national and regional newspapers, public broadcasting, the Associated Press, and the evening news television broadcasts. As described in more detail throughout this introduction, the narrative of illegality drew far more attention than the less controversial aspects of the migration story in every case.

Many of my former colleagues in the news business, including friends who are contributors to this book, insist that the narrative of illegality has been unavoidable given journalism's mission to highlight the unusual rather than to chronicle the routine. People arriving in the United States legally from abroad and successfully starting new lives do not fit the traditional definition of news, the argument goes. Meanwhile, law breaking and everything that goes with it fits naturally into the rubrics of journalism. I can accept that explanation. I can also regret it. The fact that the narrative of illegality arises from epistemological structures and professional imperatives so old that they are rarely questioned only makes the situation more grave, not less, in my view.

The current era of immigration coincides with a period of profound changes in American journalism; changes in the technology that delivers the news, in business structures, in audiences, and in some key professional norms. Among the developments has been the rise of advocacy journalism on talk radio, cable television, and the blogosphere in which news is presented overtly from an ideological stance. While departing from the values of objectivity and nonpartisanship, the new advocates have often borrowed formats and themes from the mainstream press. In the case of immigration coverage, conservative advocates adopted the narrative of illegality and eventually carried it forward to a shrill extreme. There was no countervailing narrative from either the mainstream press or progressive advocates because none existed in the repertoire of American journalism.

Starting with Lou Dobbs in 2003, then the anchor of the flagship evening news broadcast on CNN, the narrative of illegality became a topic of choice among conservative practitioners of advocacy journalism. While news coverage alone rarely produces dramatic shifts in policy or public opinion, journalism does exercise a framing function that can have a cumulative effect on the way the public interprets events. As the scholar of media and politics W. Lance Bennett defines it: "Framing involves choosing a broad organizing theme for selecting, emphasizing, and linking the elements of a story. Frames are thematic categories that integrate and give meaning to the scene, the characters, their actions, and supporting documentation."[8] The framing function can be exercised within a single story, for example, when a candidate's popularity is explained as a function of race or gender rather than by his or her positions on critical issues. Framing can have a cumulative effect; when stories about gang violence dominate coverage of crime, for instance, it gives the impression that gangs are primarily responsible for criminal violence. In addition, as Shanto Iyengar, a professor of communications and political science at Stanford, has demonstrated in studies of television news coverage, the media can portray events as singular and disconnected. "Episodic framing," as he put it, prevents audiences from accumulating a sense of context and long-term trends.[9]

The news media's framing of immigration could well have stoked the public's anxiety over illegal migration and its distrust of the government's ability to contend with it. Such attitudes contributed to a policy stalemate in the mid-2000s—a time marked by near universal unhappiness with immigration policies and practices combined with an inability to move forward decisively in any direction. At the start of the current decade, both aspects of that situation appear only to have deepened even as opposing opinions among the most fervent advocates have hardened. In some sectors, particularly those who favor tougher enforcement measures, the rhetoric has grown harsher. Three major tendencies in the coverage of immigration by the U.S. news media have produced that perceptual framework, and in examining each of them, one can search for parallels to academic depictions as well. These three tendencies are an episodic and irregular flow of coverage, an overemphasis on illegality, and a portrayal of migrants as protagonists.

. . .

The legendary newspaper editor Eugene Roberts of the *Philadelphia Inquirer* and the *New York Times* drew a distinction between stories that "break" and those that "ooze." He sought to correct what he perceived as journalism's neglect of the slowly developing but important trends in American society. Simply by virtue of operating on very short time frames, the news media, of course, are far better suited to the depiction of stories that break. Meanwhile, both the institutional structure and the vocation of the academy, especially in the social sciences, aim to capture patterns and truths that play out over the long term. Like education, health care, and some other matters of public policy, immigration produces a narrative that may be punctuated by high-profile events but is defined by the cumulative impact of many small events that go unnoticed individually.

Journalistic coverage of immigration has been notably episodic, producing spikes of coverage and then long periods when attention falls off. The spikes have been driven by dramatic set-piece events, such as the Elian Gonzalez saga, legislative debates, and protest marches. The surges in coverage have conditioned the public and policymakers to think of immigration as a sudden event, often tinged with the air of crisis. Consider, for example, that immigration coverage by the national desk of the *New York Times* averaged 102 stories a year from 1980 to 2008 but ranged from a low of 43 stories in 1991 to a high of 217 in 2006. On the *CBS Evening News* coverage of immigration in 1993 was nearly six times what it was in 1992, nearly three times as much in 2000 as in 1999.

In contrast, the academic depictions of this wave of immigration were tardy in arriving and then the scholarship was slow in gathering momentum. In the intricate hierarchy of status and prestige in the academy, immigration was a domain of very low status throughout much of the current era of migration. With the possible exception of labor economists and urban sociologists (and they never represented the cutting edge of their respective fields), immigration scholarship tended to dwell at the margins of the major theoretical and empirical enterprises that dominated the social sciences in the last quarter of the twentieth century. Until very recently, entire scholarly disciplines completely ignored the phenomenon—academic psychology, among others. There are important institutional factors at work; the time frames involved in academic production combined with the availability of data seemed to have put scholarship behind the curve through much of this era of immigration.

In the 1980s and 1990s major scholarship relied on the decennial census as the essential source for data, and the data then came in what now would be regarded as hopelessly primitive forms. As a result, major monographs, books, and articles relying on census data were typically published in the middle of the decade or even late in the decade. In a rapidly changing field, such delays inevitably diminish influence outside the academy. Many of those works are of enduring value to their disciplines but had less public impact than they deserved because the foreign-born population was growing and changing so quickly during the lag between data collection and publication. That situation improved in the early 2000s, when the American Community Survey started providing yearly data, and statistical techniques improved for combining files from the Current Population Survey to allow detailed analyses of population segments in the years between the decennial census. The cumulative effect has been a slowly gathering but now rapidly expanding pace of scholarship.

A detailed examination of the volume of scholarship on immigration is beyond the scope of this chapter, but let us take the formation of professional associations as one indication of how the academy has responded to this wave of immigration. Arguably, sociology is the discipline that has lent the most attention to this phenomenon, and yet the American Sociological Association did not organize its immigration section until 1994. That same year the Social Science Research Council organized its migration program. Similarly, the American Political Science Association organized its section on race, ethnicity, and politics in

1995 and then a Latino caucus in 1998. It took until 2010 for the American Psychological Association to establish its first Presidential Task Force on Immigration, headed by Carola Suárez-Orozco (see her contribution in this book). It is not that these dates mark the beginning of academic activity. Indeed, scholars with already well-established track records on immigration were involved in launching these activities. The formation of these bodies represented a certain level of recognition within the disciplines, and these groups served to spur much more activity in subsequent years. More broadly, the mid-1990s produced other signs of increased interest in the academy including the publication of a number of important monographs, special issue journals, and books that have laid the foundation for subsequent scholarship.

The overall trend seems quite clear: Since the mid-1990s, the volume of scholarship on immigration, its scope and quality, and the number of scholars attending to the subject have increased very substantially. All this activity came after the 1990 census chronicled a jump in the foreign-born population to 19.8 million, up from 14.1 million in 1980. It also followed the enactment of two major pieces of legislation in 1986 and 1990, and coincided with the development of an anti-immigrant backlash that became manifest in the elections of 1994 and 1996. Scholars started to pay attention to contemporary immigration only after it had become a familiar consideration in politics and policy.

Just as the volume of journalistic coverage has been marked by stark peaks and valleys, the academic output appears to present the opposite profile, arriving late on the scene and then gathering momentum slowly but surely. There is a similar contrast in the topics that have dominated the two depictions. Journalism has focused squarely on migration as a phenomenon that is supposed to be regulated by government but often isn't. Meanwhile, the academy has focused on migration as an individual and social activity with far less regard to the legal status of individuals or government policies and bureaucracies. Illegal immigrants have never constituted more than a third of the foreign-born population in the United States, and that mark has been reached only in recent years. Nonetheless, illegal immigration and government's efforts to control it have dominated the news coverage in all sectors of the media by wide margins for many years. This pattern of coverage would logically cause the public and policymakers to associate the influx of the foreign-born with violations of the law, disruption of social norms, and government failures.

For example, an analysis of 1,848 Associated Press stories on immigration topics from 1980 to 2007 showed that 79 percent fit into the framework of illegality. Of 2,614 stories on immigration in the *New York Times* over the same period, 86 percent dealt with illegality in various forms, and that included 83 percent of the coverage in Washington and 88 percent of the stories from elsewhere in the country. The news media's focus on illegality appears to stem at least in part from an institutional bias that draws attention to malfeasance. According to deeply ingrained ideas about what kind of events deserve attention in journalism, any act that violates any law is a priori more newsworthy than the observance of law. And those depictions are not unwaveringly negative. Journalistic narratives relish characters in the underdog role, and the striving illegal migrant who braves dangers to cross the border in search of a better life often fits the bill (see Patrick J. McDonnell's chapter in this volume).

Given those preoccupations, the media has inevitably tended to ignore legal immigration even when set-piece news events would have justified coverage. For example, in 1990 Congress passed the first major revision of legal immigration statutes in thirty-five years, substantially increasing migration flows and changing their composition. This legislation has altered the face of America. The *Washington Post* covered the debate leading up to enactment with a total of 2,078 words of news copy in four routine Capitol Hill stories. The bill's potential impact was not examined in Washington's newspaper of record until a week after it was passed. In contrast, when Congress produced a law dealing exclusively with illegal immigration in 1986, the *Washington Post* published ten stories about the deliberations in the month before passage and seven follow-ups in the immediate aftermath.

The narrative of illegality gained influence in the mid-2000s, when it became a major preoccupation for conservative advocacy journalists. After he took over CNN's flagship evening broadcast in 2003, Lou Dobbs reported on the federal government's failure to control illegal immigration for days on end under the heading "Broken Borders." His immigration coverage gradually became shriller and more expansive, as he accused unauthorized migrants of being responsible for a growing catalog of socials ills—from burglary to leprosy. Although a variety of immigration advocates pointed out gross inaccuracies in Dobbs's reporting, the mainstream media left him largely unchallenged. A confrontational interview with journalist Lesley Stahl on *60 Minutes* in May 2007 was the exception.

Meanwhile, other conservative advocates, such as Rush Limbaugh and Bill O'Reilly, took up the issue, often echoing Dobbs's rhetorical points particularly when policy debates were under way. Our content analysis shows a sudden spike in coverage by conservative talk show hosts and commentators during the Senate debate of 2007, when a proposal to offer a path to citizenship for the current population of undocumented migrants was successfully attacked as an "amnesty for lawbreakers." In addition to their apparent influence on public opinion, conservative advocacy journalism on immigration also increasingly succeeded in shaping the public policy agenda. For example, before he left CNN in 2009, Dobbs started a long campaign against so-called anchor babies, children whose birth was allegedly arranged to take place in the United States so that the parents—twenty-one years later—could benefit from immigration sponsorship. Despite scant evidence that this was even a minor factor in immigration flows, the claims inspired proposals to revoke the constitutional guarantee of universal birthright citizenship that were being debated in Washington and several states as of early 2011.

Meanwhile, academic depictions of immigration, not surprisingly, have focused on trends that develop slowly, on actions that involve broad social formations, and on the arc of individual human development. The process of assimilation, for example, which plays out over many years, sometimes across generations, has been a subject of notable interest (see the chapters by Mary C. Waters, Carola Suárez-Orozco, and Vivian Louie in this volume). This is also the case with other subjects of similarly long fetch, including economic incorporation (see Barry R. Chiswick's chapter in this book), transnationalism, and residential settlement patterns. Those are all stories that ooze rather than break, and they are justifiably the stuff of academic work seeking to build theory and advance knowledge. All sorts of institutional structures, from tenure trajectories to peer review, ensure that the development of these fields is deliberate, slow-paced, and incremental.[10]

Even though processes like assimilation and transnationalism are not entirely novel to this era of migration or specific to the United States, scholarship went through a process of rediscovery, as often happens in the social sciences, as a new generation of researchers updated older ideas and claimed them as their own. Scholarship moved at its own pace, but in the meantime American society had started forming its contradictory but often unhappy responses to a wave of immigration that was already a generation in the making. Immigration scholars, particularly in sociology and labor economics, started producing depictions with greater confidence, breadth, and regularity by the early 2000s and then increasingly as the decade progressed. There are now solid bookshelves of scholarship that will stand the test of time, but most of it, alas, has come *after* the American public and its policy makers had finished their voyages of discovery on this topic.

Whatever the reasons, and assuredly they are multiple and complex, the social sciences were not fully engaged participants during the first two or even three decades in which the United States was trying to come to terms with the current era of immigration. Some might argue that the academy is not well-suited to illuminating public discourse in a timely manner, and others would claim it should not even try. However, there are some important cases of scholarship about major socioeconomic developments that have informed public debates even if consensus has remained elusive. Consider globalization or the digital media revolution, for example. Even as they struggled to assess these developments scientifically, scholars produced vocabularies and conceptual frameworks that in turn shaped policy discussions in both government and the private sector. Immigration scholars have had much less visible impact. Consider, for instance, the decade and a half of important academic work that falls generally under the term *assimilation*. There has been a lively and productive debate among scholars over how immigrants and their offspring are changed by societies of destination and how they in turn produce change in those societies. But this research is rarely mentioned in policy debates.

Scholars have been further limited in their public influence because they have tended not to focus on the topic that has most preoccupied the news media. No specific information on the immigration status of noncitizens is collected in the census or other large government surveys, so scholarship has been constrained by virtue of the availability of data alone. Indeed, it was not until the early 2000s that a statistical method emerged to produce widely accepted estimates of the size of the unauthorized population and its broad characteristics at a given point in time. Large-scale, scientifically valid studies of illegal migrants living in the United States remain out of reach, especially if the intent is to understand changes in their characteristics, let alone their behavior over time. As with the focus on illegality in journalism, these preoccupations by the academy reflect habits of mind that reach back well before the emergence of the current wave of immigration in the 1970s. However, another characteristic of the academic rendering does very much reflect the era in which it developed.

The renewed attention to immigration that accompanied the current wave came at a time when the study of ethnic and racial groups had achieved unparalleled prominence on American campuses. The largest wave of immigration in American history took place in the aftermath of the great struggles for civil rights, during which race and ethnicity acquired a new salience in public policy. In retrospect, it seems inevitable that late-twentieth-century immigration would be viewed through a lens that aggregates individuals in large ethnic groups—Hispanic/Latino, Asian, and so on. Other forms of categorization—such as countries of origin—tended to be ignored. So the label "Hispanic" or "Latino" has subsumed differences between Mexicans, Dominicans, Cubans, and many other Spanish-speaking national origin groups that demonstrate differences on important traits. Moreover, the large ethnic or racial groups have overshadowed other variables that could have greater power in explaining a population molded by contemporary immigration. So all the emphasis has been on drawing comparison between the major groups: Latinos and Asians, whites and blacks. Meanwhile, less attention has gone to characteristics like English proficiency, time in country, and parents' education, which could help explain outcomes across groups. All the focus has been on the columns when the rows deserved greater attention.

In emphasizing racial and ethnic differences to the exclusion of other considerations, the academy is merely reflecting the society in which it operates. And so too by viewing nonwhites through the lens of minority group status, the academy is merely applying society's norms. But given the fact that the great majority of recent immigrants are nonwhite, this has had a profound effect. The academic depiction of contemporary immigrants as belonging to racialized groups has been as distorting as journalism's preoccupation with illegality. Public opinion has been conditioned to see immigrants not only as criminals but also as members of groups that bear grievances and that are making special claims on the majority society, even if empirically that is far from the truth (see Mary C. Waters's chapter in this book).

The third tendency in the depiction of immigration by journalism finds a clear parallel in scholarship. In both cases, immigrants have been portrayed as the protagonists of the narrative to the exclusion of other actors—especially economic players—that have exercised as large an influence, if not larger, over the outcome of that narrative. In the case of journalism, policymakers and advocates have also shared the limelight, often to the exclusion of other critical actors, especially employers and consumers. At the simplest level, this has deprived the coverage of essential context by underemphasizing the role of the U.S. labor market in determining the size and characteristics of immigrant flows and overemphasizing the role of government—especially in its failures. When their attitudes toward immigration turn negative, audiences exposed to this kind of coverage can readily view immigrants as villains and themselves as victims. Distrust of government—a seeming accomplice or an incompetent protector—is a natural by-product.

For example, an analysis of the 201 stories about immigration aired on the three broadcast networks' flagship evening news shows in 2006 and 2007 found that employers were quoted in only twelve stories. In contrast, immigrants were interviewed or made statements in fifty-eight stories. On the policy side, only seven stories made mention of sanctions against the employers of unauthorized workers, and it was a minor element in most of them. Meanwhile, twenty-nine of the stories on the evening news broadcasts were about the border and the federal government's failed efforts there. This is a substantial body of work by the three news organizations which share a platform that has the broadest reach in American society, even though the audience is much reduced from what it once was. Taken as a single narrative, this depiction would suggest that migrants—overwhelmingly unauthorized in these news accounts—were the controlling actors of the drama, fully in charge of their own destiny, with government playing a lesser and failed role in trying to block them from entering into the country.

Portrayals of immigration by social scientists have tended to emphasize the agency of the migrant if only because the portrayals are based on information gathered about individuals. Reliance on government-collected demographic data inevitably produces analysis based on the characteristics of the individuals studied. While nativity variables yield an abundance of data about immigrants, there are no variables in population surveys that permit an analysis of the employers, consumers, teachers, police officers, landlords, and foremen who exercise influence over the immigrants' lives. The danger, of course, is to assume that the characteristics of immigrants or their children have a power to determine outcomes that is equal to or even greater than the socioeconomic milieu in which they operate. Of even greater danger in the political arena is the perception that immigrants produce certain social outcomes either by choice or because of the inevitable results of their characteristics and that public policy can have no impact. Thus some in the public might be led to believe, for example, that increasing a city's Mexican immigration population by x will inevitably result in an increase of y high school dropouts twenty years later. It is as if the socioeconomic characteristics of parents inevitably trumped teachers, principals, school budgets, and education policies in shaping the learning outcomes for their children.

The context of reception has been a key concept in immigration scholarship since the great urban sociologist Robert Park studied the lives of Europeans living in Chicago in the 1920s.[11] Nonetheless, it remains extremely difficult to quantify, and during the current era of immigration, quantitative methods and models have dominated the social sciences. Meanwhile, economics should have provided contextual studies that explain critical causes and effects, but the field has been dominated by game theorists and econometricians—the labor economists who tend to study immigration remain at the periphery of power and prestige in their own discipline. Whatever the cause, contemporary economics has failed to reach a consensus on questions that have plagued policymakers for decades now: What is immigration's effect on labor markets, fiscal balance sheets, and economic productivity? For a concise overview, see Barry R. Chiswick's chapter in this volume.

. . .

Immigration has consistently generated acrimonious public debates. It is simply the kind of topic that touches a great many nerves—economic security, national security, national identity, social cohesion, and more—and it affects many different sectors of society in different ways. So there is no reason to expect that the development of immigration policy will be easy. Nonetheless, the United States has been marked by a bitter stalemate since the mid-2000s. Public opinion and the views of policymakers are fragmented along several axes, including the proper role of enforcement in reducing the illegal immigrant population, the wisdom of a legalization program for the currently undocumented, new visa allocations, and the terms of a temporary worker program, if any, to help manage future flows. Over time the social divisions appear to have become more profound and more emotional as the public policy debate becomes more sterile and ineffective. After the 2007 stalemate over comprehensive reform, Congress managed to go more than three years without having a floor debate over any significant piece of immigration legislation even as the public opinion polls showed rising anxiety over the status quo.

One need not take a stand on specific immigration policies or even on a broad direction in order to wish that this situation could be resolved. The stalemate does not benefit anyone and seems to be making a resolution ever more difficult to attain. Journalists and academics can contribute to a remedy while remaining fully loyal to their professions. Neither need make concessions about which produces a more accurate or more valuable rendering. Because they take very different approaches to the subject of migration, they may have something to learn from each other simply by observing the contrasts. Through dialogues like the one that produced this book, there is the potential, even the likelihood, that they will further inform each others' work. But in the end, both professions and each journalist and scholar individually will have to consider how his or her work is shaping public opinion and policy on a cumulative basis. Exercising social responsibility is not incompatible with an unfettered search for the truth, but it is too often left by the wayside.

NOTES

1. U.S. Congress, Select Commission on Immigration and Refugee Policy (otherwise known as the Hesburgh commission), "U.S. Immigration Policy and the National Interest: The Final Report and Recommendations of the Select Commission on Immigration and Refugee Policy with Supplemental Views by Commissioners," Education Resources Information Center, 1981, A unique accession number assigned to each record in the database; also referred to as ERIC Document Number (ED Number) and ERIC Journal Number (EJ Number). ED211612, introduction p. 3; available online at http://www.eric.ed.gov/PDFS/ED211612.pdf.

2. Ibid., 36–37.

3. Ibid., 35

4. Ibid., introduction, 10

5. Roberto Suro, "The Triumph of No: How the Media Influence the Immigration Debate," in *A Report of the Media and the Immigration Debate* (Washington, D.C.: Governance Studies at Brookings Institution, 2008). The monograph can be downloaded at www.brookings.edu/~/media/Files/rc/reports/2008/0925_immigration_dionne/0925_immigration_suro.ashx.

6. Jeffrey S. Passel and Roberto Suro, "Rise, Peak, and Decline: Trends in U.S. Immigration, 1992–2004," Pew Hispanic Center, Washington, D.C., 2005.

7. The Clinton administration angered many Cuban Americans by sending Elian Gonzalez back to Cuba, and in the 2000 presidential election thousands of Cuban Americans shifted their allegiance to the Republican Party. Without that backing, George W. Bush might have lost the Florida count on election night and the election itself.

8. W. Lance Bennett, *News: The Politics of Illusion* (New York: Pearson, 2007), 38.

9. Shanto Iyengar, *Is Anyone Responsible? How Television Frames Political Issues* (Chicago: University of Chicago Press, 1992).

10. See Howard Gardner, "How Education Changes: Considerations of History, Science, and Values," in *Learning in the Global Era: International Perspectives on Globalization and Education,* edited by Marcelo M. Suárez-Orozco (Berkeley: University of California Press, 2004), 235–58.

11. Robert Park, *The City: Suggestions for the Study of Human Nature in the Urban Environment* (Chicago: University of Chicago Press, 1925).

Immigration and the Law

In Part One of the book Nina Bernstein of the *New York Times*, Cristina M. Rodríguez of the New York University School of Law, Dianne Solís of the *Dallas Morning News*, and Peter H. Schuck of the Yale Law School debate the problem of writing about some of the most controversial and complicated topics in immigration today: raids on immigrant communities, deportations, family separations, and immigration-related ordinances at the local level. On top of a byzantine legal architecture—full of contradictions, good and bad laws—a human drama of broken family bonds, shadowed lives, and postponed dreams is unfolding.

A sample follows of the exchanges on immigration and the law that took place at the 2008 Nieman Foundation for Journalism conference.

. . .

Audience question: How has the law on the ground evolved over time? In North Carolina, where I'm from, there was a huge debate on letting illegal immigrants into the community colleges. They eventually decided to do that. What was implicit in that was the debate over whether they [illegal immigrants] should be allowed into schools, elementary schools, and secondary schools, which is pretty much settled. I'm wondering what things have changed over the last ten or twenty years that are parts of the law that maybe are not even on the books, but that are in the communities and have become settled.

Panelist Cristina M. Rodríguez: I think that's a difficult question to answer. The debate about the extent to which shifts in enforcement policies have actually changed is part of it. Whereas once ICE's [United States Immigration and Customs Enforcement's] focus was on the so-called criminal aliens, now they're more focused on the undocumented, and the mechanisms they have used have evolved over time.

On the subject of the admission to higher education, there are rumblings in a lot of states about whether or not it's (a) legal for public institutions to admit students who don't have status; and (b) whether institutions can give the reduced-rate tuition to people of undocumented status. It's another area of ferment in the states. What's settled—and the public consensus is shifting away from this, but the legal consensus is still pretty fixed—is that the equal protection clause prohibits states from keeping people out of the public schools through twelfth grade. The implication then is that you have a lot of kids who are educated in the public school system who have nowhere to go if the public colleges are not open to them. That puts a lot of pressure to open them up. In many states you've seen that happen. I suspect that's part of why North Carolina settled on the fact they [the community colleges] could be open.

As a legal matter, I don't think there's a limitation on whether or not they [illegal immigrants] have access. The question about whether the state can give reduced-rate in-state tuition is a closer legal question. The states have actually gotten around what seemed like a clear prohibition. When Congress says something explicitly, there are lots of ways that lawyers can get around it by the clever use of language; and I think they've succeeded. But that's an area where the consensus might be shifting a bit, but it might be shifting in the direction of openness as opposed to restriction because of the effects of *Plyler v. Doe* (see Rodríguez's contribution in this volume) on the system.

. . .

Audience question: [In the United States] I'm hearing the term *illegal immigrant* a lot, and I'm hearing this term from journalists and lawyers who have a great impact on public opinion. For me it's a contradiction. Back in Spain we never, ever speak of an *illegal immigrant*. A *documented immigrant* is fine. This is something that I'm struggling with. I think the terminology that we use is important.

Panelist Patrick J. McDonnell: As a journalist, I would say the more neutral the language the better. Some people find *illegal immigrants* offensive. I think most newspapers use that. It used to be *illegal aliens* and I think that's mostly been dropped. *Unauthorized*—I think that would be great if the mainstream media adopted that [term] because it comes down to the political question, in my experience. I think that *alien* is something that's not used anymore.

Panelist Edward Schumacher-Matos: There have been huge debates in every newsroom across the country on this particular issue. The AP [Associated Press] style book uses *illegal immigrant.* The *New York Times* style book uses *illegal immigrant.* The *Wall Street Journal* doesn't have the term in its style book. It uses the [various] terms indiscriminately, but it normally starts with *illegal immigrant* in stories. The National Association of Hispanic Journalists has been trying to push very hard across the country to change it to *undocumented.* Now the Pew Hispanic Center and others have begun using the word *unauthorized.* That's the word that's getting pushed more and more.

Panelist Cristina M. Rodríguez: What I tell my students when I teach immigration law is to not be inhibited by their use of language. In that sort of a setting, talking someone down because they said *illegal immigrant* or even *illegal alien* restricts debate in the classroom. As a result, it sometimes creeps into the way I speak about it too. But I also grew up in Texas, where the use of *illegal aliens* is just the way that people talk about it. That's also happening. That's not to the point of the style guides that journalists should use, but in conversation it's hard to control your language without controlling your thought.

. . .

Audience question: Dianne Solís mentioned the question of due process and calibrating our legal lenses as journalists to understand how these immigration raids are conducted. I'm not a legal affairs reporter. I have covered immigration raids. What are the parameters within which ICE agents are operating when they bang on your door and say "Police here" and then come into your house, open doors, and go through rooms? I'm interested in the perspectives of the legal scholars on advising us as journalists of where the lines are. I've run into resistance from editors who say "Well, they're here illegally." How does due process apply to them and why is this a story?

Panelist Cristina M. Rodríguez: To address the last thing you said, when someone says they're here illegally, what's the problem, the question is determining whether or not the person is here illegally. The point of due process is to make sure there's not an erroneous deprivation of someone's liberty or property interests. Before you have made a factual determination according to procedures, you don't know the answer to that question. Procedures are put in place to make sure you're most likely to get the best answer. That's why the Supreme Court imposed due process on the military tribunals and status review tribunals in Guantanamo, because you don't know that they're enemy combatants until you have a viable procedure to make the determination. I think that's the way to think about that type of question, which people commonly ask.

Panelist Peter H. Schuck: It's not just to increase our confidence in the accuracy of decision making. It's also to restrain the government by forcing it to adhere to norms of fairness and dignity. Even if accuracy were not increased, these would be important values.

Panelist Cristina M. Rodríguez: A lot of the raids traditionally use administrative warrants. This is because immigration enforcement is a civil matter, not a criminal matter, and there are lower standards for obtaining those. [There is] an important issue in the current raids: the extent to which people can consent to allow ICE into the home, people who aren't actually targeted in the investigation. There are lots of anecdotal stories of children consenting to allow ICE in. There are questions about from whom can you genuinely get consent to enter into the home, because you need consent to enter into the home without a criminal warrant. However, there are lots of ways around that. In the criminal law, if someone who is in your home consents to let the police in, the fact that person doesn't live there is not a defense.

1

The Making of an
Outlaw Generation

NINA BERNSTEIN

In the fall of 2004, my first year covering immigration for the *New York Times,* I met an eight-year-old girl named Virginia Feliz. Her last name means "happy" in Spanish, but she hated her name, she told me. She threw herself down on a couch in her family's apartment in the Bronx, beside her father, Carlos Feliz, a U.S. citizen who was born in the Dominican Republic. She declared: "I'm not happy, I'm sad. Because it's not fair that everybody else has their mom except me." In an article on the front page of the *Times*—one of the first, I believe, to highlight the breadth of this phenomenon—I wrote: "Virginia is part of the growing tribe of American children who have lost a parent to deportation."[1] Virginia's forty-seven-year-old mother, Berly Feliz, had gone to the federal immigration headquarters in Manhattan on a supposedly routine visit to renew her work authorization. But an old deportation order had resurfaced, and Mrs. Feliz, who had lived in the United States for a decade after migrating illegally from Honduras, was quickly handcuffed and placed on a plane, with no chance to say goodbye.

By all reports Virginia Feliz had been a happy child before her mother's expulsion. Two months later, doctors said Virginia had a major depressive disorder marked by hyperactivity, nightmares, bed-wetting, frequent crying, and fights at school. In a letter to the Department of Homeland Security, Dr. Victor Sierra, the director of the Child and Adolescent clinic where Virginia was treated, made no bones about the underlying problem: "Absent mother, secondary to deportation."

Virginia's case, on its own, might have made a compelling local feature story for the Metro desk, to which I was assigned. But at the time (and until mid-2006) I was the only reporter at the *New York Times* covering immigration. That fact itself may be evidence of what Roberto Suro, professor of journalism and public policy, criticizes as the episodic nature of immigration coverage. But it was also one reason I had lobbied for the beat on my return from a fellowship at the American Academy in Berlin. I knew I could use New York–based reporting as a framework for articles with national, even international, scope. My task was to put Virginia's case in a larger context.

I learned that 186,000 people were being deported from the United States in that year (2004), and 887,000 others had been required to make a "voluntary departure." In the 2010 fiscal year the annual "removals" figure reached a record 392,862. Yet no one kept track of exactly how many American children were being left behind. After consulting with demographers at the Pew Hispanic Center and the Urban Institute, however, I could confidently write that the number was in the tens of thousands. A spokesman for federal immigration services, William Strassberger, acknowledged the human fallout in a way that made Virginia's case resonate in the broader immigration debate and beyond. "There are millions of people who are illegally in the United States, and it's unfortunate, when they're caught, seeing a family split up," he said. "But the person has to be answerable for their actions." Parents had to decide whether to leave their American-born children with relatives or friends, or take them along when they were expelled from the country, he added, going so far as to evoke an image from the Nazi concentration camps: "People refer to that as a Sophie's choice situation," he told me.

Perhaps because I was steeped in the history of child welfare after writing *The Lost Children of Wilder: The Epic Struggle to Change Foster Care,* I was struck not only by the scale of this largely unrecorded phenomenon of family disruption but also by the lack of any official nod to "the best interest of the child"—a concept enshrined in family law, if not in child welfare practice.[2] There is a rich clinical literature on the psychological damage suffered by children who lose an attachment figure. More recent longitudinal studies of immigrant students offer nuanced discussions of the ways family separations caused by migration affect children who are belatedly reunited with their parents in the United States.[3] But in journalistic terms what the Virginia Feliz article really demanded was an academic study specifically tracking the impact of parental deportation on children left behind in the United States. My hurried search turned up nothing on point.

This is the classic catch-22 facing a reporter ahead of the curve: the fresher the story, the more editors want corroboration from authoritative voices and scholarly evidence—and the less likely readily available scholarship fits the bill.[4] What served me best in this instance was research on transnational migration that focused on children left on the southern side of the border, whose distress certainly echoed that of children like Virginia. Through a lucky break, I reached Leah Schmalzbauer, a social anthropologist who had conducted a two-year research project on families split between Honduras and the United States. She helped me broaden my context further: The numbers were expected to swell, Schmalzbauer noted, because families in poor countries like Honduras could no longer manage without remittances from the United States, and women were beginning to replace men as the primary migrants, filling growing demands in the United States for low-cost elder care, domestic work, and other service jobs. In an article framed by an individual narrative, this observation served to point to the larger economic forces at work. At the same time, Schmalzbauer gave me the strong quote. I needed to connect the dots to Virginia's mother, who had originally migrated to the United States when she could no longer afford to buy clothes, food, and school supplies for her son in Honduras, then thirteen.

I still needed other examples to show that Virginia's mental health problems were not an aberration. This was no easy task, given the imperatives of patient confidentiality and the stigma of deportation. Eventually I found Birdette Gardiner-Parkinson, the clinical director at the Caribbean Community Mental Health program at Kingsbrook Jewish Medical Center in Brooklyn, who described similar cases. She said, "When children lose a family member this way, even though they may have a phone conversation with them, the physical separation feels like death." To advocates of greater restriction on immigration, I noted, this illustrated the painful consequences of poor enforcement in the past and pointed to the perils of guest worker programs like one then being proposed by President George W. Bush. "Once you let the person stay in the United States, it becomes extremely difficult in our society to make them go," said Steven Camarota, director of research at the Center for Immigration Studies in Washington, arguing that a temporary worker program, if enforced, would only add to the number of families facing separation. "How are you going to keep them from falling in love, getting married and having U.S.-born children?" To critics of the sterner laws adopted in 1996, on the other hand, such cases showed that more systematic enforcement since September 11, 2001, was compounding the laws' contradictions and loss of discretion.

The case of Virginia's mother could be cited to support either side of the policy debate. Caught within hours of crossing the border in 1994, Mrs. Feliz had quickly been released on bond and then fled to New York. When she failed to show up in a Texas immigration court, she was ordered deported in absentia. But like the great majority of such orders, it was not pursued for years. And like millions of other illegal migrants, Mrs. Feliz was readily hired by Americans, first as a live-in housekeeper and then for low-wage factory work. Indeed, after her 1996 marriage to Carlos Feliz, when she applied for a green card, her lawyer said, federal immigration officials issued her an official work authorization several times and allowed her husband, as a U.S. citizen and new stepfather, to sponsor the teenage son she had left in Honduras for a visa. Now that son was a twenty-four-year-old lawful permanent resident with his own New York–born child, while his mother was back where she began, without a job or either of her children. "I don't have peace because I'm not with my little girl," she told me in Spanish, weeping in a telephone interview from Honduras. "I can't be without her—I have no life."

The article, which ran above the fold with a six-column photo of Virginia and her father, perhaps would be seen by the law professor Peter H. Schuck as framing immigration issues as "conflicts between powerless, underdog immigrants and powerful corporations and bureaucrats," instead of providing "a sympathetic explanation of the tradeoffs and of the constraints on the system." To Suro, it no doubt fits a pattern of telling immigration narratives that highlight individual agency and illegal entry, giving short shrift to pull factors.[5] But I see the piece as a personal milestone in my coverage, the point when I recognized that children and families were actually at the cutting edge of the national immigration dilemma, though still at the margins of political discourse.

The article also marked my realization that prying basic information from secretive or indifferent government enforcement agencies would absorb an inordinate amount of my reporting time. Six years later, despite formal congressional queries and newspaper articles around the country that have highlighted such family separations, there is still no reliable public count of how many American-born children have lost a parent to deportation—or how many have been, in effect, deported along with their parents. In January 2009 the inspector general of the Department of Homeland Security reported that collecting information on the U.S. citizen children of deported adults was still optional, so the agency was unable to answer a House subcommittee request for statistics on such children, whether they had been taken away or left behind, and how many had lost both parents to deportation. Even the incomplete data, however, showed that among 2.2 million people removed or deported between 1998 and 2007, more than 108,000 were parents of such children.

The legal and historical backdrop for Virginia Feliz's story, and for many of the human narratives I have told since then in the *New York Times,* was the sweeping immigration legislation enacted in 1996, which embraced harsher policies for both legal and illegal immigrants and asylum seekers, too. These Clinton administration laws, which mostly took effect in 1998, sharply curtailed defenses against deportation, severely narrowed judicial review that would allow consideration of individual circumstances, and raised civil and criminal penalties for immigration law violations. Shaped by the politics of ending welfare and by the war on drugs, the measures also barred legal immigrants from most government benefits and retroactively mandated the detention of all noncitizens who had ever committed a crime on a list of deportable offenses, which was expanded to include misdemeanors like drug possession and shoplifting. People facing deportation had no assurance of a lawyer. They could be held for years without recourse— a practice modified, though not eliminated, by the 2001 Supreme Court ruling in *Zadvydas v. Davis,* which held that indefinite detention is constitutional only if the detainee is dangerous and defined the limit generally as more than six months.

It was only after the 9/11 terrorist attacks, however, that the 1996 measures known as IIRIRA (for Illegal Immigration Reform and Immigrant Responsibility Act) were vigorously enforced. Early on, the Bush administration explicitly resorted to immigration law as a weapon in its war on terror, rounding up hundreds of noncitizens and holding them for months with little or no effort to distinguish between genuine suspects and Muslim immigrants with minor visa violations.[6] In 2003 the transfer of immigration services to a new Department of Homeland Security further blurred the boundaries between the administrative control of immigration, criminal law enforcement, and national security, and tapped billions of tax dollars to expand operations against noncitizens. In the mid-2000s the Immigration and Customs Enforcement

(ICE) arm of the department grew increasingly aggressive as Bush tried, and failed, to pass an immigration overhaul that would satisfy conflicting demands for stricter enforcement, more temporary workers, and a path to citizenship for many illegal residents.

The signs of change from the Obama administration on immigration issues remained mostly that—signs rather than substance. Despite the administration's moratorium on large workplace raids—events that had drawn widespread negative publicity—there was no decrease in deportations of unauthorized workers caught more discreetly. Overall, following essentially the same strategy that failed under Bush, the Obama administration has pushed for a record number of deportations, to prove its enforcement bona fides, in the hope of winning legislative concessions in return.[7] Though the Obama administration maintains that it wants to concentrate immigration enforcement on serious criminal offenders, it has embraced programs that are feeding record numbers of noncriminals, misdemeanants, and traffic offenders into detention and prosecuting record numbers of immigration-related offenses as federal crimes.[8] These trends clash with the promise to transform immigration detention into "a truly civil" system.[9] As this book goes to press, the midterm elections have decisively shifted the congressional balance of power toward Republicans and restrictionists, and the demise of the DREAM Act (Development, Relief, and Education for Alien Minors) has left Obama's immigration policy in shambles.[10] But well before those events, the Democrats' discussion of comprehensive immigration reform increasingly emphasized enforcement. Parts of the existing system have so permeated local law enforcement and local economies that it is hard to envision any quick reversal. Even the longer-term prospect for mixed-status immigrant families remains guarded at best.

. . .

In this chapter I use my own reporting experiences, illuminated by the work of social scientists and legal scholars, as signposts to the shifting, conflicted landscape where such families have been raising a new generation of Americans. It is a place where fear has increasingly complicated the role of journalists and academics alike. In the end, I contend, it is the landscape that we all inhabit, whether we know it or not—a version of America that challenges our fundamental understanding of human rights and raises the specter of a kind of homegrown statelessness. In my experience one of the key features of this landscape is the ballooning immigration detention system. Detainees are often held for months, shuttled across the country from one lockup to the next, with little access to legal help or proper medical care and with almost none of the due process safeguards that people who watch *Law & Order* take for granted.

Catherine Dauvergne, a professor of migration law at the University of British Columbia Faculty of Law, has summarized the vulnerability of such unauthorized migrants in all Western countries: "They are confronted with legal regimes where, generally speaking, the state agents have more powers than the police and individuals have fewer rights protections than criminal suspects." Few would contest Dauvergne's observation that we are in the midst of a worldwide crackdown on extra-legal immigration. She reads it as a response to globalized threats to national sovereignty, noting that when physical borders are not effective at bolstering assertions of national sovereignty, "a strong policy stance against 'illegals' is" because "the label 'illegal' ensures exclusion from within."[11]

In the United States, certainly, exclusion from within has become a growth industry. Immigration detention, now funded by Congress at the rate of $2.4 billion a year, is a shadowy conglomeration of profit-making prisons, county jails, and federal detention centers that holds more than 407,000 over the course of the year, churning through some 31,000 beds. That's more than triple the number a decade ago. And I would argue that the reach of detention and deportation is much greater now than even these numbers suggest. An escalating fear that their own families could be next permeates many immigrant communities across the country. Fear radiates from publicized events, like the wholesale workplace roundups that spurred public outcry, legal resistance, and recently a quiet moratorium. But just under the public radar is a much more pervasive crackdown that has not let up under Obama—in predawn home raids, traffic stops, and local sweeps that make it dangerous for members of millions of families just to drive to work, take a train, or go to sleep.[12] It can be risky, for example, simply to live in an immigrant neighborhood in a house or apartment where a previous tenant may have had an old deportation order. Immigration agents may show up at the door with a photograph of someone who hasn't lived there for years, roust people from bed to demand papers, and take away in handcuffs anyone who cannot produce the right documents. In the aftermath of such raids, relatives, employers, even lawyers have to struggle to find out where those detained are being held.

In a case I encountered myself in 2007, no one could locate Marvin

Lopez, a twenty-one-year-old seized in a dawn raid at his home on Long Island that fall, despite calls to the authorities from the *New York Times;* from his employer, Eberhard Mueller, a farmer who was the former chef of the restaurant Lutece; and from the immigration lawyer hired to find Lopez. He was a Salvadoran with no criminal record, a packer of baby vegetables and rosemary for delivery to some of the best restaurants in Manhattan. When Lopez finally surfaced two weeks later, it turned out he had been sent in shackles from a maximum security prison in Brooklyn to a detention center in Rhode Island and then to a New Jersey jail, with no chance even to call his family. To its credit, the Obama administration recently introduced a computerized locator system that is supposed to help relatives track such detainees. But it has many blind spots, including all the county jails in New Jersey where New York detainees typically are first held, and all detainees in transit, though multiple transfers among distant detention centers have become the norm.

Again and again I've found that Americans and Western Europeans who learn about this system one-on-one, through the detention of a neighbor or an employee, tend to be astounded and outraged. There is still no widespread understanding that the familiar rules of due process do not apply. Though immigration detainees are locked up in jails and prisons, often side by side with people charged or convicted of violent crimes, legally their incarceration is not considered a deprivation of liberty, let alone a punishment. Based on a line of U.S. Supreme Court decisions rooted in the nineteenth-century Chinese exclusion laws, immigration detention is considered an administrative, civil measure taken solely for the purpose of deportation. The confusion has been compounded by the growing criminalization of immigration violations without a meaningful increase in due process. The most notorious example is the filing of tough criminal charges of identity fraud against hundreds of migrants rounded up in the meatpacking plant raid in Postville, Iowa, in May 2008, followed by wholesale guilty pleas and fast-track sentencing in temporary courtrooms on a cattle fairground. Many more such migration-related criminal prosecutions take place outside the spotlight, and as the Transactional Records Access Clearing House (TRAC) at Syracuse University has documented, the explosion of such federal prosecutions has continued under the Obama administration.[13]

Legally, the result is the worst of both worlds, such law scholars as Jennifer Chacón contend. She warns that "the protective features of criminal investigation and adjudication are melting away at the edges" in such criminal cases, even as civil immigration enforcement imports the priorities and more punitive methods of criminal law but explicitly rejects its procedural protections.[14] At Immigration and Customs Enforcement officials have said that the escalation of detention and deportation are simply restoring integrity to the nation's existing immigration laws. Supporters of the crackdown have welcomed the fear it generates and say it is a crucial step toward the "self-deportation" of twelve million illegal residents. It is a mistake to underestimate or oversimplify the anger and moral panic that many Americans feel over illegal immigration. Yet when confronted with individual human consequences, I have found, many also seem to have second thoughts.

. . .

The *Times,* whose editors mostly live in New York—a gateway city visibly rescued from decay a couple of decades ago in large part by a diverse immigrant influx—was perhaps slow to get the backlash in places where immigration was more recent, less familiar, and almost entirely Spanish-speaking. But after reading *Nation by Design: Immigration Policy in the Fashioning of America,* a masterful book by the political science professor Aristide Zolberg, I set out to find a protagonist for a more nuanced, empathetic picture of resistance to the new immigration close to home.[15] In the spring of 2006, I spent several weeks reporting in Elmont, New York, a working-class Long Island suburb, where my guide was Patrick Nicolosi, a third-generation union man and former Wonder Bread truck driver who had retired in his forties after a back injury. To my eyes, the streets of Elmont still had the look of the 1950s, with single-family homes sitting side by side, their lawns weed-whacked into submission to the same suburban dream that Nicolosi's Italian-American parents had embraced forty years before. But what Nicolosi saw was America unraveling. As I wrote in a front-page article in the *New York Times* in 2006:

> When a school bus stops at the white Cape Cod opposite his house, two children seem to pop up from beneath the earth. Emerging from an illegal basement apartment that successive homeowners have rented to a Mexican family of illegal immigrants, they head off to another day of public schooling at taxpayer expense.
>
> This is a neighborhood in the twilight zone of illegal immigration, and wherever Mr. Nicolosi looks, the hidden costs of cheap labor hit home.
>
> There is the gas station a dozen blocks away where more than 100 immigrant day laborers gather, leaving garbage and distress along a residential

side street—and undercutting wages for miles, contends Mr. Nicolosi, 49, a third-generation union man and former Wonder Bread truck driver who retired after a back injury. There are the schools and hospitals filled with children from illegal apartments like the basement dwelling, which Mr. Nicolosi calls "a little dungeon, windowless."

"Two children are in school, and one is handicapped—that's $10,000 for elementary school, $100,000 a year for special education," he said. "Why am I paying taxes to support that house?"[16]

At the time, members of Congress, pressed by the Bush administration to produce a comprehensive immigration bill, were going home to their districts across the country and finding rising anger over immigration policy. The story of one man's frustration over a family in a basement was a way for me to explore that anger. And it was the economics of class, not the politics of culture or race, I found, that fired Nicolosi's resentment of what he saw in Elmont, which is as diverse a suburb as any in the United States. In the decades since Nicolosi's father, a bus driver, had moved his family there from the city, families from every continent had joined the Italian and Central European generations who settled the first subdivisions. Its population of thirty-three thousand was then roughly 46 percent white, 35 percent black, 9 percent Asian, and 14 percent Hispanic.

But like many working-class Americans who live close to illegal immigrants, Nicolosi worried that they were yet another force undermining the way of life and the social contract that generations of workers had strived so hard to achieve. "The rich, they're totally oblivious to this situation—what the illegal immigration, the illegal housing, the day labor is doing to us," he told me. "Everyone's exploiting these people—the landlords, the contractors. And now we can't afford to pay taxes. People like me who want to live the suburban dream, we're being pushed out unless we join the illegality." In the previous four years, Elmont had raised school taxes by 57 percent and added forty elementary school classrooms—partly filled, district officials agreed, by families in illegal rentals, both immigrant and native-born.

As a self-appointed watchdog, Nicolosi had tried to get local officials to investigate houses that he and his allies suspected of violations and to crack down on day laborers spilling into front yards. The house across the street was among hundreds that he and his associates had reported to officials since 2002, based on anonymous complaints collected by a local weekly. They checked the addresses for telltale signs like multiple electric meters—with no regard, he insisted, to the occupants' ethnicity or citizenship. As the immigration debate ignited nationally, the results of Nicolosi's crusade unfolded like a parable about being careful what you wish for. In the end the Mexican family was uprooted, his neighbors were unhappy, and Nicolosi was left more frustrated than ever. For me, as a journalist, the story seemed richly emblematic of the nation's immigration dilemma. It also marked a new realization of the increasing risks my presence and my questions brought to families like the one in the basement on Lucille Avenue.

The place was not, by the way, a dungeon. As the thirty-year-old mother, Ariana, told me: "If that were the case, we would have moved a long time ago." I got a glimpse of its two-bedroom finished interior enough to see that she and her husband, Placido, a mason, had made it homey for their three children: a boy of ten, a developmentally disabled girl of about six, and a year-old baby—the last two born in the United States. In Guanajuato, Mexico, Placido's best option had been a job at General Motors that at the time paid ten dollars a day. Like everyone, he said, "we came for a better life for our children." They asked that their last name be withheld from the article for fear of immigration authorities. The family was aware of past housing-code citations generated by Nicolosi's complaints. But nothing had come of those, so when I first spoke with them, they were not too worried.

As the national debate flared on television, so did Nicolosi's frustration. The neighborhood's clipped front lawns? Mowed by underpaid Latino workers. The tidy homes? Contractors hired immigrants off the books to repair roofs and replace pipes, Nicolosi said, instead of training, and decently compensating, someone like the twenty-year-old American up the block who needed a job. "They're telling us Americans don't want to do these jobs," he said. "That's a lie. The business owners don't want to pay. I know what my grandparents fought for: fair wages and days off. Now we're doing it in reverse." Connecting many dots, Nicolosi pointed to American companies in Mexico that paid wages too low to keep Mexicans from streaming north to sell their labor on American streets. He angrily denied bigotry and avowed pity for the immigrants, squeezed by low wages and high rents. "They will never, ever better themselves," he said of the Mexican family.

From the basement, what struck the Mexican couple was that Nicolosi himself did not work. "The man has nothing to do except look," the wife said in Spanish a few weeks after my first visit. Recalling the Latino workers she saw renovating his house, she added, "If we weren't here, who would do the work?"

"We all consume," Placido argued, with a gesture that took in the dining table, the television, and a picture of the Last Supper. "I'm paying the rent, so I'm paying the homeowner's taxes."

Yet upstairs that very day, their landlords, a young couple with a baby and a construction business, were deciding to evict the family. An official had called, alerting them to a new complaint by Nicolosi. This time, with heightened public attention—the *Times*'s attention—it would lead to hefty fines unless the basement was vacated. On the first Saturday in June, the Mexican family moved out. Even a neighbor who favored an electrified fence at the Mexican border said Nicolosi had no conscience. She worried about the children's schooling and wondered where they could go. Probably, she said, to another basement apartment. "For every solution," she said, "there's another problem."

Like the five people evicted from the basement apartment, about 8.8 million people in the United States are in families that include parents who are illegal immigrants and children who are American citizens, according to a recent report by the Pew Hispanic Center. The two younger children in Ariana and Placido's family are among about four million U.S. citizens who are children growing up in such households. More than 1.5 million children, like the older son, who must now be fourteen, lack legal status themselves. And that doesn't even count those who have already aged out of this calculus. Having been brought here as children, they have come of age as outlaws.

For years now, fear and uncertainty have cast a long shadow over this generation. Neither journalists nor social science researchers have done a particularly good job of tracking the impact of that shadow. In 1982 the Supreme Court held, five to four, that illegal immigrant children have a Constitutional right to free public education through twelfth grade under the Fourteenth Amendment. Only nine states, however, offer in-state college tuition for state high school graduates without legal status—that is, let them pay the same college tuition fees as legal residents and U.S. citizens in the state. About one-third of children of illegal immigrants live in poverty, nearly double the 18 percent poverty rate for children of U.S. citizens, the Pew report found. Yet researchers, like teachers and principals, generally have adopted a "don't ask" approach to immigration status.

My own reporting on the crackdown leads me to wonder whether the "don't ask" policy of schools and researchers, however necessary to protect the most vulnerable students and families, may in some ways lead to overstating the assimilation difficulties of recent Hispanic immigrants, even as it obscures the worsening problems of a generation without legal status, the consequences of growing up with parents at risk of deportation, and the broader impact on schools and communities of young people all but barred from college and career.[17] The work of scholars has been valuable in showing how counterintuitive and nuanced overall differences in student outcome can be. Some immigrant students thrive because they have *not* Americanized; some assimilate downward, caught in an undertow of race, class, and low expectations. "Princeton or prison" is the way that dichotomy has been drawn at its most extreme. A more complicated picture is offered by the Suárez-Orozcos, who studied four hundred immigrant children from Haiti, China, Central America, Mexico, and the Dominican Republic between 1997 and 2002, ages nine to fourteen when they arrived. The study identified different academic trajectories and tried to unpack the factors in school, home, and community that influenced one set of children to improve dramatically over time, another set to drop precipitously, while separate groups started out as high achievers and stayed high or began as low achievers and only lost ground.[18]

But the factors considered did not include immigration status. Why not? I asked Carola Suárez-Orozco and others involved in such research. Two main facts emerged in their replies. First, it was too hard to ask questions about legal status—institutional review boards would not approve them, or study participants would drop out. Second, the researchers had been able to find out anyway. Suárez-Orozco said that an unpublished case study analysis of seventy-five cases found illegal status had "a tremendous effect" on educational performance. "For low achievers and the precipitous decliners," she said, "where you saw them drop down, that's when they all of a sudden realized it's not going to make any difference." Researchers in a Los Angeles study found the same.[19]

Studies on achievement by the sociologist Vivian Louie (see her chapter in this volume) tease out the importance of parental engagement in their children's schools. Yet parents without papers are increasingly afraid to engage in the public sphere at all, as I witnessed during intensive reporting in 2008 in Central Falls, Rhode Island, a small, impoverished, heavily Latino city of nineteen thousand. Fear became palpable after the state governor ordered a crackdown on illegal immigrants, and a publicized raid swept up immigrant cleaning crews at state courthouses. Even at a progressive, highly successful public charter school where an atmosphere of trust and parental involvement had been fostered for years, some parents stopped attending school meetings altogether, the principal told me. Moreover, administrators there and at other public schools changed their minds about helping me in reporting that could have drawn political attention to the fallout for the children.

The eight-year-old daughter of a mechanic who had been one of the charter school's high-scoring pupils had stopped eating and speaking in school after her father disappeared into the detention system. This child and her mother, a U.S. citizen, were almost evicted from their apartment because the mother had fallen behind in the rent without her husband's wages. Yet a top education official who had been open about such adverse effects of the crackdown on the town's pupils now begged me not to write about the issue. She believed in the national importance of such articles, she said, but she was afraid that any publicity would bring raids by immigration agents to Central Falls. In good conscience, she said, she could not bear to be a conduit for bringing more fear and pain to her schools' families.[20]

These days, when some university publicists send out daily lists of faculty experts prepared to comment on breaking news, the different time frame in which academics and journalists do their best work may have blurred. But our jobs really are not the same. Scholarship is not supposed to be "of the moment." It is supposed to endure, to build on past scholarship, or to respectfully challenge it. Newspaper journalism, on the other hand, must almost by definition be about the new, or seem to be. Its influence sometimes is immediate and powerful, and it can have terrible unintended consequences, but its half-life is notoriously short. Scholarship's influence is more likely to last or to emerge in unintended ways years later, like Schuck's modulated critiques of birthright citizenship in the 1980s and 1990s, which now give legitimacy to extremist political movements seeking to strip citizenship from millions of children born and raised in the United States.[21]

At their best, journalists and academics complement each other. But our professional adjectives betray a certain tradition of disdain. To call a scholar's work "journalistic" is to insult it, to deem it superficial, shallow, and unscholarly. To call a piece of newspaper writing "academic" is to label it dull, self-important, or thick with unnecessary jargon. Yet a quote from the right professor and findings from the right academic study are often crucial ingredients in turning a compelling anecdote into an illuminating front-page story. To be quoted in the *New York Times* or the *Wall Street Journal* surely raises the profile of an academic seeking to enlighten the public—or competing for the next research grant. More important, dispatches from the front line can inform scholarship, and scholarship can help reporters see and tell what we might otherwise miss on the ground.

The problem for a reporter these days (aside from the fact that our industry is in free fall) is that fear makes it harder than ever to get people on the ground to speak at all about what is happening in immigrant families, schools, and neighborhoods. And as we try to work around the problem, the ground keeps shifting. Consider the *Providence Journal*'s commonplace newspaper feature on the first baby born in Rhode Island in 2008, with a smiling photo of her Guatemalan immigrant father and U.S.-citizen mother from Puerto Rico. Before the mother came home from the hospital with the baby (her third child), ICE agents—spurred by the article—had raided the couple's apartment and taken the father away on immigration violations, for detention and eventual deportation. Later the same day, the baby's mother and grandmother came home and found that a roommate, also an illegal immigrant from Guatemala, had hanged himself behind his locked bedroom door, seemingly in panic during the raid.

In this climate, even sympathetic coverage can draw the unwanted attention of immigration authorities who wield almost unchecked power to detain. Even no-name quotes can bring retaliation from local citizens who blame Spanish-speaking immigrants for crowded schools and hard-pressed emergency rooms, for high property taxes, budget deficits, and rising unemployment. Even the most careful, balanced coverage seems to inflame anti-immigrant rhetoric on the airwaves and the Internet and to promote the rise of local politicians who take a hard line against illegal immigration where it counts the most—in traffic stops, housing inspections, and behind-the-scenes partnerships with federal immigration agents.

In this context, how can we talk about the assimilation of the second generation without foregrounding the problem of legal status? How does a citizen child integrate into a society that rejects his mother, father, brother, or sister? How do adolescents fulfill their potential when they—or other students who create their high school's culture—are barred by law from the opportunities their teachers keep touting: college, career, social mobility? Or any mobility, since driver's licenses are now out of reach without the right visa. Are we, in effect, creating an American caste system here, one that challenges the nation's concepts of civil rights? That is the way I originally posed the question. But recently, reading an essay by Linda Kerber, a historian at the University of Iowa, I began to think that creating de facto statelessness might be a more apt description. Kerber, who also touches on the deeper history of statelessness in the United States, notes that the United Nations High Commissioner for Refugees (UNHCR) has recently expanded the definition of statelessness to include "the unprotected" and speaks of "effective nationality" and "ineffective nationality."

"In the United States now," Kerber writes, "perhaps the most chilling signal that re-conceptualization is possible is the presence of a vigorous political attack on the Fourteenth Amendment's guarantee of birthright citizenship, an attack that destabilizes one of the strongest founding principles of American identity and makes highly likely the increase of statelessness."[22] Kerber's essay is one of several in a book edited by Seyla Benhabib and Judith Resnik, *Migrations and Mobilities: Citizenship, Borders, and Gender,* that crystallized my journalistic experience with families caught at the crossroads—wanted as workers but unwelcome as citizens. We might not eliminate or cut back birthright citizenship, as Ireland did not very long ago, but already U.S. citizenship means less for some children than for others, as the human rights scholar and lawyer Jacqueline Bhabha points out in the same book, in her essay "The 'Mere Fortuity of Birth?' Mothers, Borders, and the Meaning of Citizenship."

> Arguably the most significant citizen-specific entitlement today is the guarantee of nondeportability, irrespective of criminal offenses. Even treason cannot lead to deportation of a citizen. And yet . . . if a young child's parents are forced to leave the country, so in effect is the child. This is an extremely severe sanction inflicted on an innocent party, a vivid illustration of the invisibility of the child's perspective. For what could be more devastating for a child than the loss of a parent or a home?[23]

In recent years the silence meant to protect unauthorized immigrants converged with the open hostility of programs like CNN's *Lou Dobbs* and Fox News, blurring the difference between immigrants with and without proper papers even as that difference became more crucial. The DREAM Act, legislation tailored to the most appealing members of the young outlaw generation, has languished year after year, perhaps because so many citizens are increasingly anxious about the downward mobility of their own children. There are still, of course, extraordinary cases of young people who work two and three jobs, illegally, to pay their way through public college without any financial aid, for which they are ineligible. But what then? How do you use your degree to get a job when you lack a real Social Security number? The assumption has been that a path to legalization would eventually emerge, either wholesale or case by case. But in 2008 an appeals court in California declared the in-state tuition law unconstitutional; the case is under review by the California Supreme Court. State budget crises and the politics of high unemployment make the repeal of in-state tuition programs likelier in the short term than the passage of a national DREAM Act. Meanwhile, the cognitive dissonance of enforcement continues.

While the government is deciding whether to deport the adults, the children, legal or not, are learning lessons about America. These are not the lessons taught in civics classes. Rather, they hark back to dark episodes in American history. As Kerber points out, the concept of the stateless as the citizen's "other" is deeply embedded in our national history. Quoting the American legal scholar Christopher Tomlins, she writes that slaves were "the living dead of the United States Constitution," central to the economy of the new republic, "and their absence from its protections central to the agreement—the three-fifths compromise—that made the federal constitution possible."[24] The 1882 Chinese Exclusion Act and the quotas of 1929 continued what Dauvergne, the professor in British Columbia, calls the long, "dichotomous relationship in which the liberal discourses of equality and inclusion are left to citizenship law while immigration law performs the dirty work of inequity and exclusion."[25]

In *Deportation Nation: Outsiders in American History,* Daniel Kanstroom, a law professor who also directs human rights programs, shows that deportation law shifted in the early twentieth century from border control to social control, dropping the statutes of limitation that had made amnesty routine earlier in our history and seeking to send away those deemed not to be "true" Americans. "The formalistic exclusion of deportable noncitizens from our rich traditions of constitutional discourse also risks the creation of a caste from a 'discrete and insular minority,'" Kanstroom warns. "It facilitates irrational discrimination against the noncitizens who live, work, pay taxes, raise children and participate in communities alongside citizens every day. And practices that take root against noncitizens may provide models for actions against citizens."[26]

In 1931, during the Great Depression, the fear tactic now embraced by some as a deterrent to illegal immigration was called "scare heading." It worked to send millions of Mexicans and Mexican-Americans, including citizen children, back across the border. In 2006, I wrote a *Week in Review* piece about this recurrent pattern of deliberately leaving the back door open for Mexican workers and later expelling them out the front door, a feature of U.S. immigration policy since 1890. "The basic dynamics do not change," Aristide Zolberg told me. "Wanting immigrants because they're a good source of cheap labor and human capital on the one hand, and then posing the identity question: But will they become Americans? Where is the boundary of American identity going to be?"[27]

. . .

Over the last three years much of my reporting energy has been absorbed not by the outlaw generation, but in the investigation of deaths and substandard care in immigration detention.[28] And as I read Kerber's discussion of Hannah Arendt's writings about statelessness, I realized why these cases of death in detention compel me so. Hannah Arendt, who was stateless herself for a decade, wrote of the inalienable rights that proved to be unenforceable, of those who had lost the right to have rights. Perhaps as journalists and academics focused on border-crossers, we can agree that the ultimate human boundary is between the living and the dead. The sign and obligation of our common humanity across that final border is that the living count and name the dead. As law and practice in the United States erases the rights of some residents to have rights, and as the common parlance of television and Internet sites dehumanizes millions as "illegals" and "criminal aliens," perhaps nothing more clearly points to the danger of statelessness than the uncounted, unnamed dead in immigration custody.

The *New York Times,* which may be destined to be remembered someday as the last, best embodiment of independent journalism in the service of democracy, sometimes lets me feel like a catalyst of change, if only case by case. On its front pages in 2008 and 2009, I managed to rescue two detention casualties, Boubacar Bah and Tanveer Ahmad, not from death, of course, but from oblivion.[29] And back in 2004, when a headline in the *New York Times* perhaps had more clout, a happy Virginia Feliz got her mother back in time for Christmas.[30]

NOTES

1. Nina Bernstein, "A Mother Deported, and a Child Left Behind," *New York Times,* November 24, 2004. Unless otherwise attributed in these notes, the quotes throughout this chapter are from this *New York Times* article by Bernstein.

2. Nina Bernstein, *The Lost Children of Wilder: The Epic Struggle to Change Foster Care* (New York: Pantheon, 2001).

3. See Carola Suárez-Orozco, Marcelo M. Suárez-Orozco, and Irina Todorova, *Learning a New Land: Immigrant Students in American Society* (Cambridge: Belknap Press of Harvard University Press, 2008), 56–70.

4. A 2010 study by the University of California law school on the impact of deportation of lawful permanent resident parents is the kind of research that I was seeking but that did not exist at the time (see http://www.law.berkeley.edu/6838.htm).

5. This article and most of the others I wrote as a Metro immigration reporter (see http://topics.nytimes.com/topics/reference/timestopics/people/b/nina_bernstein/index.html?scp=1-spot&sq=%22Nina%20Bernstein%22&st=cse) were not included in Suro's count of *New York Times* coverage, which was limited to articles originating in Washington, D.C., and the national bureaus. While accepting Suro's larger points about episodic coverage that emphasized illegal immigration, and the "operatic" influence of cable shows like that of Lou Dobbs, I would argue that it is precisely in local, culture, and lifestyle sections of major newspapers, which the surveys omitted, that Suro would find immigrants treated as part of the social fabric. In those sections, too, readers are more likely to catch a story that "oozes" rather than breaks.

6. U.S. Department of Justice, Office of the Inspector General, "The September 11 Detainees: A Review of the Treatment of Aliens Held on Immigration Charges in Connection with the Investigation of the September 11 Attacks," June 2003, and supplemental report, December 2003. Nearly all of the detainees were eventually cleared of ties to terrorism and deported.

7. Record deportation numbers—392,862 in fiscal year 2010—were assailed by immigrant advocates without ever being accepted as genuine by restrictionists. It seems both administrations cut corners to inflate their enforcement numbers without any legislative payoff. See Andrew Becker, "Unusual Methods Helped ICE Break Deportation Record," *Washington Post,* December 6, 2010 (www.washingtonpost.com/wp-dyn/content/article/2010/12/05/AR2010120503230.html).

8. Dora Schriro, "Immigration Detention Overview and Recommendations," *New York Times,* October 6, 2009; see Nina Bernstein, "Report Critical of Scope of Immigration Detention," *New York Times,* October 6, 2009 (www.nytimes.com/2009/10/07/us/politics/07detain.html).

9. John T. Morton, director of Immigration and Customs Enforcement, as quoted in Nina Bernstein, "U.S. to Reform Policy on Detention for Immigrants," *New York Times,* August 5, 2009.

10. See Julia Preston, "Immigration Vote Leaves Obama's Immigration Policy in Disarray," *New York Times,* December 18, 2010 (www.nytimes.com/2010/12/19/us/politics/19dream.html?ref=juliapreston).

11. Dauvergne's essay is "Globalizing Fragmentation: New Pressures on Women in the Immigration Law-Citizenship Dichotomy," in *Migrations and Mobilities: Citizenship, Borders and Gender,* edited by Seyla Benhabib and Judith Resnik (New York: New York University Press 2009), 349.

12. See Nina Bernstein, "Border Sweeps in North Reach Miles into U.S.," *New York Times*, August 29, 2010.

13. See "FY 2009 Federal Prosecutions Sharply Higher: Surge Driven by Steep Jump in Immigration Filings," *TRAC Reports*, December 21, 2009 (http://trac.syr.edu/tracreports/crim/223/).

14. Jennifer M. Chacón, "Managing Migration through Crime," *Columbia Law Review*, December 12, 2009.

15. Aristide Zolberg, *Nation by Design: Immigration Policy in the Fashioning of America* (Cambridge: Harvard University Press, 2006).

16. Patrick Nicolosi as quoted in Nina Bernstein, "On Lucille Avenue, the Immigration Debate," *New York Times*, June 26, 2006.

17. Research on the assimilation of the children of immigrants rarely distinguishes between families with legal immigration status and those without. Such differences are obscured, for example, in national educational statistics that showed a 22 percent dropout rate among Hispanics in 2005 and 2006, much higher than among blacks (10 to 10.7 percent), whites (6 to 5.8 percent), or Asians/Pacific Islanders (3 to 3.6 percent) (see U.S. Department of Education, National Center for Education Statistics 2010, "The Condition of Education 2010 [NCES 2010-028], Indicator 20"). One can only guess that it underestimated the graduation rates of Latino students from legal immigrant families. By the same token, no one would dispute the importance of parental income as a factor in educational outcomes; yet we know that many parents stuck in poverty cannot command better wages and working conditions because they are unauthorized immigrants.

18. Carola Suárez-Orozco, Marcelo M. Suárez-Orozco, and Irina Todorova, *Learning a New Land: Immigrant Students in American Society* (Cambridge: Belknap Press of Harvard University Press, 2008)

19. See Rubén G. Rumbaut, Frank D. Bean, Leo Chávez, Jennifer Lee, Susan K. Brown, and Louis DeSipio, "Immigration and Intergenerational Mobility in Metropolitan Los Angeles," Russell Sage Foundation (www.russellsage.org/research/Immigration/IIMMLA).

20. The resulting article is Nina Bernstein, "City of Immigrants Fills Jail Cells with Its Own," *New York Times*, December 27, 2008.

21. Perhaps it is not so unintended after all. In an op-ed piece in the *New York Times*, when the campaign against birthright citizenship had erupted in the Republican mainstream, Schuck embraced the cause, using the language of moderation and compromise to advance a change so radical that it would create whole new categories of stateless children born in America and a new bureaucracy responsible for judging them for possible citizenship as ten-year-olds. See Peter H. Schuck, "Birthright of a Nation," *New York Times*, August 14, 2010 (www.nytimes.com/2010/08/14/opinion/14schuck.html).

22. Linda Kerber, "The Stateless as the Citizen's Other: A View from the United States," in Benhabib and Resnik, *Migrations and Mobilities*, 76–126, 86.

23. Jacqueline Bhabha, "The 'Mere Fortuity of Birth?' Mothers, Borders, and the Meaning of Citizenship," in Benhabib and Resnik, *Migrations and Mobilities*, 187–227, 192.

24. Kerber, "Stateless as the Citizen's Other," 90–91.

25. Dauvergne, "Globalizing Fragmentation: New Fragmentation."

26. Daniel Kanstroom, *Deportation Nation: Outsiders in American History* (Cambridge: Harvard University Press, 2007), 18.

27. Aristide Zolberg as quoted in Nina Bernstein, "A Hundred Years in the Back Door, out the Front," *New York Times,* May 21, 2006.

28. For an overview, see "In-Custody Deaths (Immigration Detention)," *New York Times,* http://topics.nytimes.com/top/reference/timestopics/subjects/i/immigration_detention_us/incustody_deaths/index.html?scp=1-spot&sq=in-custody%20death&st=cse.

29. Nina Bernstein, "Few Details on Immigrants Who Died in Custody," *New York Times,* May 6, 2008. Bernstein, "Immigrant Detainee Dies and a Life Is Buried Too," *New York Times,* April 2, 2009. Bernstein, "Piecing Together an Immigrant's Life the U.S. Refused to See," *New York Times,* July 5, 2009. Boubacar Bah was a fifty-two-year-old Guinean tailor who died after suffering a skull fracture at a privately run detention center in Elizabeth, New Jersey; he had been left in an isolation cell without treatment for more than thirteen hours. Officials rebuffed inquiries about his case when he was comatose, but secretly discussed sending him to Guinea to avoid the cost of his care and media exposure. Tanveer Ahmad, a forty-three-year-old Pakistani, was a longtime New York cabby who had overstayed a visa. In the New Jersey immigration jail where he was held, a fellow detainee wrote a letter complaining that Ahmad's symptoms of a heart attack had gone untreated until too late. The difficulty of confirming his very existence showed that deaths could fall between the cracks in immigration detention. See Bernstein, "Officials Hid Truth of Immigrant Deaths in Jail," *New York Times,* January 9, 2010, and Bernstein and Rob Harris, video, "What Really Happened to Boubacar Bah?" (http://video.nytimes.com/video/2010/01/09/nyregion/1247466467222/what-really-happened-to-boubacar-bah.html?ref=incustodydeaths).

30. Nina Bernstein, "Deported Mother Gains Permission to Return," *New York Times*, December 9, 2004.

2

The Integrated Regime of Immigration Regulation

CRISTINA M. RODRÍGUEZ

State and local laws designed to address immigrants and immigration have proliferated in recent years,[1] and many of these measures have inspired considerable media scrutiny. In most of their assessments of this trend, commentators have juxtaposed a description of the local activity with either a causal account stressing the federal government's failure to enact comprehensive immigration reform, or with a quasi-normative statement that states have stumbled into the federal government's jurisdiction by adopting measures designed to control immigrant movement. This assumption of federal exclusivity—that immigration ought to be handled solely by the federal government through uniform policy—shapes both the legal doctrine and political debates governing immigration regulation. The presumption of exclusivity therefore dominates inquiries into the validity or desirability of state and local activity in the area. But as a device for evaluating the strategies political actors have adopted to address immigration and the change it provokes, the exclusivity assumption obfuscates more than it illuminates.

As a general matter, state and local immigration measures should not be regarded as presumptive usurpations, but rather as expressions of the profound interests state and local governments and their constituents have in how public and private institutions manage immigration and integration. To be sure, state and local laws that conflict with federal law are invalid, or preempted, and therefore unconstitutional. But, as the Supreme Court itself has made clear, not every subfederal regulation that touches on the subject of immigration creates the sort of conflict that runs afoul of the Constitution's Supremacy Clause.[2] More important, failing to move beyond the exclusivity premise prevents us from discerning what motivates state and local immigration activity. The failure to grapple with these motivations, in turn, prevents us from addressing the economic and sociocultural challenges presented by immigration with the broadest institutional options available.

This chapter provides a conceptual framework for moving beyond the conventional zero-sum formulation of the federal-state-local dynamic in immigration regulation. I accept the integration of the three tiers of government as a given, while acknowledging that points of conflict must be resolved, either through federal supremacy or the recognition of state autonomy. I also emphasize the possibilities for intergovernmental cooperation that simultaneously advances federal and local interests. Though such cooperation may itself give rise to tensions, as federal and local priorities diverge, some variation is inevitable in a federal regime and therefore should be negotiated rather than papered over.

I begin by considering a crucial and underreported dimension of the state and local phenomenon—the sheer diversity of immigration-related measures considered in the fifty states and in numerous localities. This diversity underscores a singularly important point—that when it comes to the subject of immigration, the public does not speak with one voice. Demands for uniformity in regulation therefore belie the complexity of the issue. That diversity exists does not of course obviate the need to build consensus, nor does it justify unconstitutional laws, or moot the pursuit of uniformity where uniformity is genuinely necessary to promote efficient regulation. Instead, the presence of such diversity should prompt the federal government to respond actively to state and local interests and encourage lawmakers more generally to consider seriously the different forms that federal-state-local cooperation might take.

REGULATORY DIVERSITY

State and local participation in immigration regulation hardly represents a new phenomenon, nor is it likely to disappear from the regulatory landscape if and when Congress acts to reform the system, even if it diminishes in intensity. In the 1970s and 1980s, for example, state legislatures sought to limit immigrant access to various social benefits and institutions, including the public schools.[3] By 1986 as many as twelve states had passed laws sanctioning employers who hired those unauthorized to work in the United States—laws Congress preempted when it enacted the federal employers sanctions regime that year. In the 1990s the federal-local dynamic framed the immigration debate even more poignantly. California voters passed Proposition 187, which would have denied unauthorized immigrants access to a broad range of state services, again including public schooling. New York City defended and revised its sanctuary policy, which restrained police and other civil servants from inquiring into and reporting on the immigration status of those with whom they came into contact. Congress sought simultaneously to curtail and expand state authority—by preempting certain sanctuary policies and limiting certain benefits extensions on the one hand and authorizing the devolution of policing powers and benefits-granting authority to local officials on the other.[4]

To frame recent trends as novel, then, mischaracterizes the political economy of immigration regulation. The federal-local dialogue represents a perennial and even necessary feature of the system, with states signaling their concerns and disagreements to Congress, and Congress responding, through both legislative action and inaction. The recent profusion of state and local legislation therefore simply provides a new opportunity to reassess the federalism dynamic. Rather than dismissing this subfederal activity as ultra vires, we ought to take it seriously, as a valuable window into the American public's views on the immigration issue—a view far more complete and complex than one based on the failure of comprehensive immigration reform in Congress and public opinion polls taken during congressional debates.

Commentators in the public sphere have succeeded in reporting on the sheer number of state and local measures considered in recent years. In 2007 alone, state legislatures considered more than a thousand laws regulating immigrants in some way, and activity in 2006 and 2008 reached similar levels.[5] The lion's share of media analysis of this trend has focused on those laws that purport to crack down on illegal immigration (see Roberto Suro's introduction in this volume) either by sanctioning private actors, such as employers and landlords, or by empowering public law enforcement officials to engage in immigration-related policing, sometimes with federal authorization and sometimes without. These stories tend to provide colorful local officials as dramatis personae. Mayor Lou Barletta of Hazleton, Pennsylvania, and Sheriff Joe Arpaio of Maricopa County, Arizona, have claimed to be "standing up" to the federal government but with rhetoric easily categorized as anti-immigrant, much as the Proposition 187 debate in the 1990s served up a contentious political fight with easy politician villains (or heroes) and exasperated voters.

The media's overwhelming focus on laws that address illegal immigration makes a great deal of sense. The presence of high numbers of unauthorized immigrants—approximately eleven million, even in the face of a deep recession—fuels the intensity of the debate at the state, local, and federal levels. Illegal immigration exacerbates the perception that immigration generally has compromised the rule of law and spiraled out of control, even though the number of illegal entries has dropped substantially and consistently since the mid-2000s. Commentators' focus on enforcement also corresponds to important trends; laws that either punish employers or engage local law enforcement in immigration policing represent the most common measures introduced, debated, and passed of late.[6]

The full scope of the state and local phenomenon has been obscured, however, by this tendency to highlight enforcement-oriented laws and conclude that their profusion is the result of the federal government's failure to reform a "broken" regime, for several reasons. First, some empirical evidence suggests that enforcement-oriented measures, as well as laws that restrict benefits available to immigrants, pass at higher rates in jurisdictions that have experienced the most rapid growth in their immigrant populations.[7] This correlation suggests that subfederal regulation of immigration emerges from public concerns over rapid demographic change as well as confrontation with the unfamiliar[8]— a hypothesis whose implications go underexplored when the response to the state and local laws is to pressure the federal government to act.

More important, though many lawmakers do legislate to abate immigration, others seek to come to terms with changing demographics through laws and institutional reforms designed to protect immigrants from exploitation and integrate immigrants into the communities where they have settled. In many instances, measures in this vein do not distinguish between authorized and unauthorized immigrants, though a number of localities in particular have deliberately extended benefits and protections to the unauthorized. Even some enforcement-based efforts to address illegal immigration recognize the dangers of state and local involvement in this arena and include mechanisms to prevent government abuse. The attorney general of New Jersey, for example, issued an executive order in 2008 that directed police to inquire into the immigration status of persons detained for the commission of certain offenses, but also emphasized that victims and witnesses reporting crimes would not be subject to similar screening—a qualification designed to address the concern that status inquiries by police would chill the reporting of crimes and diminish trust in the police.[9]

The diversity and texture of the state and local phenomenon is revealed by various collections of bills introduced in the state legislatures since 2004, by organizations such as the Migration Policy Institute and the National Council of State Legislatures.[10] In 2006 and 2007 the two most pronounced trends in the protection of immigrants' rights involved prevention of exploitation, regardless of immigration status. To combat fraud and misrepresentation, legislators considered laws prohibiting notary publics from holding themselves out as "*notarios*," which in Spanish connotes legal authority, and requiring immigration service providers to register with the state. Anti-trafficking measures also were debated and enacted into law across the country.[11] Many of these measures not only devote resources to studying the scope of the trafficking problem; they also establish criminal sanctions and extend benefits to victims of trafficking regardless of status, though trafficking laws do simultaneously provide a basis for apprehending unauthorized immigrants.

In addition to these protective law enforcement measures, several state legislatures have at least considered extending in-state tuition benefits at public colleges and universities regardless of immigration status. Approximately eleven states to date have enacted such policies. In some states, such as New York, legislators have sought to remove citizenship as a qualification for licensing in certain trades and professions, such as veterinary medicine and medicine generally. And still other states have chosen to create integration-related task forces—Illinois and New Jersey represent two high-profile examples[12]—designed to make public institutions and benefits more accessible to immigrants, and to devise integration policies that include language education as well as job and citizenship training.

The media have not wholly ignored this dimension of the federalism story and have highlighted particularly prominent nonenforcement initiatives by state and local actors. The decision by the city of New Haven, Connecticut, to create an identification document available to all persons regardless of status received broad coverage. The city designed the identification to enable unauthorized immigrants to open bank accounts and use certain public goods, such as libraries, thus making life easier and more stable for immigrants regardless of status. But the antiexploitation, integrative phenomenon runs much more deeply and broadly than the reporting on such isolated examples suggests and has not been documented with the same degree of detail or level of frequency as enforcement-oriented activity.

Perhaps the most important unrecognized dynamic is not the mere existence of this diversity, but rather the fact that in each of the fifty state legislatures, lawmakers have introduced and debated measures that are both enforcement-oriented and integration-oriented. Within the states themselves, broad diversity of opinion exists and has found open expression in the lawmaking process. Even in states that have become notorious for adopting harsh enforcement laws, such as Arizona and Oklahoma, bills designed to protect immigrants from exploitation have been a part of the legislative agenda. Many of the more extreme enforcement measures have not succeeded in attracting a majority of support in most states. The same is true for many integrative measures, however, and the New Haven example certainly deserves notoriety for its almost unique, affirmative, and formal embrace of unauthorized immigrants as members of the community. This diversity within states mirrors the fact that localities within states also take divergent positions from one another, with some cities choosing, for example, to cooperate with the federal government in immigration policing and others opting to protect unauthorized immigrants from official inquiries into their status.[13]

Ambivalence marks immigration policy within governments as well. Legislators who must respond to public opinion directly tend toward a more punitive direction than administrative officials, whose relative political insulation shifts their focus to pragmatic policies that emphasize public health and safety, which means ensuring that the state's institutions serve all people.[14] In some instances, state legislatures have sought to flatten out this disagreement by adopting laws that prohibit certain local practices. Many legislatures have considered banning localities from adopting sanctuary laws, and California Governor Arnold Schwarzenegger made news when he signed a statute that prohibits localities from adopting Hazleton-type ordinances to prevent landlords from renting to unauthorized immigrants.[15] Whether this state-initiated imposition of uniformity is desirable—I have argued elsewhere that it has costs worth acknowledging[16]—the important point to grasp is that multiple vectors of conflict and multiple points of deliberation exist within the regime that governs immigration.

The fact that these varied local stances on how best to confront immigration reflect genuine and legitimate disagreement does not, of course, justify state and local laws that clearly conflict with federal statutory law or other provisions of the Constitution, such as the due process and equal protection clauses. Where such infirmities exist, local preferences must yield. All government action is subject to rights-based constraints. In addition, the federal government has a profound interest in ensuring compliance and consistency with all of its laws, including immigration laws, though conflict between federal and local interests can be difficult to concretize and should not be presumed every time local law regulates differently from federal law. Litigation challenging both enforcement and integration-oriented measures is, in fact, in various states of completion, based on preemption as well as individual rights claims. Whether the lawsuit challenges the authority of the state of Arizona to direct all police to inquire into the immigration status of those with whom they come into contact, or rescind employers' licenses to do business if they have been found to have hired unauthorized immigrants,[17] or the authority of the state of California to extend the in-state tuition benefit, each case turns on whether the state law interferes with federal objectives and otherwise violates the constitutional interests of affected parties. The individual rights claims, which motivate much of the opposition to state and local legislation, may be difficult to win; the scope of rights protection for unauthorized immigrants has never been clearly defined, and the impact of many local immigration laws on citizens and lawful immigrants is theoretically and anecdotally apparent but difficult to substantiate. But even in the absence of court victories, appreciation of the human costs of state and local legislation must be part of the debate.

Whatever the outcome of this litigation, however, the fact of disagreement makes it crucial from a political perspective to understand what motivates this regulatory activity, not simply to diffuse the assumption that immigration ought to be handled exclusively by the federal government, but also to heighten the federal government's sensitivity to state and local interests. As I have written elsewhere, the states and localities that have passed immigration-related measures in recent years are searching for various types of control over the change immigration prompts. Lawmakers, responding to public pressure, expressly claim to be trying to protect the health, safety, and welfare of their populations, including immigrant populations, and to address the fiscal costs imposed by immigration—whether perceived or real. Much of their activity also reflects a desire for a more elusive sort of control—over the pace of cultural and social change.[18]

That local lawmakers feel compelled to respond to constituents' concerns by actually legislating (as opposed to posturing) ultimately reflects the political salience of the immigration issue. But the intensity of the state and local interest in immigration is also structural in nature. The interest stems largely from the fact that states and localities run the major institutions directly affected by immigration—namely public schools, hospitals, and social service agencies—but have been subjected to federally imposed constraints in managing these institutions. In 1982, in *Plyler v. Doe,* the Supreme Court made clear that the Constitution restrains states from denying unauthorized immigrant children access to the public schools—a decision that has been remarkably resilient, despite the fact that its reasoning has been vigorously criticized and tested by such enactments as Proposition 187. The Supreme Court also has substantially limited state and local actors from denying noncitizens access to publicly funded services in such cases as *Graham v. Richardson.* When Congress amended the welfare laws in 1996 to deny even legal immigrants access to federal public benefits, it still prohibited states from denying even unauthorized immigrants access to emergency medical services, disaster relief, in-kind assistance, and other very basic forms of support.[19] In other words, states and localities are responding to a set of background rules or conditions set by federal institutions themselves, thus underscoring the highly integrated nature of the regulatory regime.

THE LIMITS OF UNIFORMITY

Once the diversity of regulations and interests has been recognized, the question becomes whether and how to assimilate this diversity into some form of détente among the levels of government. The oft-heard appeal to uniformity will not suffice, because it masks deeper concerns about state and local regulation and sidesteps the important task of coming to terms with some form of state and local involvement. The cynical explanation for appeals to uniformity is that they provide a seemingly neutral cover for policy disagreement with the state or local law being critiqued. More charitably, the appeal to uniformity may reflect a national interest in promoting free travel and an integrated market. When different states and localities treat immigrants differently, they effectively exert power to control the movement of people by creating incentives or disincentives for immigrants to remain in a particular location. Not only would such states and localities be imposing externalities of a sort on their neighbors, they might also be interfering with the basic and constitutionally protected right to freedom of movement.[20]

And yet these sorts of effects on internal migration are the inevitable result of a federalist system, where different states naturally adopt different regulatory postures. These differences, in turn, lead to disparate treatment of similar classes of people based on the state in which they find themselves, thus prompting movement across state lines. In some instances federal baselines may be necessary and appropriate, and barriers to entry ought to be struck down accordingly, but those cases must be specified rather than assumed.[21] What is more, diversity extends to the federal system itself; regional actors within the federal government often implement policy directives in distinct ways from one another and in a different manner than the central bureaucracy might, were it in sole control. Uniformity therefore amounts to a false promise.

Perhaps the best explanation for appeals to uniformity is that they stand in for calls for governmental accountability, predictability in policy implementation, and respect for due process of law. Both federal and state laws that permit state and local officials to participate in immigration enforcement,[22] for example, can be critiqued for their failure to ensure a uniform enforcement standard across jurisdictions. In reality, however, the substantive concerns about the program, which revolve around increased risks of racial profiling and sowing distrust in immigrant communities, sound more in the need for accountability and supervision of local actors to prevent the rise of these negative consequences.[23] Similarly, the claim that the landlord ordinances made famous by Hazleton threaten the federal interest in a uniform immigration policy masks the underlying and far more important human rights concern—that the law denies people access to basic housing, perhaps with a disparate impact on Latinos. Demands for rigidly enforced centralization of all immigration law and policy address these substantive concerns only obliquely; each of the concerns may be addressed through federal direction, and in some cases through outright federal prohibition of certain practices, but resolution need not always depend on uniform outcomes across jurisdictions.

The debate over how best to respond to state and local variation would be better served if advocates, litigators, and commentators were more specific when invoking uniformity—what exactly ought to be uniform, and why is uniformity necessary? Again, federal leadership or supervision will often be crucial, particularly when what is at stake is the application of the legal standards for who has the right to enter and reside in the United States—standards that ought to be centrally defined for the sake of coherence and to provide adequate notice to interested parties. But such specific articulations of uniformity's desirability must be accompanied by efforts to structure the federal-state-local relationship in a way that promotes the broader goals of the system.

Even the need for uniformity of standards does not necessarily mean that state and local officials cannot participate effectively in the application of those standards, or that their desire to participate must be eschewed, or even that the federal government can go without state and local support.[24] Indeed, when the federal government does not have a clear agenda in mind, or the capacity to address all of immigrations' implications, we must expect states to act to address their own interests. More to the point, vague calls for federal leadership will not be a panacea because no complete solution is available to challenges such as illegal immigration or even long-term immigrant integration. The transnational dynamics that produce immigration are such that the federal government will never quite be able to fully control illegal immigration, and the issue will rise and fall in salience, rather than disappear. Because no amount of federal action will flatten out the underlying differences in public opinion reflected in the legislative activity described earlier, those differences must be taken into account in policy formation.

FORMS OF COLLABORATION

A complete response to the diversity I have described ultimately demands consideration of how and in what contexts the federal government ought to be attentive to state interests and vice versa. Given the breadth and depth of the subfederal interest in immigration, it may well be that federal immigration policy would benefit from collaboration and coordination with states and localities. The question we should be asking is not how to set up a high wall of separation between the federal and state governments, but rather, when might state involvement advance federal regulatory goals as well as the more general interest in bringing the country to terms with immigration-generated social change?

This sort of collaborative relationship defines the federal-state relationship in countless other regulatory contexts. The academic literature on regulatory federalism has taken a turn toward exploring the nature of the interaction among the levels of government, as an alternative to attempting to delineate separate spheres of activity.[25] Only the hoary reference to federal exclusivity prevents the same from being accepted as true for immigration. As with consumer protection, environmental law, health care, and countless other areas, it is important to imagine ideas and energy flowing in two directions—from the federal governments to states and localities and vice versa—and to consider the possibility of states participating to fill in the federal regulatory regime.[26] The general values ascribed to collaborative forms of federalism—such as resource sharing, leveraging state institutional advantages, taking advantage of state and local expertise concerning local conditions, and diffusing tensions within the public at large by allowing diversity of opinion to be expressed—pertain to the immigration context as much as any other.

We can begin to concretize an integrated, collaborative agenda in a few ways. First, in several areas, federal law governing the scope of state authority is not clear, and the courts that have addressed the explicit reach of federal law have thrown the ball back into Congress's court, giving federal lawmakers the opportunity to clarify their intent (should they want to). The leading example in 2010 of such ambiguity involves the provision of the Immigration Reform and Control Act of 1986 that preempts state employer sanctions laws but permits states to use their licensing authority to regulate—a provision the Supreme Court soon will address. What Congress meant by authorizing reliance on local licensing authority is neither clear on the face of the statute nor in the legislative history, but states such as Arizona have exploited this ambiguity to adopt laws that would deny employers who hire unauthorized workers a license to do business in the state—a potent tool for regulating immigration. By late 2010 two courts of appeals had upheld this sort of state action, one had struck it down, and the Supreme Court had added the case to its docket.[27] The battle that was waged in the California courts about whether a federal statute preempts state authority to make in-state tuition available to unauthorized immigrants who have graduated from a state high school presented a similar opportunity for clarification. The California Supreme Court upheld the in-state tuition law.

Beyond the outcomes of these cases, but particularly if disagreement emerges among courts and among states and localities, Congress might seek to refine its positions. In some instances the federal government might be better off occupying the entire regulatory space; if state licensing sanctions overburden employers or lead to discrimination against Latino job seekers, thus upsetting the balance Congress seeks between policing illegal immigration and promoting economic growth and preventing discrimination, then Congress has the power to reset the federal-state relationship. If the California courts or other courts uphold existing in-state tuition laws, concluding that the federal statute on point does not cover the types of laws the states have adopted, Congress again has the power to act to clarify its position. But with respect to both examples, the preferences expressed by the states through the laws they have adopted represent evidence relevant to Congress's deliberations.[28]

The second way of giving content to a collaborative, integrated conception of the regulatory regime would involve treating the intensity of the immigration debate at the state and local levels as a signal of the need for the federal government to step in with greater federal aid to those jurisdictions whose institutions bear a heavier fiscal burden as the result of high rates of immigration. States such as Texas and California have sought but failed in the past to force this sort of redistribution through litigation, but an honest appreciation of the challenges states face might turn federal resistance into federal support. Indeed, in the new immigration destinations in the Southeast and the Midwest, federal financial and technical assistance is likely to be of heightened importance because of the novelty of the regulatory challenges these states face, including educating large numbers of non-English-speaking school children—a novelty that is contributing to the churning in the legislative process.

A third dimension of an integrated regime would grow from the observation that the diversity of state and local laws sometimes suggests that the federal government should perform a coordinating function rather than a substantive or directive function. This formulation of the federal-local relationship is particularly salient when it comes to devising mechanisms for immigrant integration. The federal government is well positioned to disseminate information regarding best practices and to support innovation but not to serve as the main engine in the formulation of integration policy. The fact that the United States does not have an integration policy is often lamented, but this assumption ignores perhaps the most important insight to emerge from empirical investigations into the state and local phenomenon—that states and localities do the work of integration. The absence of a national integration policy really represents a feature, not a bug, of our federal system.

This feature, far from being dysfunctional, revolves around an important logic. Not only are states and localities more likely to run and/ or interact with the institutions through which integration actually occurs—such as the public schools, local workplaces, and community centers—but, more to the point, different parts of the country also will approach the question of assimilation in different ways and with different resources. Rather than trying to formulate a federal language policy, for example, states and localities ought to be permitted to experiment with how best to provide English-language instruction for children and adults alike. Federal support in the form of grants, or the creation of national networks of service providers, will be crucial. But the integration process is anything but centralized and homogenized in practice, and so integration policy ought to exploit diversity rather than obscure it.

The final dimension of an integrated regime might involve the creation of opportunities for genuine, affirmative cooperation between the federal government and the states, in a manner that mirrors programs such as Medicaid, the State Children's Health Insurance Program (SCHIP), and other cooperative schemes. Various examples of affirmative collaboration have been proposed as well as implemented in the past decade. In the late 1990s, for example, Governor Tom Vilsack of Iowa proposed a scheme that would have involved state agencies in the setting of employment visa levels—a proposal that did not gain traction but that might be worth considering, as other states, such as Colorado and Arizona, have considered adopting guest worker programs of their own. Canadian law provides something of a model along these lines by requiring that the federal government consult with the provinces on immigration matters, as a way of integrating local expertise and preferences into the process of selecting new entrants.[29]

Another much-publicized collaborative program has grown out of a provision enacted by Congress in 1996, authorizing state and local law enforcement to enter into Memoranda of Agreement with federal immigration authorities to enforce federal immigration law. These so-called 287(g) agreements provide for the training and deputization of state and local police to either engage in immigration policing and investigation or to check the immigration status of inmates in their prisons and jails. The state of Florida signed the first 287(g) agreement in 2002, and over seventy agreements have been signed to date, mostly after 2006.

The program arguably provides benefits for federal and local actors alike. It can function as a force multiplier, helping the federal government to advance its enforcement agenda. And it performs a valuable political function for the states by providing them with an opportunity to address a problem seen as serious by their constituents, thus diffusing anxiety about illegal immigration by giving localities the ability to assert control over the immigration issue.

Opposition from immigrants' rights advocates and many police associations has been intense, however, and anecdotal reports of racial profiling and the use of 287(g) authority to arrest and deport immigrants who have committed only minor traffic infractions have been invoked to argue that the program as a whole ought to be scrapped.[30] To the extent that the program has become an entrenched feature of the enforcement landscape, the relevant question becomes whether something inherent in the structure of state and local police departments makes them ill-equipped to perform this function. If so, perhaps structural solutions to potential due process problems can be devised. Instead of worrying about whether it is appropriate to have state and local law enforcement involved in policing at all, lawmakers should work to articulate clear federal and state objectives, and to create structural mechanisms to ensure accountability and adherence to those objectives. In other words, rather than eschew cooperation because of its potential costs, we should be focused on how to improve the mechanisms of cooperation to advance the objectives of the system while protecting individual rights and acknowledging the needs of immigrant communities.

Because of the limited attention paid in public commentary to the diversity of state and local immigration-related practices, the real texture of the immigration debate in the United States has been hidden from view. The sometimes alarmist tone that accompanies discussion of state and local regulation fuels the outmoded principle of federal exclusivity by highlighting immigration as a problem to be solved by the federal government. The issue instead should be framed as part of an ongoing federal-state-local dialogue about how best to respond to immigration and its implications, which include fiscal challenges and tests of social tolerance. These implications underscore that immigration is much like any other regulatory issue, in that subfederal governments have legitimate interests at stake, as well as institutional capacities that can be put to good use, even when federal resolution or control might be desired. As I have written elsewhere, conflict among the levels of government may be inevitable, and even desirable. But the federal government ultimately depends on states and localities to manage aspects of the immigration phenomenon writ large—to assist our society as a whole with the process of adjusting to demographic change—and so we must learn to think of immigration regulation as a task for an integrated regime.

. . .

CASES, STATUTES, AND ADMINISTRATIVE ORDERS CITED

Chicanos por la Causa, Inc. v. Napolitano 544 F.3d 976 (9th Cir. 2008)
De Canas v. Bica, 424 U.S. 351 (1976)
Graham v. Richardson, 403 U.S. 666 (1971)
Lozano v. City of Hazleton, 620 F.3d 170 (3rd Cir. 2010)
Lozano v. City of Hazleton, 496 F. Supp.2d 477 (M.D. Pa. 2007)
Plyler v. Doe, 457 U.S. 202 (1982)
Saenz v. Roe, 526 U.S. 489 (1999)
8 U.S.C. § 1611(b) (2006)
8 U.S.C. § 1357(g) (2006)
Attorney General Order No. 2353-2001, 16 Fed. Reg. 3612 (January 16, 2001)
California Assembly Bill 976 (2007)
Executive Order 78 (N.J. August 6, 2007)
Attorney General Anne Milgram, New Jersey Law Enforcement Directive no. 2007-03 (August 22, 2007)

NOTES

1. For an empirical analysis of measures considered by the 50 state legislatures in 2007, see Laglagaron, Rodríguez, Silver, and Thanasombat (2008).

2. For an elaboration of this holding in the context of a case in which the Supreme Court remanded a preemption challenge to a California law that sanctioned employers who hired unauthorized workers, see *De Canas v. Bica* (424 U.S. 351).

3. For Supreme Court cases in which such restrictions were struck down, see *Graham v. Richardson* (403 U.S. 366), in which the Court held unconstitutional laws that restricted lawful permanent residents' access to public benefits, and *Plyler v. Doe* (457 U.S. 202), in which the Court struck down a Texas law that restricted unauthorized immigrant children's access to the public schools.

4. For a discussion of local sanctuary policies, see Rodríguez (2008, 600–605). For a discussion of devolution, see Rodríguez, Chishti, and Nortman (2009).

5. See Laglagaron, Rodríguez, Silver, and Thanasombat (2008, 3).

6. See ibid. (2008, 5, fig. 1).

7. See ibid. (2008, 17–18, fig. 7).

8. It has become common but still crucial to note that, though traditional immigrant-receiving states such as Texas, California, New Jersey, New York, and Florida still receive the majority of new immigrants, the geographic distribution has changed substantially in the last decade, with millions of immi-

grants moving to new destination states, such as North Carolina, Georgia, and Tennessee. For collections of essays exploring this new distribution, see Massey (2008); Anrig and Wong (2006).

9. Attorney General Anne Milgram, New Jersey Law Enforcement Directive no. 2007-03 (Aug. 22, 2007).

10. Migration Policy Institute data are available at http://www.migration information.org/datahub/statelaws_home.cfm.

11. For 2007 data on these measures, see Laglagaron, Rodríguez, Silver, and Thanasombat (2008, 7, fig. 2).

12. For New Jersey, see Executive Order 78 (N.J. Aug. 6, 2007). For Illinois, see Illinois Coalition for Immigrant & Refugee Rights (2006, 1). For a discussion of similar initiatives by Washington and Massachusetts, see Jordan (2008).

13. For analysis of this phenomenon, see Rodríguez (2008, 637).

14. For a discussion of this divergence in North Carolina, see Rodríguez (2008, 584–85).

15. Cal. Assem. Bill 976 (2007).

16. Rodríguez (2008, 571–72, 580).

17. For the Ninth Circuit opinion upholding the Arizona employer sanctions law, see *Chicanos por la Causa, Inc. v. Napolitano* (544 F.3d 976). For the Third Circuit and federal district court opinions invalidating the Hazleton ordinance, using slightly different reasoning, see *Lozano v. City of Hazleton* (620F.3d170, 2010 WL 3504538); (496 F. Supp.2d 477).

18. Rodríguez (2008, 582–609).

19. 8 U.S.C. §1611(b) (2006). The Attorney General maintains a list of in-kind services deemed to be necessary to protect life or safety. It includes child and adult protective services; programs addressing weather emergencies and homelessness; shelters, soup kitchens, and Meals on Wheels programs; and certain medical services. U.S. Department of Justice Notice, "Final Specification of Community Programs Necessary for Protection of Life or Safety Under Welfare Reform Legislation," A.G. Order No. 2353-2001, 16 Fed. Reg. 3612 (Jan. 16, 2001).

20. This right has been protected most recently in *Saenz v. Roe* (526 U.S. 289), in which the Supreme Court struck down a California state law that imposed a durational residency requirement on access to public benefits, on the ground that it violated the right to travel inter-state.

21. This observation is certainly complicated by the fact that we are generally talking about persons who do not have a recognized right to be in the United States. Nonetheless, the federal government might claim exclusive control over where they may reside, thus obviating states' authority to pass laws that might pre-determine the question. And yet, the federal government is hardly determining where immigrants settle, and the immigrant population is hardly spread out equally across the states, so appeals to a federally managed distribution to control state regulatory activity seems a bit odd (Rodríguez 2008, 638-40).

22. 8 U.S.C. §1357(g) (2006).

23. The General Accounting Office recently released a report analyzing a

portion of existing 287(g) agreements and concluded that the absence of over-sight, which made it difficult to determine whether the programs were operating as intended, was one of the major flaws of the program (GAO 2009, 10–19).

24. Roderick Hills has emphasized that the Supreme Court has "thoroughly repudiated" the idea that the federal government should not rely on the states to carry out federal responsibilities, noting the broad range of federal programs carried out by states in the contexts of the environment, worker safety, health insurance, and historic preservation (Hills 1997, 853). He notes, as well, that "the notion that there can be only a single federal rule promulgated by a single national agency is a prejudice born of habit rather than legal or practical necessity" (Ibid. 881).

25. Metzger (2008, 2101–4); Galle & Seideman (2008).

26. The federalism literature suggests two ways in which states might participate in advancing federal regulatory goals: state agencies can develop federal rules, or state rules can be used to fill in a federal regime (Weiser 2003, 732). For a broad and deep historical account of the jurisprudential origins of cooperative federalism and an argument that the federal government should enlist state governments using financial incentives, see Hills (1997). Another scholar more pointedly argues that cooperative federalism was replaced in the '70s and '80s with coercive mandates from the federal government, undermining "governmental responsibility and public accountability." As a result, a new consensus needs to be forged from "elements of cooperative equity, competitive efficiency, and dual accountability" (Kincaid 1990, 937).

27. For a detailed analysis of the legal claims in the licensing and other cases, see Rodríguez, Chishti, and Nortman (2007).

28. Elsewhere I have argued that Congress ought to adopt a presumption against preempting state action in the immigration context, or at least take account of state interests in the immigration arena as legitimate, rather than inappropriate, before restricting state authority to regulate (Rodríguez 2008, 630–32).

29. For a discussion of these collaborations, see Rodríguez (2008, 588–90, 632–36).

30. For a constitutional and policy critique of the devolution of authority, see Wishnie (2001).

REFERENCES

Anrig, Greg, and Tova A. Wong, eds. 2006. *Immigration's New Frontiers: Experiences from the Emerging Gateway States.* New York: New America Foundation.

Galle, Brian, and Michael Seidenfeld. 2008. "Administrative Law's Federalism: Preemption, Delegation, and Agencies at the Edge of Federal Power." *Duke Law Journal* 57, no. 7, 1933–2022.

Greve, Michael S. 2000. "Against Cooperative Federalism." *Mississippi Law Journal* 70: 557–623.

Hills, Roderick. 1997. "The Political Economy of Cooperative Federalism: Why State Autonomy Makes Sense and 'Dual Sovereignty' Doesn't." *Michigan Law Review* 96, no. 4: 813–944.

Illinois Coalition for Immigrant and Refugee Rights and Office of New Americans Advocacy and Policy. 2006. "For the Benefit of All: Strategic Recommendations to Enhance the State's Role in the Integration of Immigrants in Illinois." Joint summary. Chicago: Illinois Coalition for Immigrant and Refugee Rights.

Jordan, Miriam. 2008. "Some States Seek Integration Path for Immigrants." *Wall Street Journal,* August 15.

Kincaid, John. 1990. "From Cooperative to Coercive Federalism." *Annals of the American Academy of Social and Political Science* 509, no. 1: 139–52.

Laglagaron, Laureen, Cristina Rodríguez, Alexa Silver, and Sirithon Thanasombat. 2008. *Regulating Immigration at the State Level: Highlights from the Database of 2007 State Immigration Legislation and the Methodology.* Washington, D.C.: Migration Policy Institute.

Massey, Douglas, ed. 2008. *New Faces in New Places: The Changing Geography of American Immigration.* New York: Russell Sage Foundation.

Metzger, Gillian. 2008. "Administrative Law as the New Federalism." *Duke Law Journal* 57, no. 7: 2023–109.

Rodríguez, Cristina. 2008. "The Significance of the Local in Immigration Regulation." *Michigan Law Review* 106, no. 4: 567–642.

Rodríguez, Cristina, Muzaffar Chishti, and Kimberly Nortman. 2010. "Legal Limits on Immigration Federalism." In *Taking Local Control: State and Local Immigration Policy Activism in the U.S.* Edited by M. Varsanyi. Palo Alto, Calif.: Stanford University Press.

———. 2007. "Testing the Limits." In *A Framework for Assessing the Legality of State and Local Immigration Measures.* Washington, D.C.: Migration Policy Institute.

U.S. General Accounting Office. 2009. "Better Controls Needed over Program Authorizing State and Local Enforcement of Federal Immigration Laws." U.S. General Accounting Office, Washington, D.C.

Weiser, Philip. 2003. "Cooperative Federalism and Its Challenges." *Michigan State DCL Law Review* 3: 727–39.

Wishnie, Michael J. 2001. "Laboratories of Bigotry: Devolution of the Immigration Power, Equal Protection, and Federalism." *New York University Law Review* 76, no. 2: 493–569.

3

What Part of "Illegal" Don't You Understand?

DIANNE SOLÍS

In the national shouting match over immigration, we are often asked, "What part of 'illegal' don't you understand?"

The answer isn't easy.

Immigration is one of the most complex and knotty areas of law (see Cristina M. Rodríguez's and Peter H. Schuck's chapters in this volume). It's rapidly fusing with criminal law and known as "crimmigration" law. Due process issues crop up with frequency. The dragnet of the toughest crackdown in decades is even sweeping up the lives of U.S. citizens and legal permanent residents. New cases in the federal courts increasingly involve the use of criminal prosecutions for cases previously handled with administrative immigration law. That rise—a doubling of criminal prosecutions from fiscal year 2007 to fiscal year 2010, according to a Syracuse University–based tracking project—raises questions about legal triage and what *didn't* get prosecuted because of a new emphasis on immigration.

Add to the mix the fact that so many in policy circles on both sides of the debate insist they believe in the rule of law, except for the laws they want to change. The law is now braided with contradictions. Undocumented immigrant children have a constitutional right to a free public education but cannot take a job legally when they graduate from high school. Mixed-status families live with both the fruits of citizenship and the risk of deportation. Illegal presence in the United States is an administrative matter but illegal entry can be prosecuted criminally.

And illegal entry can also be handled as an administrative infraction of immigration law. Some groups, such as the Federation for American Immigration Reform, call for a crackdown on "anchor babies"—those children born of illegal immigrants—and question the Fourteenth Amendment and its real intent. Did the following passage of the U.S. Constitution *really* mean to cover the children of an illegal immigrant?

> All persons born or naturalized in the United States, and subject to the jurisdiction thereof, are citizens of the United States and of the State wherein they reside.

As some activists and politicians try to revive a large overhaul of the nation's immigration laws, the crackdown continues against a population estimated to be about 10.8 million. Deportations or removals of those in the United States unlawfully have quickened in volume during the presidential administration of Barack Obama (see Nina Bernstein's chapter in this volume). Nearly 400,000 persons were removed in each of the fiscal years of 2010 and 2009. That's an increase from about 246,000 in the opening year of the Bush administration and about 360,000 in the last full year of the Bush administration.

My tribe—journalists—would be well advised to make sure our legal lens is well calibrated. We must recognize that the essence of the writer's craft is often finding the humanity in the story. We must change the camera angle frequently to take our audience inside the lives of various kinds of protagonists: municipal cops, clinic directors, school principals, factory owners—as well as the child whose father was just deported. The issues are as complex as they are cinematic. We've seen powerful narratives put to screen—from *The Visitor,* a story of the music-based friendship between a college professor and a Syrian immigrant, to *Crash,* a fast-paced tale of cultures that clash and crash with a car accident in Los Angeles. Both films, like good narrative journalism, got at the deep plate tectonics of change shaping a new America.

CHEECH AND CHONG

An old comedy with a simple plot also comes to mind: *Born in East L.A.,* by Richard "Cheech" Marin and Tommy Chong. Two decades ago, the script was parody: Cheech is deported to Tijuana despite his assertions of U.S. citizenship in English. Today, we hear more and more stories like this in real-time dramas from North Texas to South Texas, California to New Mexico. It's yet another chapter in the story of the most significant crackdown in decades. There has been a growing incidence of U.S. citizens and legal permanent residents getting caught in the dragnet of federal immigration agents. And with that comes legal challenges alleging violations of due process and federal torts claims. For illumination and interpretation, scribes turn to lawyers in law firms and law schools and research houses and advocacy centers of varying stripes. They animate the law with recent cases, with their own research projects, and with their cogent arguments or interpretations of faulty reasoning. Lawyers can be story protagonists or their clients may be. My story in May 2008, for example, in the *Dallas Morning News* on the rising complaints among U.S. citizens and those with legal residency was rooted in roundups at residences and at Pilgrim's Pride in the East Texas town of Mount Pleasant. It also came from the raids at the Swift & Co. plants in December 2006.

> U.S. Immigration and Customs Enforcement, an agency within the Department of Homeland Security, contends that such arrests are rare and that when it does happen, citizens are immediately released. But across the U.S., reports of arrests and detentions of U.S. citizens and legal permanent residents have increased. Lawyers and immigrant-defense groups said such incidents will continue to rise as the federal government deepens its crackdown against illegal immigrants—one of the broadest such actions in fifty years.
>
> Raids have intensified in the last two years—a get-tough approach in the absence of comprehensive immigration legislation.

And then Juan Manuel Carrillo, an eighteen-year-old at the Mount Pleasant Pilgrim's plant, retold his story of being arrested in a dragnet that began before dawn. Some three hundred Immigration and Customs Enforcement (ICE) agents and other personnel arrested forty-six workers—a six-to-one ratio. Carrillo said he told officials that he was a U.S. citizen. "I said I was born in San Diego, and they said they didn't believe me," he recounted, in Spanish. "I said I was telling the truth. They said I was working with another's Social Security number." Carrillo said that when his seventeen-year-old brother, Marco Antonio, brought him his U.S. passport, immigration agents insisted the pair were lying and asked him where he bought the passport. Carrillo had been taken to Mexico as a toddler by his Mexican-born parents; he lived there for fifteen years before returning to the United States about a year before this incident. He speaks little English.

The "he saids" and "she saids" continued when Alicia Rodriguez was detained in a routine traffic stop. In August 2007 the Mansfield, Texas tax preparer was held for sixteen hours before she was able to convince authorities she was a U.S. citizen. Authorities mistook her for an illegal immigrant deported three years earlier, who had insisted she was a U.S. citizen. "They were pretty belligerent in not believing me," said Rodriguez, who is a monolingual English-speaker.

How serious is all this? In the summer of 2009, U.S. Senator Robert Menendez (D-NJ) reintroduced legislation to protect U.S. citizens and lawful permanent residents from being unlawfully detained and deported by the Department of Homeland Security. The Protect Citizens from Unlawful Detention Act would establish minimum standards of procedure and treatment for U.S. citizens, lawful permanent residents, and immigrants who are caught up in immigration enforcement and detention operations. In its March 2009 report, "Jailed with Justice," Amnesty International said it had identified more than a hundred cases in the past decade in which U.S. citizens and lawful permanent residents have incorrectly been placed into removal proceedings. That same report cites another research agency, the Vera Institute of Justice, which identified 322 persons in detention with potential claims to U.S. citizenship in the calendar year of 2007.

Since 2005, the Vera Institute of Justice has worked with the Justice Department's Executive Office for Immigration Review (EOIR) and nonprofit legal service providers to offer a legal orientation program that informs immigrant detainees about their rights, the immigration court, and the detention processes. Adding to the confusion is the fact that in a criminal proceeding, the accused has the right to an attorney paid by the U.S. government. In the United States individuals in deportation proceedings have the "privilege" to secure counsel but at no expense to the government. From fiscal years 2006 to 2010, 51 percent to 57 percent of individuals in removal proceedings didn't have a lawyer, according to the Justice Department's EOIR.

HISTORY AND HISTORIANS

An echo in history can be found in these episodes that pick up U.S. citizens and those immigrants in the United States lawfully. There were mass deportations in the 1930s and the 1950s, when Mexican-Americans were swept up in raids. In the 2007 book *Decade of Betrayal: Mexican Repatriation in the 1930s,* we learn that the number of returnees might have been a million. It's unclear how many of those were actually Mexican-American adults or the U.S. citizen children of immigrants. *Decade of Betrayal*, published by the University of New Mexico press, was written by Francisco Balderrama, a professor at California State University–Los Angeles, and Raymond Rodríguez, a professor emeritus at Long Beach City College in California.

In 2006 then U.S. Representative Hilda Solís (D-CA) pushed for federal legislation to form a commission to study the "deportation and coerced emigration" of Mexican-Americans from 1929 to 1941. The bill got twenty-one sponsors but never made it out of committee. "American society hasn't realized what happened from that time frame. It is almost like an exodus that occurred," said Solís in a 2008 interview with the *Dallas Morning News*. "People from as far away as Chicago were gathered up and taken to Mexico and just dumped there."

Changing the camera angle to Mexican soil is helpful in understanding the history of deportations, or what is sometimes called repatriations. What happened to those deported in past decades? I've researched the topic in the archives of the Mexican Foreign Ministry and in presidential archives in Mexico City.

In the 1930s during the Great Depression it is not known how many of those who left for Mexico were actually *illegal* immigrants, rather than legal immigrants or United States–born children. Many who left were coerced to do so, according to the scholars. At least one Mexican consulate in the 1930s was paying particular attention to U.S. citizen children of Mexican immigrants and to those of Mexican ancestry who had no proof of citizenship. This comes from documents in the archives of the Foreign Relations Ministry written by Mexican consul Rafael de la Colina in Los Angeles: "I recognize fully the right that the authorities have in this country to make foreigners leave under these conditions, but I consider that in this work they ought to use methods that don't hurt those who reside here legally."

Newspaper accounts filed in the archives of Mexico's Foreign Ministry document abuse and thefts on the trains carrying Mexicans and Mexican-Americans. "In Mexico, Worse Treatment," reads one headline. In late 2008, I interviewed Fernando Saúl Alanís, a professor in San Luis Potosí, about the Mexican government's limited care for those returning citizens and their children in the past wave of deportations. Mexicans make up nearly a third of the foreign-born people living in the United States, overwhelming other nationalities. The treatment of the returnees and the limited care for the returnees is reflected in Alanís's book's title, which translates to "Let them stay over there." According to Alanís, newspaper stories from that period show that adjustment for the returning families was difficult, as Mexico's economy was reeling too. "Sooner or later, they go back," Alanís added, ". . . And because some were U.S. citizens, they could return easily to the United States." He continues: "It is like a vicious circle. . . . In moments of crisis, they are deported."

Rather than split up her family, United States–born Marty Parson Acuitlapa decided to move to Mexico when her husband, José Acuitlapa, was barred from entry into the United States, while trying to fix his immigration status at the U.S. consulate in Juárez. There is no special reentry program for the Acuitlapas, and their three children have had to adjust to life in the southern village of Malinalco about two hours from Mexico City. Culturally, this mountain village couldn't be more different than Parson Acuitlapa's native Warner Robins, where only about 5 percent of the population is Hispanic. Leslee, the eight-year-old, once drew pictures of an airplane and a sun with beams of tears. "I had to leave," her caption read. Her brother, thirteen years old when he arrived in Malinalco, found school easy. Among his classes: English as a second language. And the pushback in Mexico against those who help illegal immigrants, from Central America, is now so great that in late 2010 the Mexican Catholic Bishops Conference instituted a monthly surveillance program. Each month, advocacy agencies are called to check on any threats or harassment experienced at the agency or to clients.

CRIMMIGRATION

The rise of such criminal charges as aggravated identity theft could be seen in December 2006 with the raids at the Swift meat plants in Texas and several other states by Immigration and Customs Enforcement (ICE), an agency within the Department of Homeland Security. It didn't begin in Postville, Iowa, at Agriprocessors Inc., when Guatemalans, Mexicans, and a translator collided in a fast-tracked justice system. Before these dragnets and raids, immigration matters were usually handled using administrative law. U.S. attorneys, busy doing a sort of legal triage in the everyday workload, were not bothered with immigration matters unless they involved crimes of violence or had clearly defined victims. With the criminal charges of aggravated identify theft, there were affidavits that listed real victims whose social security numbers had been taken in the Swift case. Getting to their story in the Swift drama was rather easy once the legal trail was established.

The issue was significant enough that the United States Supreme Court weighed in on it in May 2009. This came as circuit courts were divided over the standard of proof in establishing aggravated identity theft. A big question: Must there be knowledge that the identity belongs to another person? People who use false documents can be jailed, the court said. But, the court ruled unanimously, they cannot be convicted of the more serious crime of "aggravated identity theft" without proof that they knew the identification number belonged to someone else. In recent years Congress stiffened the penalties against those who stole identities. It called for a mandatory two-year prison term for aggravated identity theft. False use of a social security number, however, is also a felony but doesn't call for such a mandatory sentence.

Some past grievances have been addressed. As reports picked up in the *Los Angeles Daily Journal,* the *Washington Post,* and the *Dallas Morning News* on the sedation of deportees with a powerful anti-psychotic, ICE moved to change its procedures. They will now seek a federal judge's permission, according to a policy change issued in 2008. Officials must show deportees have a history of physical resistance to being removed or are a danger to themselves. Among the coverage was a *Dallas Morning News* report on nearly 400 persons who had been sedated over a six-year period. Of that amount, 354 had received the drug Haldol. The report was based on data released under the Freedom of Information Act and is believed to be the fullest accounting to date of the government's past process of sedation.

Law and Justice and Mutual Exclusivity and Going Forward

Distinctions between law and justice go back in time to the trial and death of Socrates, the crucifixion of Jesus, and the denial of a front-row seat on a bus to Rosa Parks. As journalists, we write about such mutual exclusivity. The story lies in the contradiction between these two ideas and how real people live lives mangled by laws, or contradictory laws. We now live in a time where the United States Supreme Court, under a 1982 decision known as *Plyler v. Doe,* has ruled that all children, with or without legal authorization for U.S. residency, be given a free, public education until high school (see Cristina M. Rodríguez's chapter in this volume). But the same government yanks away the fruits of that education when those students graduate and can't earn a living because they lack authentic work documents. This issue is addressed in so many of the stories on immigration and has played out in student walkouts in 2006 in such cities as Dallas, Houston, and Los Angeles.

For the past several years, legislation has been introduced—the Development, Relief, and Education of Alien Minors Act (the DREAM Act)— to provide legalization to those college students in the United States without proper authorization. The stories are gripping: one potential beneficiary who graduated from a Texas high school is now at Harvard. During the walkouts, he took to the school's public address system to tell students not to walk out as it would send a damaging message. Behind the scenes at Harvard, he is lobbying Capitol Hill. Around the nation, as in Washington, dozens of students unlawfully in the United States came out to push for passage of the DREAM Act in the final days of 2010. Some of them boldly gave their full names.

And there are more challenges to families of mixed citizenship. By 2009 there were four million children with U.S. citizenship born of at least one parent in the United States without papers. More families must choose whether they live divided or in the homeland of the foreign-born parent. Changes in immigration law in 1996 reduced defenses against removals for those who had substantial ties to the United States, including spouses and children. These changes allowed for more easily placed ten-year bans on those trying to legalize who had come into the country illegally in the first place. The federal government's position has been clear: "We recognize that children are impacted by enforcement of the law," said ICE spokesman Carl Rusnok in a 2009 *Dallas Morning News* article. "However, ultimately parents, who are in violation of the law, are responsible for the negative impact to their families."

In January, at the request of a congressional committee, Homeland Security's inspector general found that more than 108,000 parents of U.S. citizens had been deported over the decade ending in 2007. New legislation, called Uniting American Families, might address some of the more vexing issues for these mixed-status families. The pace of the growth among U.S. citizen children has been fast. In 2003 there were 2.7 million U.S. citizen children living in mixed-status families. By 2009 there were 4 million children. But, like all proposed immigration legislation, it's unclear what kind of traction it will receive in the four-year Obama term.

Recession and Looking Ahead

Therein lies one of the more difficult questions of the Obama administration. How can it address the legal contradictions, the legal ambiguities, the legal dilemmas for mixed-status families when there are so many economic problems with the native-born workforce and their families? Hispanics now make up 16 percent of the U.S. population, according to the 2010 census. Hispanics of Mexican origin in the United States comprise 10 percent. Mexico is reeling from its own economic problems. The Mexican government's census agency says immigration is down about 40 percent. It is the most significant contraction in decades, after a demographic trend that reshaped the United States. "The change was driven largely by unauthorized immigrants; flows of legal permanent residents have been steady this decade," says a 2009 Pew report, using Mexican data.

Studies by the nonpartisan Migration Policy Institute and El Colegio de la Frontera Norte suggest that those here in the United States illegally aren't returning in massive numbers to Mexico. Mexico's former consul general in Dallas, Enrique Hubbard Urrea, said that immigration to North Texas was flat—"not growing, but not shrinking." He also noted that immigrants were coming to North Texas from other parts of the United States, possibly because the economy isn't as bad here as it is elsewhere. The observations are significant for the nation: North Texas had the third largest population of foreign-born Mexicans in the country, according to 2007 Census estimates. Mexican officials at the national and state levels are fairly uniform in denying that a large or "massive" return migration is occurring. But a trickle, at least, is returning. Anecdotal evidence from Mexico shows some are returning to such states as San Luis Potosí, according to a 2009 report from the *Dallas Morning News*.

In Cerritos, San Luis Potosí, a wave of return migration has sparked an increase in crime "by desperate youth" and the creation of temporary jobs programs by the government.

Mayor Salvador Martínez Sifuentes said that about one-third of the town's twenty-five thousand people are in the U.S. at a time, and that hundreds if not thousands have returned recently as a result of the U.S. recession.

"We don't have numbers," he said, "but one parameter that we use is the closing of the exchange houses. Their financial transactions have dropped by 50 percent in the buying and selling of dollars, and that gives you an idea of what the situation is like."

And then, there is the violence along the border. Such violence makes it more and more difficult to cross, even with the traditional mom-and-pop coyote. Mexico's drug cartels are now expanding their product lines to include migrants. Consider my 2007 *Dallas Morning News* interview on the dangers of crossing in the Sonoran desert.

> Isaac Catalan would love a job in construction in the Carolinas, he says. But the Arizona border is now "tapado por la mafia"—closed by the mafia, says Catalan, who tried to cross three times and lost more than $3,000 in the attempts.
>
> "There's too much vigilance, too much," says Catalan, who comes from Mexico's southernmost state of Chiapas. "And it's not the Border Patrol."
>
> One U.S. law-enforcement official blamed the migration violence on the drug capo known as Chapo Guzman. "Chapo's ambition is nothing short of taking control of the Mexican border," said one U.S. law-enforcement official who's been on Guzman's trail for nearly a decade and agreed to speak only on condition of anonymity. "He's a crafty drug trafficker and ruthless killer who also happens to be a brilliant businessman. And there's nothing more lucrative on the border than control of vital transit border routes."

That story continued through 2010. Mexican officials believe the drug cartel known as the Zetas were behind the summer slaughter of seventy-two migrants in northern Mexico, ninety miles from the Texas border. Drug cartels even steal rival gangs' migrants, using them for ransom or forcing the migrants to become "drug foot soldiers" of the cartel, said Mexico's ambassador, Arturo Sarukahn, in a 2010 interview in the *Dallas Morning News*.

In the meantime, how long can President Obama postpone an overhaul of the nation's immigration laws? What tasks will he undertake, and are those measures likely to be piecemeal and more focused on enforcement? Enforcement-training pacts are increasing between local police and the Department of Homeland Security. Immigration officials say it gives them a "multiplier effect." Others say it dilutes the goodwill that police need to inspire among potential witnesses and victims of crime when they know those same officers might turn them over to federal immigration authorities. The crackdown—in some respects—is shifting from the workers to the employers. It mirrors the late 1980s. That's when the U.S. Congress established under the Immigration Reform and Control Act that employers could be fined for knowingly hiring a worker unauthorized to labor in the United States. Such a crackdown is obviously less confrontational, less disruptive, and less likely to sweep in the native-born and legal permanent residents.

Tensions burst open in 2010 in Arizona. That border state passed the toughest immigration law ever. Parts of the law, known as Senate Bill 1070, are on hold, pending court review.

Then there are those, like Roberto Suro (see his introduction in this volume), who say the news media has dwelled too much on the issue of *illegal* immigration. But a crackdown of this scale, ongoing confrontations over basic constitutional issues, and the holding of large groups of people in detention, often without bond, is the essence of news. Likewise, the breaking of immigration laws by so many is also news. In the interim, tensions will spike over the Fourteenth Amendment and who precisely deserves birthright citizenship, over the spread of copycat legislation like that in Arizona, and within the broader relationships of nations trying to cohabit in our shared globe.

4

Some Observations about Immigration Journalism

PETER H. SCHUCK

The topic of immigration journalism is of the utmost interest and public importance but it is seldom, if ever, systematically examined. Bringing academics, policy analysts, and policymakers together with journalists who cover immigration is a splendid idea whose time has come. Moreover, it has provided me the opportunity to interact with Nina Bernstein and Ginger Thompson of the *New York Times*—whom I read regularly and gratefully.

All Americans, of course, have a large stake in being well informed not only about immigration policy issues but also about the lives, struggles, achievements, and disappointments of immigrants, who truly are essential to the quality of American life. By this, I do not simply mean the economic, cultural, and other contributions that immigrants make to American society. I also refer to the pride that the vast majority of Americans take in the country's immigrant past and in the spirit of enterprise, sacrifice, courage, and freedom that immigrants continue to infuse into the nation's public philosophy. That this pride is common ground is partly due to the work of immigration journalists in helping to keep the continuing immigration drama on center stage, where it most definitely belongs. I salute the journalists' contributions to our collective understanding and appreciation of immigration, and I look forward to more such writing despite the parlous state of print journalism today. (Incidentally, a 2009 piece by *Slate* editor-at-large Jack Shafer recounts the many premature obituaries to newspaper journalism written over the past seventy years and predicts that it will continue to flourish, albeit in different forms. Let us hope so.)

This chapter opens with some observations about immigration law. After offering these thoughts, however, I shall turn to the handiwork of immigration journalists who write in the elite newspapers that I read daily (the *New York Times* and the *Wall Street Journal*). I shall pick a few bones with our journalist friends in the spirit of my high school football coach, who emphasized to his charges that we were often better served by constructive criticism than by praise, even when (as is true of the journalists but not of my juvenile athletic efforts) high praise is eminently warranted. Let me begin with immigration law. Professor Cristina M. Rodríguez (see her chapter in this volume) reviews the subject exceedingly well, as she always does. To supplement her discussion, I provide a slightly different perspective on the law—one that is more structural or schematic. I distinguish, as legal scholar and later Harvard Law School dean Roscoe Pound did a century ago, between "the law on the books" and "the law in action," and I pay special attention to the part of the law in action that consists of immigration politics and administration.

The first thing to say about immigration law on the books is that it is extraordinarily complex (see Dianne Solís's chapter in this volume). The long and detailed Immigration and Nationality Act has become in many ways like the Internal Revenue Code. I do not intend this comparison as a compliment to either statute. But there is a large and very consequential difference between the immigration statute and the Internal Revenue Code. The immigration statute is pervaded by grants of broad bureaucratic discretion that the tax code, which seeks to promote private transactions and planning through clear rules, attempts to minimize. This congressional grant of broad discretion to the immigration bureaucracy, now embedded in the Department of Homeland Security, certainly reflects the need for the agency to deal with the remarkable, apparently unending variation in the circumstances of individual immigrants. Indeed, given this extraordinary variability, the statute may not provide all the discretion that is needed. The very important 1996 amendments to the statute stripped the agency of much of the discretion that it previously could use to avoid apparent injustices by adapting the law to take individual and family exigencies into account. Many close observers and practitioners of immigration law think that most, if not all, of the earlier discretion ought to be restored, and I agree.

Most of the immigration law on the books is in the form of statutory provisions, published regulations, and guidance issued by the immigration agency. They tend to be intricate, technical, and self-referential. They are grist for lawyers, not laypeople—much less for immigrants, who tend to be unfamiliar with such things. Because the politics surrounding immigration is so difficult and convoluted, Congress only intermittently musters the will to change the immigration law on the books. Accordingly, the law's responsiveness to changes on the ground is very episodic. Although the Obama administration has announced its support for so-called comprehensive immigration reform, the complex politics surrounding such reform efforts have pushed any serious efforts into the future, perhaps even after the 2012 elections. Although some elected politicians find it advantageous to raise such divisive and politically costly issues, the president and many members of Congress manifestly prefer to defer these bitter debates as long as politically possible.

The last feature of immigration law on the books that I will mention is the importance of judicial review, which is designed not only to correct routine bureaucratic errors but to ensure that our rule of law values, including constitutional principles, are protected as they apply to immigrants. Yet the volume of immigration cases that are pending in the federal courts today is so great and constitutes so large a share of their caseloads that many federal appellate judges of all ideological persuasions have warned of a crisis and have denounced in no uncertain terms the quality of bureaucratic decision making that has generated many of these appeals.

The law in action differs from the law on the books in all areas of the law, but these differences may be particularly great with respect to immigration. Immigration law in action is largely a matter of embedded bureaucratic routines and the working out of often narrowly conceived bureaucratic incentives. Deportation provides perhaps the clearest example. It is the ultimate formally available weapon for the agency, but it is seldom used. Of the estimated eleven million unauthorized immigrants in the United States, a very small percentage, perhaps 2 to 3 percent, are formally deported. This percentage constitutes a relatively small share of those who are subject to final orders of deportation. A larger fraction of the unauthorized population, but still no more than 10 percent, choose to leave "voluntarily" because it is more advantageous for them to do so than to undergo formal removal by the agency. Enforcement, then, is both sporadic and highly ineffective. For this reason, the size of the unauthorized population has grown steadily, at least until the current recession made job-related migration less attractive.

This is not to say that full enforcement of the immigration laws would necessarily be optimal. Indeed, I have written elsewhere that the optimal enforcement level is likely to be much lower than this, though probably not as low as the only marginal level of enforcement that actually prevails today.[1] This is perhaps an obvious point but one that is seldom discussed or acknowledged in immigration policy debates. If immigration enforcement were the only value that society believed in and its only policy goal, then full enforcement might be desirable. But of course it is not our only value or goal—far from it. Our society has countless other fish to fry—health, education, national defense, housing, justice, transportation, research, and so forth—all of which require scarce resources that would otherwise be consumed by costly, less-valued immigration enforcement. Another reason why full enforcement is not optimal—although it is a reason that official rhetoric is seldom willing to acknowledge—is that many unauthorized immigrants make positive contributions to American society, which might justify permitting them to remain. In short, a rational government must determine the optimal level of enforcement and then try to implement it. I do not claim to know what the right level is, but it is certainly far less than the 100 percent that many politicians, who probably know better, seem to be demanding.

I have already noted the great importance that the law on the books places on judicial review. In contrast, however, the law in action reveals that despite the historically large number of immigration cases now pending in the courts—almost 250,000 in June, 2010, according to one estimate, producing an average waiting time of fifteen months for these cases to get to court—they still constitute a small percentage of the total of agency administrative decisions that determine immigrants' legal status. In this important sense, judicial review, when viewed as part of the large agency-governed immigration system as a whole, is actually sporadic and relatively insignificant. (This is true even though many judicial decisions have precedential effects that extend their influence beyond the specific case being decided.) When judicial review does occur, of course, immigration lawyers and law professors read those decisions carefully and use them to advise clients, analyze the law, and often propose legal changes. Nevertheless, the effect of these decisions on the vast majority of immigrants in the United States whose legal status is at issue is marginal at best.

The last aspect of the law in action that I mention here is that the key players in the system are the private immigration lawyers. Their job is to advise and represent their clients as effectively as they can. The quality of this representation is very mixed. Professor Dan Kanstroom's clinic at Boston College Law School and our immigration clinic at Yale Law School are unusually conscientious and well-staffed, as law school clinics tend to be. They devote a great deal of time to their individual clients and serve them well, with generally good results and at no fee. But this is not at all typical of the experience of immigrants with private immigration lawyers, when they are lucky enough to be able to afford to hire them. Again, there are many admirable exceptions in the private immigration bar, but the general quality of representation is notoriously poor and, as Professor Richard Abel has shown, often breaches even baseline professional ethical standards.[2]

The politics of immigration policy, as I noted earlier, is central to the law on the books as well as to the law in action. Immigration politics is also quite Byzantine, which is all the more reason why we need fine journalists to explain it to us. I can think of no area of public policy in which there are stranger political bedfellows than there are in the immigration field. For example, the views of the editorial page of the *Wall Street Journal* are congruent with those of many left-wing Democrats and agricultural interests that favor vastly increased, if not unlimited, immigration. Many liberals—some labor unions, professional organizations of high-tech workers, and some environmental and population control groups—tend to favor immigration restriction. Blacks are an especially interesting example: although the rank-and-file have traditionally opposed increased immigration, some black organizational leaders, who must work with broader-based coalitions to secure liberal public policy goals, have worked to avoid the stigma that attaches to anti-immigration positions among Latinos and other liberal coalition members.

As Rodríguez has noted in her chapter, and as some of my research has also emphasized, the effects of immigration on local communities are much more important and varied than much of the media coverage suggests. Tip O'Neill famously said that "all politics is local," and although this is something of an exaggeration, it is certainly at least as true of immigration politics as of other politics. This is one reason for the spate of local and state laws that seek to augment the federal enforcement efforts and limit in-state tuition and other benefits to unauthorized immigrants are under challenge in the courts on Supremacy

Clause and other legal grounds. The Hazleton, Pennsylvania, case and the litigation over Arizona statutes enacted in 2010 are only the most prominent examples.

Public opinion about immigrants is quite complicated. Survey data about many public policy issues often seems puzzling or even incoherent, of course. Attitudes concerning immigration are no exception. This data is sensitive to the respondents' own perceptions about economic and social conditions, the specific wording of the question being asked, and the respondents' willingness to share strong sometimes stigmatized feelings with interviewers who are strangers. But the data is also hard to interpret because of Americans' markedly ambivalent views about immigration, and because respondents tend to draw subtle but important distinctions. They tend to think very differently about different categories of immigrants.

According to the survey data, for example, Americans like immigrants more than they like immigration, they favor past immigration more than recent immigration, they prefer legal immigrants to undocumented ones, they prefer refugees to other immigrants, and they support immigrants' access to educational and health benefits but not to welfare or Social Security. Not surprisingly, they tend to admire the immigrants whom they know (including undocumented ones) while often stereotyping those whom they don't know. They feel that immigrants' distinctive cultures have contributed positively to American life and that diversity continues to strengthen American society today. At the same time, they overwhelmingly resist any conception of multiculturalism that discourages immigrants from learning and using the English language.[3]

The attitudes toward immigration held by Latinos in the United States are also complex and, perhaps surprisingly to some observers, are not very different from the attitudes of other Americans. Writing in 2005, Roberto Suro, a former journalist and former director of the Pew Hispanic Center (PHC), found that "although an overwhelming majority of Hispanics expresses positive attitudes toward immigrants, relatively few Hispanics favor increasing the flow of legal immigration from Latin America and a significant minority, concentrated among native-born Latinos, is concerned that unauthorized migrants are hurting the economy. One hotly debated means to discourage unauthorized migration—laws that deny driver's licenses to people who are in the country illegally—draws support from a majority of the native born, according to a survey of the Latino population in the United States conducted by the PHC."[4]

Americans' bottom line about immigration policy has been fairly consistent over many decades: only a small fraction of respondents favor an increase in immigration levels, while the vast majority want either fewer immigrants or no change. Fluctuations generally reflect changes in the unemployment rate. My reading of the data is that most Americans are what I call "pragmatic restrictionists." That is, they do not oppose new immigration in principle or in general. They might even be prepared to support it if they can be persuaded, for example, that immigrants actually create jobs rather than taking them away from native workers, that they are mastering the English language without undue delay, and that they do not exploit the welfare system or otherwise threaten social cohesion. But many Americans have serious doubts about whether these claims are true.

Immigration politics reflects these public attitudes, but the law often does not. In my recent work, I have shown that both the law on the books and especially the law in action are considerably more generous to immigrants than the public opinion data, much political rhetoric, and private immigration lawyers would suggest.[5] This is true (though certainly to a lesser extent) even of undocumented immigrants, a disfavored category. As I noted earlier, only a small fraction of them are actually placed in proceedings and removed. This reality—the very low probability of being detected and deported—is well known in immigrant communities. Needless to say, this does not necessarily negate the anxiety among undocumented immigrants who fear that they will be the unlucky exceptions and may be ethnically profiled, but the strong odds in their favor constitute an overwhelmingly important fact of life for them. This fact enables them to go about their daily business and relationships, albeit with one ever-vigilant eye out for the immigration law enforcers. Another important fact that marks the law in action with respect to the undocumented is that many of the states where most of them live have made them eligible for certain social benefits. Indeed, some localities like New York and especially San Francisco have defied or declined to cooperate with federal enforcement by creating bureaucratic sanctuaries for the undocumented, making it more difficult for the federal agents to find and remove them.

Where immigration politics, the law on the books, and the law in action converge most closely is in the case of those immigrants who commit crimes in the United States, even relatively minor offenses. The law has become much harsher over the past few decades, depriving such immigrants of many procedural and substantive rights to which they were previously entitled and facilitating their summary removal from the country. But even here, the law in action is a far cry from the law on the books. In a study published in 2000, my coauthor and I found that the immigration agency had failed to actually remove most of these convicted criminals—even those who were already under lock and key or other law enforcement supervision.[6] Since then, the number of deportable criminals who are actually deported has increased substantially, but for a variety of reasons a large number still remain in the country.

The number of immigrants incarcerated in federal facilities increased from approximately forty-two thousand in 2001 to approximately forty-nine thousand only three years later. By mid-2009, according to recent federal data, a reported 94,498 immigrants were held in federal and state prisons.[7] Immigrants represent more than a quarter of the federal prison population, roughly 4 percent of the total state prison population, and they occupy significant space in local jails as well.[8] I hasten to add that despite these large numbers, the data indicate that immigrants are significantly less prone to crime than citizens, particularly if one excludes Puerto Ricans, who have far higher crime rates but are U.S. citizens.[9] The Immigration and Customs Enforcement (ICE) agency today manages to remove more of these criminals in terms of absolute numbers than ever before—128,000 in 2009, almost 30 percent of them for dangerous drug offenses. Nevertheless, the number of those who are actually deported remains a relatively small percentage of the much larger total, estimated by ICE to be up to 450,000 a year, who are under criminal justice supervision, most of whom are unlikely to have significant legal defenses to deportation.[10]

. . .

I now turn to the coverage of immigration by journalists. The journalists' work included in this volume—and a few others, including Julia Preston of the *New York Times* and Miriam Jordan of the *Wall Street Journal*—are my heroines. I don't know why there are only heroines and not heroes. An exception is Barry Newman, who used to cover immigration for the *Wall Street Journal*. Perhaps there is an interesting story there about journalism in general or immigration journalism in particular. In any event, the best immigration writers whom I read these days are women.

In an important sense, journalists and academicians have the same job. I presume that we are all deeply sympathetic to immigrants and to the challenges that confront them here, and we value their contributions to American life. This leads me and many other students of immigration, including journalists, to favor (setting the all-important details aside for now) an expansive legal immigration policy, a generous "earned legalization" program, fair treatment of guest workers, more high-skill admissions, and so forth.[11] But as a professional matter, our job is not to advocate for immigrants or what we conceive to be their interests. (We may, of course, do so in our nonprofessional capacities as citizens.) Instead, our duty as professionals is to educate our readers about a very complex, multifaceted immigration system.

It is complex in part because the system must somehow balance many conflicting but important individual and social goals. At the most basic level, we all want an immigration system that is scrupulously fair to the individuals and families who are affected by the immigration law by protecting their personal dignity, substantive interests, and procedural rights. This is no simple task because immigration law is inevitably a system of mass justice and, more specifically, mass *adjudication*—a term of art in administrative law that refers to decisions, analogous in many (but not all) respects to judicial adjudications, that should be tailored to individual facts and circumstances rather than decisions determined through general rules and policies. In such a system of mass adjudication, the cost of administering the elephantine decision process necessarily constitutes a very severe constraint, for this process must provide millions of noncitizens with *individualized* status determinations and adjustments, documentation, employment and travel permissions, and many other services. At the same time, some nine million to ten million undocumented immigrants, if apprehended and placed in proceedings, have a legal right to *individualized* adjudications of their status. All of this adjudication requires an immense bureaucracy that is governed by extensive standardized procedures and routines.

Assuring individualized adjudications and due process to immigrants, however, is by no means society's only end in administering the immigration law system. Equally important is that the system be effective in achieving its policy goals. These systemic goals include limiting and regulating immigration in the ways that Congress has prescribed. This means maintaining the integrity of the law on the books that governs all noncitizens in the country (and the citizens who interact with them). Maintaining the integrity of the system depends on the effective achievement of at least three other, related goals. The first is deterrence. This requires that those who might consider whether to game or evade the system believe that the sanctions are sufficiently credible—that is, sufficiently severe and likely to be actually imposed against violators—that they will decide not to take their chances.

A second related goal is swift enforcement, which is especially important in immigration policy—and is a major source of its failure. After all, for out-of-status immigrants who want to remain in the United States, delaying enforcement is ultimately the name of the game. Delay enables them to build "equities" by establishing new relationships that may suffice to attain a more secure legal status and defeat the agency's efforts to remove them. Delay also gives them more time to earn money in the United States, which is the main goal of almost all undocumented migrants. Beating the system of immigration law is a game that almost any resourceful immigrant equipped with authentic-looking false documents and a reasonably competent lawyer can hope to win. This raises a third related goal—minimizing fraud—which is also a major source of policy failure. The law on the books penalizes document fraud ever more severely, yet the immigration system remains notoriously rife with it—and no remedy for this fraud is on the horizon given the widespread, and in my view excessive, resistance to a secure national identification card carried by all residents.

What has this to do with immigration journalism? My strong impression is that those who cover immigration for the elite newspapers are excellent at expressing and arousing public indignation about the failures of this system at an individual level. Almost any piece by Nina Bernstein illustrates this probing, admirable, crusading, edgy, disturbing, shoe-leather journalism; her front-page article in the July 23, 2010, edition of the *New York Times,* entitled "No Immigration Papers, No School, Many New York Districts Say," is a classic example of her energetic sleuthing. The skill of the best immigration journalists reflects several factors: an aptitude for tenacious digging into the messy details of a complex human story; a passion for narrating the drama of individual lives; and a sympathy for vulnerable, hard-working people caught up in what often seems like a Kafkaesque morass. I am making an educated guess here, but I believe that their work also reflects a liberal social-political ideology that tends to perceive and frame immigration issues as conflicts between powerless underdog immigrants and powerful corporations and bureaucrats; between admirable individuals and a mindless, soulless system; and between a concept of undocumented immigrants that views their illegal status as a mere technicality and the brute formalism of the law that imposes stigma and demands enforcement.[12] Immigration lends itself to this kind of story, and journalists like Nina Bernstein are the true masters of the genre.

Where journalism does a less effective job, if I may respectfully so say, is in filling out the rest of the picture—in providing lay readers with a balanced, sophisticated understanding of what that system seeks to do, its multiple and conflicting missions, the constraints under which it operates, and the policy trade-offs that the Congress has struck in enacting the law on the books. Let me be clear: I am emphatically not defending this law and the way it is elaborated and executed by the agency. There is much to criticize on both scores and an army of justified critics in the media, the professoriate, and the general public. Indeed, one is hard put to find an outside defender of ICE. This is hardly surprising, and is a newsworthy story of its own. After all, any system of mass administration generates enormous inefficiency, frequent errors and fraud, and too many arbitrary injustices. These pathologies are especially endemic in a system that combines service, enforcement, and adjudication functions; whose individual clientele consists largely of people who cannot vote, fear sudden removal, and are often poor and ignorant of the country's language and customs; and where the immigrants' stakes in getting a favorable decision are extremely high—in the case of refugees, perhaps a matter of life or death.

That said, what I think even the best immigration journalists fail to provide is a sympathetic explanation of the trade-offs and the constraints on the system that administers them. By "sympathetic explanation," I certainly do *not* mean one that excuses or extenuates that system's errors, follies, and injustices. Rather, I mean an account that takes these trade-offs, multiple missions, and constraints seriously rather than ignoring or obscuring them in the interests of telling the always compelling and indignation-stirring story of individual suffering, victimization, and injustice. For example, an ineffective immigration enforcement system—one that fails to deter, proceeds slowly, and is plagued by fraud—does more than provide more breathing room and opportunity for relief to individual immigrants who are caught in the great maw of the immigration bureaucracy. It also creates what I would call *invisible victims*. These are individuals who may be equally or more vulnerable and worthy of protection than the ones whose stories journalists so effectively and dramatically tell but about whom they seldom write.

Who are these invisible victims? There are many categories, but I shall mention only a few. First are the millions of deserving people who want to come to the United States and who would otherwise qualify to enter legally but who cannot do so because of the political backlash aroused by public perception of ineffective enforcement at the border and in the interior. All politicians who hope to expand immigration or provide amnesty for the undocumented fear this backlash and must proceed gingerly to avoid its force. This almost always means promising tighter control as a (usually *the*) top priority, a strategy reflected in President Obama's initial immigration reform proposals and in Senator John McCain's before him.

A second kind of invisible victim consists of those legal immigrants whose wages are reduced by competition from undocumented workers. Labor economists disagree about precisely what those wage effects are, but they all find that the clearest wage-reduction effects are felt by other immigrants who came earlier; the effects on native workers are secondary. A third group of invisible victims consists of the genuine refugees whose ability to convince the government of their credible fear of persecution is undermined by the high incidence of fraud committed by many asylum-seekers and others, many of whom have compelling personal stories, who seek to dissemble their way inside the gates. This fraud is encouraged by the government's inevitable difficulty in refuting the underlying factual allegations about persecution in the claimant's country of origin. Its notoriety has generated a general skepticism about the veracity of asylum claims, a skepticism that increases the likelihood that genuine ones will be rejected. A fourth kind of invisible victim consists of those who are held in detention because this is seen as the only way to ensure that they will appear for their hearings in immigration court. (An experiment run by the Vera Foundation some years back suggests that there may be other, better ways to ensure the appearance of these people in some cases, but that was of course merely an experiment and the cost implications of moving to a new system of mass, routinized administration were not entirely clear.)

Journalists largely ignore other aspects of the immigration system that not only create many invisible victims but would also help to explain to the reading public why the government adopts policies that might otherwise strike the uninformed observer as perverse. Journalists, by failing to explain their rationale, often depict these policies as more perverse than they are in the real, inevitably compromised world of mass administration. Some aspects of the system seldom if ever appear in our elite newspapers. For example, studies demonstrate that 80 percent of immigrants who are deportable but not detained decide to abscond before their hearings and melt into the population. This is a huge proportion. Think about what this absconding rate does to an enforcement system. It practically forces the agency to detain such people rather than leaving them at large, with all the restrictions on personal liberty and large detention costs that this entails.

Another pattern that attracts little journalistic interest (to which I referred earlier) is how hard it is for the government actually to deport somebody—that is, to apprehend the person, obtain a formal deportation order (usually simple, albeit plagued by delay, once he or she is placed in proceedings), and then actually put the person on the plane or take him or her to the border and make sure that the person leaves the country. As immigration professionals know, a high percentage of immigrants under deportation order respond to the government's instruction to appear at a certain place and time with their baggage so that they can be removed by disappearing, never to be seen again. These instructions are known in the trade as "run letters."

A third story that I don't see much written about—Rodríguez alludes to it and I have written about this for a long time—is what I call the severe fiscal mismatch between the revenues from immigrant activity and tax payments, which (with the exception of sales taxes) go largely to Washington, D.C., and the enormous cost burdens imposed by immigrants, especially undocumented ones, which are borne at the state and local levels. Indeed, I view as scandalous the federal government's failure to reimburse localities for these costs as Congress promised to do more than twenty years ago, costs for public services—schools, hospitals, prisons, and so forth—that federal enforcement failures have thrust on states and localities. This fiscal mismatch, by the way, is perhaps the main reason why some states and localities have adopted arguably unconstitutional laws attempting to enforce the immigration laws themselves rather than relying entirely on federal enforcement. Speaking of prisons, another story that elite newspapers seldom cover concerns the very high percentage of those held in state and local prisons and jails who are deportable undocumented immigrants but are not promptly deported—a phenomenon mentioned earlier in this chapter.[13] Journalists could easily write about this disturbing pattern without suggesting that immigrants are more prone to crime than American citizens, which is not the case.

Yet another story that needs to be told concerns the administrative burdens that almost any legalization program (that is, amnesty) would impose on the already overwhelmed Department of Homeland

Security. I can think of no immigration expert who does not acknowledge that some form of amnesty program is both necessary and politically inevitable—if not now, then some day. Even many conservative politicians accept this fact while insisting that many specific preconditions be met. But any precondition that the law requires an undocumented immigrant to meet to qualify for amnesty will require detailed paperwork, documentation, verification, agency adjudication, and in many cases, administrative and judicial review of bureaucratic determinations. So complex is this process that the provisions of the 1986 amnesty, for example, were still being litigated almost twenty years later. If we favor a politically viable amnesty—and I know of no immigration journalist who does not—then we must admit that a process of this kind will be at the heart of it. After all, to will the end is to will the necessary means to that end. Again, however, I have never seen an explanation of this fact in the pages of the *New York Times* or the *Wall Street Journal.*

Nor do immigration journalists compare the U.S. and European immigration systems. Such a comparison would reveal that our system, for all of its inequities, is more benign and less harsh toward immigrants than those of other affluent liberal democracies. It would provide readers with a more sophisticated context to help them assess and reform our own policies. Another interesting fact about the system that has large implications for how Americans view immigration, but that journalists seldom mention, is that more than half of the people who get green cards each year already live in the United States, often in illegal or temporary legal status. This is not the conventional image of the admissions process.

An important "structural" story that I have never seen in the papers, one that illustrates the great chasm between the law on the books and the law in action, is this: Immigration enforcement is driven less by the law than by a mundane administrative constraint visible only to officials at the local level—the number of beds that are available for detaining immigrants whom the government wishes to deport. If beds are available in a district, the agency will arrest more deportable immigrants. If not, they will look the other way. This factor alone is a major driver of immigration enforcement at the local level, where it really counts.

Another fascinating story that has received less attention than it deserves from immigration journalists is the long virtual war between the federal courts and the Board of Immigration Appeals (BIA) in the U.S. Department of Justice.[14] For years, eminent appellate judges led by

Richard Posner have rebuked the BIA for its often arbitrary decisions, its inadequate fact-finding, and its general indifference to the rule of law. This should be red meat for immigration journalists; after all, the facts of these cases are compelling, the courts' jeremiads against the government are colorful, and the insight that they afford of the larger system would be instructive to readers.

I have also never seen a story that explains how immigration enforcement actually works in detail and on the ground. In fact, the enforcement system begins, and depends entirely, on decisions made by front-line inspectors at the ports of entry and by our consular officials abroad—generally recent college graduates on their first assignments in the Foreign Service—processing visa applications. These inexperienced officials must make very rapid decisions with essentially no information other than what the documents in the dossier reveal. With applicants lined up outside around the block (and perhaps around the clock), and with their bureaucratic superiors pressuring the visa officers to meet daily quotas to satisfy *their* bosses, these officials are supposed to determine in several minutes which of the hordes of applicants might carry certain risks: of overstaying their visas, of wanting to stay in the United States, of seeking public benefits, to national security, to public health, and so forth. How would you make those kinds of decisions in their situation? You might inevitably—and rationally—resort to stereotypes and profiling simply because you would have no other choice, given your severe informational and time constraints.

I have also seen nothing in the newspapers that explains the intriguing work of sociologists like Mary C. Waters (see her chapter in this book) on the attitudes of black immigrants from the Caribbean and from Africa toward American blacks and other minorities, particularly in the workplace. Waters paints a vivid and disturbing portrait of immigration-driven discrimination *within* racial groups. The final example of immigration stories seldom told relates to the intriguing and far-reaching phenomenon that has been mentioned by Eduardo Porter in the *New York Times* and studied more systematically by Harvard political scientist Robert Putnam in his recent work.[15] One might call this the dark side of immigration-based diversity—the negative effects of this diversity on Americans' (and Europeans') eagerness to participate in politics and communal life and their willingness to support wealth redistribution within their societies.

. . .

Readers need to know and think about these more structural and systematic aspects of the immigration experience, not just the always exalting stories of immigrant success and the infuriating stories of immigrant victimization at the hands of incompetent bureaucrats, callous enforcers, exploitative employers, inveterate racists, and other scoundrels and fools who populate the immigration world, like all worlds.

NOTES

1. Peter H. Schuck, "Law and the Study of Migration," in *Migration Theory: Talking across Disciplines,* 2nd edition, edited by Caroline Brettell and James Hollifield (New York: Routledge, 2008), 249–50.

2. Richard L. Abel, "Practicing Immigration Law in Filene's Basement," in *Lawyers in the Dock: Learning from Attorney Disciplinary Proceedings* (New York: Oxford University Press, 2008).

3. Jack Citrin, "Political Culture," in *Understanding America: The Anatomy of an Exceptional Nation,* edited by Peter Schuck and James Q. Wilson (New York: Public Affairs, 2008), 153–54.

4. Roberto Suro, "Attitudes Toward Immigrants and Immigration Policy," August 16, 2005, Pew Hispanic Center, available online at http://pewhispanic .org/reports/report.php?ReportID=52.

5. For example, Peter H. Schuck, "Taking Immigration Federalism Seriously," *University of Chicago Law Forum* (2007): 59–67.

6. Peter H. Schuck and John Williams, "Removing Criminal Aliens: The Pitfalls and Promises of Federalism," *Harvard Journal of Law and Public Policy* 22, no. 367 (2000): 367–463.

7. In June 2009 states reported having 64,053 immigrants in their prisons, and federal prisons reported having 30,445 immigrant inmates in custody; see Heather C. West, "Bureau of Justice Statistics, Prison Inmates at Midyear 2009—Statistical Tables 23," U.S. Department of Justice, June 2010.

8. As of August 28, 2010, noncitizens represented 26.2 percent of the federal prison population; see Federal Bureau of Prisons, "Quick Facts about the Bureau of Prisons," U.S. Department of Justice, available at www.bop.gov/news/quick .jsp. At midyear in 2008, 2,363 of approximately 2,829 jail jurisdictions nationwide reported on the number of non-U.S. citizens in their custody to the Bureau of Justice Statistics's annual midyear survey of the nation's jails. The reporting jurisdictions reported that 47,934 non-U.S. citizens were in their custody, or 9 percent of their total population. Although the same basic annual survey was conducted for 2009 as well, in that survey jails were not asked to report on the number of non-U.S. citizens in their custody. See Todd D. Minton and William J. Sabol, "Bureau of Justice Statistics, Jail Inmates at Midyear 2008, Statistical Tables 6," U.S. Department of Justice, 2009. It should be noted, however, that these population statistics represent a snapshot in time and do not reflect the total number of non-U.S. citizens that are incarcerated per year, particularly at the county level due to the relatively short sentences.

9. See Robert J. Sampson, "Rethinking Crime and Immigration," *Contexts* 7 (Winter 2008): 28–33.

10. U.S. Senate Committee on Appropriations, "Fact Sheet: Enhanced Border and Immigration Security," 2010. The total detained criminal immigrant population in fiscal year 2007 was estimated to be approximately 630,000 nationwide, with an additional 275,000 immigrants in the United States illegally but not in detention. See *Department of Homeland Security, Appropriations for Fiscal Year 2007: Hearings before a Subcommittee of the Senate Committee on Appropriations*, 109th Congress 453 (2006).

11. For example, Peter H. Schuck, "An Immigration Reform Window Opens," *Los Angeles Times*, January 30, 2011.

12. One close and highly critical observer of the *New York Times* castigates the paper for having, in pursuit of this ideology, "either ignored, miscovered, or muted the less appealing realities of immigration—especially those involving the illegal immigration that has threatened to swamp the southwestern part of the country in recent decades." William McGowan, "Immigration and the *New York Times*," *Backgrounder*, Center for Immigration Studies, January 2011.

13. For an extensive discussion of the barriers to prompt deportation of such criminals, see Peter H. Schuck, "Immigrant Criminals in Overcrowded Prisons: Rethinking an Anachronistic Policy," unpublished manuscript, 2011. A very short version of this manuscript is Peter H. Schuck, "Do Not Go Directly to Jail," *New York Times*, December 6, 2010.

14. The *New York Times* did run such an article by its legal correspondent; see Adam Liptak, "Courts Criticize Judges' Handling of Asylum Cases," *New York Times*, December 26, 2005, online at www.nytimes.com/2005/12/26/national/26immigration.html?_r=1&ref=adam_liptak.

15. Eduardo Porter, "The Divisions That Tighten the Purse Strings," *New York Times*, April 29, 2007, page BU4; and Robert D. Putnam, "E Pluribus Unum: Diversity and Community in the 21st Century," *Scandinavian Political Studies* 30 (2007): 137–74.

Covering Immigration

From Stepchild Beat to Newsroom Mainstream

PATRICK J. McDONNELL

For the better part of two decades, I covered the U.S.-Mexico border and immigration issues for the *Los Angeles Times*. I watched the rapid growth of illegal immigration in the 1980s, witnessed the buildup of forces and barriers along the border, and was on the ground in California for the emergence of the immigration "backlash" movement, the groundswell of discontent that culminated in Proposition 187 and later spread throughout the country. I covered immigration "reform" laws and sundry efforts to alter refugee and asylum policy. I tracked demographic changes and wrote about conflicts linked to the migratory flow. I traveled to "sending communities" in Mexico and Central America to see how migration played out there. I've since observed the issue in other international incarnations: Bolivian apparel workers exploited in Buenos Aires sweatshops; disenchanted Muslim migrants who turn to fundamentalism in the gritty neighborhoods of London, Kuwait City, and Dubai; desperate Iraqis forced to flee their shattered homeland. Reporting on immigration and refugees has been both exhilarating and frustrating. I hope to convey some of that texture in this chapter.

Throughout my days on the beat, I always felt it took a little extra work to get stories about immigrants into the newspaper. One basic challenge was how to get attention for stories about immigrants and refugees, a population generally little known in the newsroom, despite deep preconceptions about who they are. A related issue was how to make the stories compelling for a U.S. readership. And, finally, there was always the concern of how to write without being perceived as an advocate—a radioactive label in mainstream journalism. These are probably dilemmas faced by everyone who explores this emotion-laden topic—be they journalists, scholars, bloggers, and so on.

A few thoughts about the immigration beat. First, it's like no other beat. There's no City Hall, no cop shop, generally no press room, to mention a few typical news-gathering venues. The whole issue is a lot more dispersed and amorphous, often a matter of interpretation and perception. It lacks the cache of more traditional beats, like covering politics or law enforcement, though it has both political and enforcement elements. When I began writing about immigration, there was little sense of an institutional memory of past coverage, a blueprint to follow. With immigration's emergence as a signature issue, however, a lot of this has changed, and the beat has taken a more prominent place in many newsrooms. I should add that the ethnic press, with its immigrant base, has always stressed the issue.

Coverage of immigration in the mainstream press still tends to be episodic, driven by crises—a new immigration law; a sweatshop exposed; smuggled migrants lost in the desert or at sea; a spate of raids of workshops or homes. All at once, newsroom antennae are raised and editors are demanding copy about something that had been way off their radar. Most stories tend to focus on the phenomenon of illegal immigration, not the much larger population of legal immigrants. Of course, this is where the controversy is, drawing journalistic scrutiny. Immigration's status as a kind of stepchild beat has its merits and demerits. It can be advantageous because it gives enterprising reporters a lot of liberty to seek out offbeat tales far from the madding crowd of pack coverage. One can generally be free to wander about and find stories that are timely and original. The assignment generally lacks the imperative for a daily drumbeat of copy. A reporter can jump between regulatory and legal developments to personal stories of immigrants. There is no shortage of human drama.

But framing stories can be tricky. My experience is that most editors in the mainstream press are several generations removed from the immigrant experience and worldview. The storyline is often an exotic one for news managers, something from the distant past, more Ellis Island than Tijuana, evoking history texts and half-remembered stories from long-departed grandparents. While every city editor will know the name of the police chief or the mayor, and will likely consider coverage of these personages vital to the daily report, they are less likely to be familiar with the local immigration director. They may be unaware of the nearby immigration lockup, though they surely know all about the local jails. The convoluted intricacies of immigration law inevitably elicit a yawn. The "human" feature pieces often tend to sound the same. All this poses challenges for "selling" stories, framing often complex issues to get them into print. Immigration sometimes feels like a foreign beat, but lacking the vogue of being abroad.

. . .

I would venture to guess that most reporters who cover immigration are sympathetic at some level to the plight of immigrants. Standing up for the underdog is a hallowed journalistic tradition. And the immigration saga arises from a fundamental human drama: people's desire to escape confining (and sometimes life-threatening) circumstances and find a better life. It bespeaks a yearning for betterment. On some level, it's the basic human story since our ancestors walked out of Africa all those millennia ago. Immigration is an experience that tends to mark one for life, as one weaves between the idealized world of the Old Country and this dynamic but often exasperating nation. This holds true both for immigrants and their offspring. I am also the child of immigrants, who emigrated to the United States in the 1920s and 1930s. My parents didn't face the hurdle of being "illegal" and weren't fleeing death squads. But in many ways their life trajectories mirrored those of today's low-wage immigrants from Latin America, Asia, and elsewhere. They fled from an impoverished, largely rural nation suffering postindependence traumas of development and identity. They settled in urban ethnic enclaves (in New York City), stayed fiercely loyal to family and church and culture, were wary of outsiders, and stressed education and upward mobility for their children. So some sense of empathy came naturally to me.

However, as a reporter for a mainstream publication, the *Los Angeles Times,* I had to draw a line between identification and any sense of advocacy. I know colleagues who have also faced this challenge, notably Latino journalists reflexively assigned to what some have disparagingly labeled the "taco beat," only to have their "objectivity" questioned. Once or twice I was summoned to meet with editors in glass offices, where my superiors counseled me on the need not to be viewed as favoring one side or another. The experience made me redouble efforts to be as bias-free as possible, as difficult as that is, considering the social and cultural contexts that have shaped all of us, journalists and everyone else. Absolute objectivity is an illusory goal, but a dedication to fairness and accuracy—to listening to all sides—are bedrock values of the craft. The lesson served me well as the immigration issue became ever more combustible—and later, as a war correspondent in Iraq, where each sentence about an unpopular war was subjected to intense scrutiny.

. . .

I first began covering the U.S.-Mexico border in San Diego in the mid-1980s, a heyday for illegal immigration in the area. In those days, thousands gathered nightly at strategic spots along the northern tier of Tijuana and the southern strip of San Diego County. This extraordinary tableau was pretty much regarded as a given, accepted by all. But for me it was always a jarring spectacle. I had previously worked as a reporter in El Paso, where there was a natural boundary (the Rio Grande), and folks waded or used some kind of boat or flotation device to cross. In San Diego, though, the numbers were exponentially higher. Groups of a hundred or more often set out together.

I sometimes accompanied them on their nocturnal jaunts. Once our group included a mariachi band bound for a gig in San Diego; this was their weekend commute. On another occasion, I and a photographer colleague were "busted" by the border patrol, who swooped down on us with four-wheel-drive Blazers and a helicopter. The next day, the regional Immigration and Naturalization Service commissioner denounced us as irresponsible lawbreakers. Once I got a mini-scoop: Ensconced amid a group waiting to cross from *la linea* in Tijuana, I witnessed a group of border patrolmen using their loudspeaker equipment to broadcast epithets to the crowds waiting to venture to the U.S. side that evening. The broadcast was a reckless and inflammatory act in that tense milieu. My article prompted an internal investigation and a disciplining of the agents involved.

What we were seeing in those days was a snapshot of the mobile population that was transforming the makeup of California, and the country. The border had become a kind of demographic launching pad, sending forth these multitudes to towns and cities across the United States. I listened to accounts of migrants' far-flung destinations—tobacco fields in Tennessee, chicken farms in Maine, delis in New York, fishing fleets in Alaska, and, of course, all kinds of enterprises in Los Angeles. I wondered a lot about how these people were changing their adopted homes. Here, it seemed to me, was evidence that the United States remained a land of great opportunity, a place that held out the hope of social mobility so absent in much of the world. Certainly that was the prevalent perception. Most of these people were not desperate; the great majority could have survived back in Mexico or wherever they came from. But they wanted something better, the chance for improved "horizons," as I was often told. Even fierce critics of illegal immigration may concede a fundamental nobility of purpose for many.

Several staging areas in San Diego led directly to a labyrinth of U.S. freeways converging on the border. Huddled groups could regularly be seen heading north on foot along the freeway shoulders and medians, sometimes amid the traffic lanes, dodging cars and trucks as the vehicles sped by, oblivious. They often took shelter on the median rail in the midst of eight or ten lanes of traffic. I spent a lot of time hanging out at the border freeways, observing and questioning. I befriended *coyotes,* or smugglers, and guides who work with them. While demonized by U.S. law enforcement, coyotes see themselves a bit like contemporary Robin Hoods, helping the little guys outwit *la migra,* despite their sometimes exorbitant fees and links to often vicious people-smuggling rings and other nefarious activities. It turned out that the coyote utilized the freeways in a very purposeful manner. The border patrol, wisely, was hesitant to try to detain anyone trekking amid the traffic, since they might bolt into the oncoming vehicles. Ditches, ramps, and patches of brush along the freeways became gathering points, temporary safe-havens and passageways. The coyote was familiar with all the drainage tunnels and other entrances and exits. Strategically placed lookouts could keep a close eye on the traffic and any sign of the law. The freeway became the migrants' way.

The problem was, this arrangement was risky in the extreme. Immigrants were being run down daily and ending up maimed or killed—their deaths seldom meriting more than a one- or two-line "brief" in the paper, much like the classic newspaper filler items of buses plunging from treacherous Third World roads. Wasn't this a bigger story? I wondered. Editors would typically shrug and say they'd it heard it all before, not much interest. From one editor, I detected an attitude that seemed to suggest, "What did they expect, crossing a freeway—at night, no less!" A photographer friend and I were aghast and irritated at this attitude. At the time, the story of alleged abuse of an elephant in a Southern California zoo was making headlines. What if these were elephants being mowed down. Or whales? Would that make the carnage a better story? Would our readers be engaged then?

It wasn't just a border phenomenon. More migrants were being mauled by vehicles along Interstate 5 some fifty miles north near the Orange County line, another strategic grid where the border patrol operates a vigorous checkpoint, a kind of second frontier: Once migrants were past it, they were basically home free to Los Angeles, and the rest of the United States, melding into the fabric of U.S. society and unlikely ever to be caught. To circumvent the checkpoint, smugglers devised alternative routes, often involving a death-defying dash on the highway. Migrants were regularly scampering across the eight-lane thoroughfare, where traffic was cruising at seventy miles an hour or more. The last thing drivers expected to run into were pedestrians, often entire groups traveling at night.

Working with U.S. and Mexican authorities, along with hospital and morgue records, I began tracking down the relatives of migrants killed—and also motorists unfortunate enough to have hit them. I recall one mortified woman telling me how she had bumped into something on the freeway one evening, stunning her. Once at her home, she checked the underside of her car, where she made a grisly discovery: blood and tissue were spattered about and a severed human arm was still attached to the bottom of the chassis. She never saw her victim but was traumatized by the incident. Police extracted the macabre evidence. I suspect the gruesome memory still gives her the chills, two decades later. I also talked to families of immigrants struck along the freeway as well as to survivors of such accidents. The story became more human, more accessible for U.S. readers. It began to gain traction with the press and public.

Eventually, the slaughter on the freeways in San Diego drew national and international media interest. U.S. authorities were forced to act: officials erected modified speed bumps, fenced off freeways, and came up with some singular warning signs, featuring a silhouette of a family running across the freeway—an image that soon turned iconic, seeming to capture a sense of desperation. Of course, the entire border zone near San Diego eventually became heavily fortified, forcing the human traffic to the parched expanses to the east and an even deadlier hazard—dehydration and exposure in the deserts of California and Arizona. All this is to say that it sometimes took a lot of digging to get stories about immigrants into the paper. But one way to succeed is to produce compelling narratives based on original reporting.

. . .

The freeway casualties were front-line victims in a larger drama of transborder trafficking and the movement of people. This is a vulnerable population caught in the middle of conflicting forces—U.S. immigration policy and people's drive to improve their lives and often to be reunited with family members. We as reporters strive to personalize the dilemmas we write about; it's our natural response. The deaths of immigrants on freeways and in the deserts are especially vivid examples. But the same template applies to more quotidian situations. Mainstays of the genre are the tales of hard-working immigrants or refugees caught up in the maze of U.S. law. Some examples: the mother being deported while her U.S. citizen children remain behind; the young man facing expulsion back to an unfamiliar homeland he hasn't been to since he was a child; needy families denied health care or in-state tuition; the refugee locked up for months or years as his or her case works its way through the system. All make for gripping human tales.

In the run-up to Proposition 187, the 1994 California ballot initiative targeting immigrant benefits, I wrote a number of pieces about how the proposed new restrictions could impact people. I examined issues that still resonate today: immigrant use of health care and other public services; the prevalence of "mixed" families, including both legal and unlawful residents, in immigrant communities; local police attitudes toward enforcing federal immigration law; and the "anchor baby" phenomenon. I recall one story about a woman whose mother, an undocumented immigrant with advanced dementia, was living in a nursing home, the tab paid by federal and state monies. The desperate woman didn't have a clue what she would do if her mother was kicked out because of an inability to pay—one of the likely consequences if Proposition 187 had become law. The story generated a lot of reaction: some folks were sympathetic, others outraged that taxpayer dollars were funding an "illegal's" time in a care facility.

But I reached a point where I questioned the wisdom of writing so many stories that turned on a similar trope: immigrants as victims. Were such accounts bolstering a negative stereotype or giving a distorted picture of immigrant life? In fact, the vast majority of immigrants are not victims. They are by and large industrious, positive-minded people who get by on a lot less than most people. Immigrants tend to be among the most ambitious, industrious residents of their home communities, those imbued with a desire for improved horizons, and a sense of adventure. Many seldom seek any kind of public assistance. This reality of immigrant life was brought home to me when a new study appeared documenting how Mexican immigrants in California were rapidly moving into the middle class. It was a big societal story that we had somehow missed, though it was evident all around us. The relentless focus on the spectacle of the border and the struggles of illegal immigrants had obscured this "good news" story. There was a lack of drama, and of victimhood, about a hard-working group that obeys the law and doesn't engender many headlines. Other studies documented rising immigrant home-buying, business ownership, savings, etc. It seems academics, more sheltered from the exigencies of the daily deadline than journalists, can sometimes be better-equipped to take the long-term view, not miss the forest for the tree. I made an effort to focus more on the broader demographic changes associated with rising immigration. A major example in California was the dramatically evolving nature of the electorate as more and more immigrants became citizens. That development was to have far-reaching impact on California politics, as Latino votes were courted and newly elected Latino lawmakers wielded great clout.

. . .

It was at the end of the 1980s, while I was covering the U.S.-Mexico border for the *Los Angeles Times* in San Diego, that I heard the first stirrings of widespread discontent with the large-scale immigration that was then remaking California and the nation. A group of activists had begun staging protests along the border in San Diego. They would park their cars and trucks near the boundary and turn on their headlights. They dubbed the movement Light up the Border, and its aim, they said, was to dramatize their dissatisfaction with galloping illegal immigration. At first, the whole thing seemed quixotic, absent the embittered, bellicose tone that would soon dominate.

"There's hardly any fence here at all," Muriel Watson, the movement founder, told me one afternoon as she gestured toward Tijuana. She was a Republican Party activist whose late husband had been a border patrol chief.[1]

The movement touched a nerve. Word got out around the state. Livid protestors started arriving from all over to express their vexation. This, of course, was before the days of cable TV personalities, radio talk-show hosts, and bloggers who vent on immigration. It became pretty clear that this was about something bigger: It was an insurrection targeting the demographic explosion that had transformed a state, where a kind of Midwestern Protestant ethic had long held sway, despite California's deep ties to Mexico and its long history as a destination for immigrants. It turned out that the protestors blamed illegal immigrants from Mexico for almost every contemporary shortcoming—from substandard schools to shoddy hospitals to crowded freeways, street violence, and even environmental degradation. Many protestors despaired at the proliferation of the Spanish language, wondering if English would be eclipsed—or, indeed, whether Mexico was in the process of la Reconquista, silently reclaiming California and the Southwest. Others worried about the infiltration of gangs and even terrorists, though this was more than decade before the September 11, 2001, attacks.

"Something has got to be done at this border," Gordon Jones, a retired Navy chief driving a pickup, told me at one Light up the Border event. "There are all kinds of people coming across. How many Iraqis are out there?" he asked. "How many Libyans?"[2] Later, of course, the coupling of illegal immigration with terrorism would become a standard tactic of those seeking to reduce new entries. The Light up the Border rallies became ever more boisterous and began to garner national press attention. Representatives from rights groups, Latino organizations, churches, and other "pro-immigrant" sectors began showing up, denouncing the Light up the Border militants as ill-informed and bigoted. The two factions exchanged diatribes. Some folks tossed rocks.

Race and ethnicity were of course significant backdrops to the escalating controversy. Most of the immigrants drawing ire were poor folks from Mexico and Central America. Most of those complaining were non-Latino whites, along with some African Americans and U.S.-born Latinos. For immigrant advocates, caricaturing the Light up the Border crowd as a bunch of stereotype-spouting racists became standard practice. But this too struck me as overly simplistic. I grappled with how to cover this phenomenon, this fast-expanding rage about large-scale immigration and the changes it had wrought. I knew something about how disquieting rapid demographic change could be.

I was reared in a mostly white-ethnic patch of the South Bronx that had undergone jarring ethnic shifts beginning in the 1960s. The children of the old immigrant families moved out; new folks moved in, many from the Caribbean and the U.S. South. This was the era before the word *diversity* became fashionable and political correctness tempered debate. Our streets saw lots of conflicts, as did many other working-class urban neighborhoods. Those old ethnic enclaves were tribal in a way: people of similar ancestries banded together and mistrusted outsiders. It had been many generations since our churches were burned or our "kind" wasn't welcome. But those collective memories, however distant, still inform a community. Tension was in the air in that era of urban riots, political assassinations, and the Vietnam War. And when crime and arson came to decimate our streets, it was easy enough to blame the new arrivals.

The polemics from all sides in the immigration debate prompted me to reconsider my coverage. I saw a need to try to explain how California had come to this nasty precipice. Coverage of the immigrant-backlash issue, I concluded, must be as scrupulous as reporting on immigrants and their concerns. Dismissing immigration critics as simply cranks or bigots didn't add much to a debate that begged for rational analysis. Polls showed deep dissatisfaction among U.S. citizens with large-scale immigration. I began to spend a lot of time chatting with the immigrant-control crowd, attending meetings in homes, social clubs, school auditoriums, and other venues. One day I ventured into a suburban community and spoke with a young mother involved in the movement. She struck me as a pleasant and even reasonable person, though she was clearly enraged about what was going on around her.

This woman sat in her neatly appointed living room in the exurbs of San Diego and pointed to a dirt track beyond her front yard. "That's the path they use," she told me. "Every day." Indeed, migrant laborers lived in a rough camp in the chaparral a half-mile or so away. Each morning and evening they walked by the home where she lived with her husband and children. On weekends, when the migrant laborers weren't working, they sang, drank beer, and roasted meat on open fires. From her standpoint, these unkempt visitors from another world represented a kind of alien invasion, a mocking of her own version of the American Dream. I could understand her sense of discomfort and even fear, just as I sympathized with the plight of the migrant workers, many of whom I had gotten to know. The reality that the immigrant workforce helped subsidize the comforts of Southern California suburban living was a difficult notion to transmit. Many cherished their household help—their maids and nannies and gardeners—but couldn't connect beloved "Maria" and trusty "Juan" with what they regarded as the border-jumping rabble.

. . .

Unquestionably, a disturbing leitmotif of intolerance and xenophobia animated some recesses of the immigrant-backlash movement. It had been seen before in U.S. history, during past efforts to limit immigration of Chinese, Japanese, southern and eastern Europeans, as well as assorted "cosmopolitans," a euphemism much in vogue early in the last century. Some dubbed the new protestors the "neo-nativists," a reference to an earlier generation of restrictionists. Conspiracy theories about the Reconquista of California proliferated. Unfortunately, the harsh rhetoric fueled some ugly acts.

In November 1988, on a semirural San Diego street called Black Mountain Road, two young Mexican migrant workers were gunned down with a high-powered rifle. Both were homeless farm workers sleeping in the rough. The murders of Hilario Castaneda Salgado, age twenty-two, and Matilde Macedo de la Sancha, age nineteen, remained unsolved for months. Then one day a guilt-ridden young man confessed to an Army recruiter about how he had participated in the slayings. A friend of his, he told investigators, had fired at the two migrant workers with an assault rifle from the back of a pickup truck. His friend, who had subsequently joined the Army and was in training to be a paratrooper, had professed his hatred of "Mexicans" and shouted "Kill! Kill!" as he squeezed the trigger. Prosecutors pronounced it a hate crime. Both participants in the murder were sent to prison. Sadly, the murder along Black Mountain Road would not be the last such incident.

The challenge: How to separate legitimate concerns about the social and economic costs of immigration from such hateful manifestations, while also not losing sight of immigrants' many contributions. This was never an easy story to cover intelligently and fairly. From my standpoint, reporters covering contemporary immigration and refugee issues are in the vanguard of modern social documentation. Time-honored journalistic principles like fairness and a dedication to accuracy often get a bad rap in an era of plummeting newspaper circulation and the free-for-all of the Internet. But my experience observing immigration in its many manifestations has helped convince me that those much-mocked old journalistic values stand society well. I'm pleased to see a new generation of young journalists, many immigrants themselves, or the sons and daughters of immigrants, engaged with the story.

It is a story that keeps coming back, notwithstanding the desire of many politicians that the immigration debate go away. The Obama administration seems incapable of delivering the comprehensive immigration "reform" that the president professes to favor, a goal that many Democratic Party constituencies demand. The fierce debate surrounding the immigration law passed in 2010 in Arizona was, in some ways, a replay of the Proposition 187 affair in California years earlier, although there are of course many differences. Children whom I saw crossing the border years ago with their parents are now often fully "Americanized," English-speaking adults—yet multitudes remain undocumented, barred from careers because of their status and facing potential expulsion back to homelands they hardly recall. Few issues seem to divide like immigration. Yet the worldwide movement of peoples, and the changes and tensions and complications associated with that movement, are central themes of the modern era. People keep crossing borders, even as economies stagnate. As journalists, we endeavor to make some sense of it all, transcending to some extent, we would like to believe, our own preconceptions and innate biases. In my case, writing about immigration and being the son of immigrants has led me to places—physical, emotional, philosophical—to which I would never have traveled otherwise. I can only hope I have added some modest insight to this defining issue of our times.

NOTES

1. Patrick McDonnell, "Protestors Light Up the Border Again," *Los Angeles Times*, August 24, 1990.

2. Ibid.

Immigration and the Economy

In Part Two of the book, Edward Schumacher-Matos, formerly of the *New York Times* and the *Wall Street Journal* and now at the Kennedy School of Government at Harvard, and Barry R. Chiswick of George Washington University address the various socioeconomic claims and counterclaims that have informed the increasingly contentious debate about the economic causes and consequences of large-scale immigration. The economic firestorm that began on Wall Street in mid-2008 and raged through Main Streets all over the country, rapidly devouring large sectors of the economy, sets a new stage for examining the general relationship between the economy and large-scale immigration. How are we to think about immigration in an era of economic anxiety and peril? Has the economic collapse made immigration redundant or, worse, a threat? Is the periodic nativism at the heart of our basic ambivalence about immigration now to define the debate moving forward? What are the myths that are likely to continue to inform and misinform the debate over immigration and the economy in the foreseeable future? Below is a sample of the exchanges generated on immigration and the economy at the conference convened by the Nieman Foundation for Journalism at Harvard University.

. . .

Convener Marcelo M. Suárez-Orozco: My question is, Can immigration make or break the U.S. economy? Am I wrong, or is the impact of immigration on the thirteen trillion dollar U.S. gross domestic product relatively minor?

Panelist Barry R. Chiswick: The point that immigration will neither make nor break the American economy is absolutely right. If we had zero immigration, the American economy would still—except for the current financial crises—chug along very well; but the American economy has chugged along much better because of the long history of immigration. One of the effects of immigration has to do with the effects on capital flows. The large historical immigration to the United States has also attracted a lot of foreign capital, so it gets very difficult to disentangle the effects of immigration per se from some of the other effects that are a consequence of the immigration flow.

Panelist Eduardo Porter: I would also say that it's not always the case that an immigrant is competing against a domestic worker. After the Bracero program ended in the mid-1960s in California, perhaps you could have expected that agricultural labor would become more native, that American native workers would go into that field; but actually that did not really happen. What you did see was a move by farmers, by growers, to put more capital investment into the fields to reduce their use of labor.

· · ·

Audience question: Illegal immigrants are much less likely to impose a net fiscal cost because they're much less likely to seek benefits, so that may be one of the reasons why we [employers] have a preference for an illegal immigration system as opposed to legal immigration. That [reality] raises the exploitation problem, and so it starts to become very difficult to think about how you would come up with a rational immigration policy given the sources of public opposition and all these different impacts it has. So I am curious how you would reconcile the competing moral and economic concerns related to the fiscal problems.

Panelist Barry R. Chiswick: When we give amnesty to illegal aliens, their impact on the fiscal system changes. It's not only that they have become public, they now become eligible for a lot more in the way of benefits; but they also have rights to legally bring in family members from the country of origin, and that increases the negative fiscal impact. The 1996 welfare reform that tried to remove a lot of immigrants from the income transfer system was a direct result of the 1986 amnesty, which added officially nearly three million but actually many more because of dependent family members that just came in. You've articulated the dilemma beautifully.

Panelist Jess Benhabib: A discourse in ideas and rational thinking about it matters and, whichever side you come on about the actual cost—you are right. Illegal aliens may pay social security but don't collect. It's also the case that we have to look over the whole life, not just at the particular instant [of immigration]. This discussion may help, but the political economy of it is very different, and it'll depend on the economic conditions at the time. So, yes, discourse helps, discussion helps; but ultimately I think it's economic conditions that drive sentiment, and we have seen this throughout history.

. . .

Audience question: I'd like to follow up the question on legal versus illegal [and the economy]. The big question mark is around how you count the cost of educating children. Really what it comes down to is, Do you count that as an investment or as a cost?

Panelist Barry R. Chiswick: If the children are not in the United States, you don't have that expense. If the children are in this country, then that is part of the fiscal burden. There may be benefits down the road but, if the question is in the current situation, what are the taxes they contribute, what are the benefits that they and their family members receive? I think it's important to include the cost of education as well as the cost of health care. Now, routine health care they will probably not get; but when there is emergency health care, they will have access to public hospitals and that is also part of the cost. That cost is greater if they have more family members here.

. . .

Audience question: Just how much of a problem is it in the United States, the exploitation of the illegal immigrants?

Panelist Barry R. Chiswick: Whenever you have a population that is operating to some extent outside the legal system, they're going to be subject to this kind of ill treatment by their employers because the workers are vulnerable. They're afraid to report inappropriate behavior by employers whether it's violation of labor laws or sexual harassment or other inappropriate behavior. That's one of the consequences of having a large illegal alien population. You essentially encourage and sanction—not explicitly but implicitly—behavior that violates the law and behavior that violates social norms.

Panelist Jess Benhabib: This is absolutely true. It's an important point. The question is, What do you do about it? Do you legalize the immigrants, or do you expel them because there seems to be a logic here that says, If we care about them, that they're exploited, let's just send them back. But that stops short a little bit. What happens when they do go back? After all, they are here willingly. So it does become a question of values. It does become a question of excluding people from our labor market. Sometimes it's couched that it's for their good that we're not allowing them [to remain in the United States].

Panelist Barry R. Chiswick: But getting a subnormal wage in the United States may still be a wage far higher than they can get in the country of origin, and the working conditions may be appalling by American standards but may be very good by the standards in the country of origin. That's part of the dilemma, because we have certain standards that we want to hold here. The illegals may be willing to work for jobs way below those standards because it's much better than their alternative. That's part of the dilemma.

5

Consensus, Debate, and Wishful Thinking

The Economic Impact of Immigration

EDWARD SCHUMACHER-MATOS

At the heart of the battle over immigration is an issue that all sides claim as their own but on which few agree: What is the economic impact of immigration on the nation? Since the early 1980s, economists and advocates have been waging an often fierce battle over the effect immigrants have had on jobs, taxes, and national income. One side argues that immigrants—legal and illegal, low- and high-skilled— have damaged all three. Others maintain the opposite. Which is it?

Getting the answer right is crucial. Since the beginning of the republic, three factors—humanitarian refuge, family reunification, and labor needs—have driven the country's policy toward foreigners. Of them, labor need is in the widest national interest, affecting all Americans. In 2009 immigrants made up an estimated 15.5 percent of the workforce—or almost one of every seven workers (CBO 2010). Almost one in twenty—5.4 percent of the American workforce in 2008—was here illegally (Passel and Cohn 2009). Such large numbers suggests that a powerful demand by American businesses is attracting these workers. In this chapter I survey the economic literature and government statistics to lay out what we know and don't know. I also explore the resulting policy implications. Of what we don't know, there is much. Unlike in trade and finance, few economists actually study immigration. The field is dominated by a handful of labor economists. The subject's political sensitivity—and the lack of national and global regulatory institutions that might support research—keeps many others away.

Noneconomists reading this should keep two truths in mind. The first is that no economist knows the truth. Most rigorous studies seldom use conclusive language. *Suggests, implies, indicates, appears, estimates, assumes*—these are the sorts of words that economists lace throughout their work, and for good reason. Their conclusions are generally extracted from models and experiments. This makes it important to understand the methodology used, the assumptions made, and the context placed within existing theory. The second truth is that for all the sound and fury among the economists in the debate, the differences among them are in fact relatively minor.

TAXES: BEGGARING THY NEIGHBOR

Let's begin with the fiscal impact, as it would seem to be a straightforward accounting chore and thus the easiest to measure: you add up what immigrants pay in local, state, and federal taxes and compare that to what they receive in services. No one has been able to do this. Methodologies among local and state governments and among federal programs vary widely. So, too, do their demographic sources and definitions, the services they provide, and the types of taxes they collect. Researchers have had to fall back on estimates and on controversial assumptions. Many of these are value judgments.

A central question is how to count the fiscal costs related to children born in the United States to parents who are here either illegally or on temporary work visas. Under American law these children are birthright citizens. Yet, obviously, they wouldn't be here if not for the parents. Should the costs associated with the children be accounted as an immigrant cost? Or should the costs be lumped with all citizen children and seen as an investment in the nation's future? The children are almost all culturally American; few return to the homeland of their parents. Similarly, how do you apportion an accounting of the taxes and services related to the households of these children? Or of households in which some of the adults are unauthorized and others aren't? More than a third of the unauthorized immigrants in 2008 lived in such mixed-status families in which, on average, half the family members were legal residents or American citizens (Passel and Cohn 2009).

Complicating matters is that the income and spending habits of immigrants—particularly unauthorized ones—is sketchy. This affects any estimation on how much they pay in sales and income taxes. There is not even consistent, reliable information on many government expenditures. No one really knows, for example, how much the government spends on unauthorized immigrant children in specialized language classes in public schools. Such classes carry additional costs for school systems. And how should you count discretionary expenditures that some communities choose to make and others don't? Are they a burden imposed by immigrants if, arguably, the expenditures aren't necessary? This applies to many state and local police costs. Some states and communities choose to more readily arrest and jail unauthorized immigrants than others. Similarly, some states go in the other direction and are more generous in offering health and welfare benefits to immigrants.

In counting fiscal costs, activists conveniently pick the assumptions that most support their point of view. Still, some objective conclusions can be drawn from a critical review of the literature and from original government sources. The main points are:

- **State and local governments suffer the brunt of a short-term negative impact, but it is not negative for all, and the impact varies widely among them.**

Education is the largest single fiscal cost caused by immigrants, which is why state and especially local governments bear the lion's share of the fiscal cost related to immigration. In 2008, one out of every five of the nation's school children in kindergarten through twelfth grade was the child of an immigrant (Pew Hispanic 2010). One of every fourteen was the child of at least one illegal immigrant parent (Passel and Cohn 2009). The cost to educate a student who lacks English proficiency is variously estimated to be between 20 percent and 40 percent more than for a native-born student fluent in English (CBO 2007).

Health costs are also significant, in part because immigrants tend to be underinsured. In 2008, 24 percent of legal immigrants and a whopping 59 percent of unauthorized ones had no health insurance at all (Passel and Cohn 2009). Extrapolating from Los Angeles County data in 2000, one academic study estimated that national public health spending by all levels of government on all immigrant adults between the ages of eighteen and sixty-four was eighty-eight billion dollars (Goldman, Smith, and Sood 2006). Unauthorized immigrants received an estimated 1.2 percent of that.

But these numbers require some perspective. Immigrants as a group are mostly healthier than Americans. This is largely because they are demographically younger and come from countries with healthy life-styles. Once in the United States, the government spends less on them *per person* than for native-born Americans. Between 1999 and 2006, for example, in northeastern states—where government services are more generous for immigrants than in other parts of the country—non-citizens averaged receiving $780 a year in public health expenditures, compared with $1,200 for native-born Americans (Stimpson, Wilson, and Eschbach 2010). For all the public hoopla about immigrants' use of hospital emergency rooms, a study in *Health Affairs* found that in 2003, noncitizens had seventeen fewer emergency room visits per one hundred people than citizens did (Goldman, Smith, and Sood 2006). In a 2005 study by the University of California–Los Angeles, Mexican migrants who had been in California less than ten years were only half as likely (about 10 percent) to have visited an emergency room than U.S.-born whites (20 percent) (Zuñiga et al. 2005).

For the education and health of unauthorized and low-income immigrants, moreover, what often is overlooked in local debates is that the federal government offsets much of the state and local cost. In general, the federal government pays for about 10 percent of all K–12 education. This includes underwriting school lunch for low-income students, regardless of immigration status. Part of the funding also goes specifically to teaching English-language acquisition under the No Child Left Behind program (CBO 2010). Health reimbursements vary more broadly, because of the wide difference in restrictions that the states themselves have over patient eligibility. Depending on the state, the federal government historically pays 50 percent to 83 percent of the emergency health-care costs for low-income patients in general (CBO 2007). On top of this reimbursement, the feds since 1996 have provided extra Medicare funds to states for the treatment of low-income unauthorized immigrants. The federal government, for example, made one billion dollars in such funds available to states between fiscal years 2005 and 2008. The money covers childbirth. It also covers the treatment of individuals age sixty-five or older, youths under nineteen, caregivers, and the disabled. Often referred to as "emergency Medicaid," this program only covers services until the patient is stabilized.

State and local governments have some immigration enforcement costs too. Because enforcement of immigration law is a federal responsibility, however, Washington picks up most of the tab. Under the Justice Department's State Criminal Alien Assistance program, for example, state and local governments received $394 million in 2009 for jailhouse salaries (but not meals or overhead) related to unauthorized immigrants who commit crimes that are not immigration related (U.S. Department of Justice 2010).[1] The Department of Homeland Security (DHS) trains and enables local police to check arrests against immigration data banks under two other programs: Secure Communities for anyone jailed and 287g by police more generally. The 2010 DHS appropriations bill includes $200 million for Secure Communities and $5.4 million for 287g. The government's goal is to roll out Secure Communities to every local jail in the country by 2013.

In return, all immigrants pay state and local sales, excise, and property taxes—the latter if only as part of their rent. Between a half and three-quarters pay income taxes in those states that have such a tax. So they hardly receive a free ride. Still, local governments appear overall to suffer a negative impact, mostly because of education costs. State governments do better. Some, such as those in Texas, Arkansas, and Nebraska, have run surpluses because of immigrants, even from unauthorized immigrants (see Decker, Deichert, and Gouveia 2008; Capps et al. 2007; and Strayhorn 2006). These states do not offer generous public benefits in general, however, which may explain the accounting. A legislative report in Colorado, another less-than-generous state, suggested that in 2006 the state ran an immigrant-related deficit between twenty-three million dollars and sixty-six million dollars (CBO 2007b). That was 0.15 percent to 0.4 percent of the state budget, hardly enough to break the bank.

Perhaps the most insightful comparative study remains one done by the National Research Council (NRC 2007).[2] It included citizen children as an immigrant cost and looked in-depth at two states: California in 1994–95 and New Jersey in 1989–90. Updating in 1996 dollars, the NRC found that the average household headed by an immigrant in California received $3,463 more in state and local services than it paid in taxes. The figure for New Jersey, however, was much less: $1,484. California has the nation's largest immigrant population, proportionally and absolutely. California also is more generous than New Jersey, though the latter is hardly tight-fisted, particularly compared with many southern and western states. But what may have been the most critical factor explaining the difference between the two was that New Jersey has many more highly educated, high-tax-paying immigrants in its immigrant mix.

- The federal government, on the other hand, receives a net
  fiscal benefit. But it does incur a deficit for one subgroup—
  the unauthorized.

The federal government makes money off of immigrants. The study by the National Research Council estimated that in 1996, the federal surplus for the average immigrant household was $120 in California and $520 in New Jersey (NRC 1997). Since then, under a law passed that year by Congress, federal welfare benefits for immigrants have been reduced. In one change most immigrants entering the United States must become naturalized citizens or live at least five years as a legal permanent resident before they are eligible for most federal benefits. These benefits include food stamps, supplemental security income, and much of Medicaid. Refugees are among the few exceptions. Adult unauthorized immigrants are never eligible for need-based federal programs such as food stamps, Temporary Assistance for Needy Families, and most of Medicaid. Not counting the federal reimbursements to state and local governments, explicit federal spending for unauthorized immigrants is limited to little more than emergency disaster relief, some immunizations, treatment for communicable diseases, some access to soup kitchens, and limited housing assistance to those already receiving it before 1996.

But if citizen children are included, families headed by an unauthorized immigrant parent appear to receive more from the federal government than they pay. In addition to the education costs for all immigrant children—legal or not—the citizen children are eligible for food stamps and other need-based welfare benefits. Using the NRC methodology, Steven A. Camarota of the Center for Immigration Studies (CIS) estimated that in 2002, households headed by an unauthorized immigrant parent cost the federal government a balance of $10.4 billion. This amounted to $2,700 per unauthorized immigrant household (Camarota 2004). CIS advocates restricting immigration, but Camarota's study was transparent and widely accepted in its general thrust (though other advocacy groups make wildly different estimates, in both directions).

Still, accepting Camarota's numbers, these federal costs were 46 percent less than those incurred by the average American household, public perceptions to the contrary. A major factor in the deficit is that while unauthorized immigrants received less in services, they paid only about a quarter as much in federal taxes (Camarota 2004). In part, this is because they earn less. In 2007, for example, the median household income for an unauthorized immigrant was thirty-six thousand dollars, well below the fifty thousand dollars for U.S.-born residents (Passel and Cohn 2009). Many unauthorized immigrants also work off the books. Camarota assumed that the proportion that don't was 45 percent—a defensible assumption, though the Congressional Budget Office estimates that the number falls in a range, between 25 percent and 50 percent (CBO 2007b). Many unauthorized immigrants pay federal taxes using an Individual Taxpayer Identification Number (ITIN) for noncitizens that doesn't ask immigration status. The numbers were created in 1996 precisely to collect these payments. More unauthorized immigrants could be paying taxes than what Camarota estimated, in other words.

All this raises a counterintuitive policy implication: if unauthorized immigrants are legalized, their net cost to the government is likely to go up. Freed from the shadows, they probably would earn marginally more and have a higher tax compliance rate, as seen by the experience following the 1986 amnesty. But they also would be eligible to receive more benefits, as well as earned income tax credits. The Congressional Budget Office and the Joint Committee on Taxation estimated in a report to Congress, for example, that legalization under the 2007 comprehensive immigration bill that was being considered would increase the "on-budget" deficit—mandatory spending versus direct taxes outside Social Security—by an estimated fourteen billion dollars over the 2008–12 period. The deficit would grow to an estimated thirty billion dollars over the 2008–17 period, largely as eligibility for federal welfare programs increasingly phases in (CBO 2007a).

- An impending funding crisis in the Social Security Trust Fund would be more imminent and deeper, were it not for a surplus from immigrants, including unauthorized ones.

The Social Security Trust Fund is the centerpiece of the American social welfare system, but it faces a solvency crisis. The fund is projected to have persistent cash flow deficits by 2015, and its reserves likely will be exhausted by 2037. At that point tax collections at the current rate will cover only about 78 percent of scheduled benefits (U.S. Social Security Administration 2010). The fundamental problem is that the number of beneficiaries is growing faster than the number of workers who support them. Americans are living longer and having fewer children. In addition, a huge baby boom cohort is entering retirement. The nation will sooner or later have to cut pensions, delay retirement ages, or raise Social Security taxes. But how much it will have to do any or all of these will be greatly influenced by immigration levels.

Immigrants help fill the demographic gap. They represent not just more workers but also workers who tend to be in their twenties when they arrive and thus have a long work life ahead of them. The labor force participation of foreign-born men in 2009, for example, was 80 percent, versus 70 percent for native-born men. American-born women outworked foreigners by a margin of 60 percent to 55 percent, but the impact of this is muted because fewer women work overall (U.S. Department of Labor, Bureau of Labor Statistics 2010). Meanwhile, immigrant women, more of whom stay home to raise children, produce more babies and thus more workers for the Social Security system. In 2008, 9.1 percent of immigrant women between the ages of fifteen and forty-four gave birth to a child, compared with 6.6 percent of native women (Pew Hispanic Center 2010).

Each year, the Office of the Chief Actuary of the Social Security Administration forecasts high, low, and likely immigration trends for the next seventy-five years and what they mean for the trust fund. In 2008 there were thirty-one beneficiaries per one hundred paying workers in the United States, or more than three to one. If total immigration—legal and illegal—continues at roughly today's levels, the actuaries forecast that the ratio likely will go up to forty-six by 2030 and keep rising slowly to fifty-two by 2085, or slightly less than two workers for each beneficiary (U.S. Social Security Administration 2009). Under the high scenario, immigration was assumed to be roughly 29 percent greater. The dependency ratio in seventy-five years became thirty-nine beneficiaries per one hundred workers. Under the third scenario, immigration was cut by roughly 26 percent from today—say, in the event of a public backlash against immigrants—and the ratio became sixty-nine per one hundred. That is almost 1.5 workers per beneficiary (U.S. Social Security Administration 2009). Under this last immigration level, the burden on workers would be extraordinary.

This is not to say that immigrants will "save" Social Security, as some pro-immigrant activists claim. Today's young immigrants will someday retire themselves and receive benefits. The projected "likely" scenario of the actuaries is based on an eventual level of 1,065,000 immigrants. An increase of 250,000 immigrants, legal or illegal, on top of this would reduce the seventy-five-year actuarial deficit projection in Social Security by 5 percent (Feinlab and Warner 2005). A reduction of 250,000 presumably would do more or less the opposite. In a fund so huge a movement of 5 percent or so in either direction in the seventy-five-year deficit projection is significant but doesn't rescue the country from having to take other measures to shore up Social Security.

One group of immigrants, however, has been a major, clear benefit for Social Security. They are, ironically, the politically derided unauthorized ones. An estimated 5.6 million unauthorized workers were paying into the system in 2007. Roughly half used a Social Security card that does not match their names. The number could have been invented or belonged to someone else. The other half have real cards in their legally registered names. Some got the card years ago by using a counterfeit birth certificate (something that is now difficult to do). More commonly, these unauthorized workers got a Social Security card legally when they entered the country under a temporary work visa. They illegally stayed after the visa expired.[3]

By 2007 the cumulative net contribution made by the unauthorized was somewhere between $120 billion and $240 billion, according to the fund's actuaries. That represented an astonishing 5.4 percent to 10.7 percent of the trust's total assets of $2.24 trillion that year.[4] The cumulative contribution is surely higher with each passing year. Unauthorized immigrants paid a net contribution of $12 billion in 2007 alone.[5] This cumulative net is after payouts. There were some. In 2007 an estimated $1 billion was paid to 180,000 unauthorized immigrant retirees or beneficiaries who fraudulently managed to get or keep real numbers. The Social Security Administration claims it has pretty much closed the loophole for more such fraudulent claims.[6] In other words, the overwhelming number of unauthorized workers is unlikely to receive benefits, ever. About the only way under current regulations will be if they become legalized and had paid the taxes in their correct name. The terms of a legalization bill could change this, however.

Were it not for these net contributions, according to the chief actuary of the Social Security Administration, the fund's persistent shortfall of tax revenue to cover payouts would likely have begun in 2009, or six years earlier than estimated. The projected reserves would be exhausted a year earlier, in 2036.[7]

- **In sum, in the short term—and including all children—today's immigrants as a group use more in federal, state, and local services than they pay in taxes, but the amounts are small.**

The National Research Council pulled together the local, state, and federal balances. Extrapolating from its two state studies, the NRC estimated that if the country were like New Jersey, the household of the average immigrant would have used $1,613 more in local, state, and federal services in 1996 dollars than it paid in all taxes. If the country were like California, the net fiscal burden would have been $2,206 per immigrant household (NRC 1997). The deficit is covered by American taxpayers. The total estimated burden borne by native households as a result of immigrants was $229 in New Jersey and $1,174 in California. This presumably has gone up as the number of immigrants has increased, though the cut in federal benefits has tamped the total impact.

Additional perspective is required. Birthright children are included as an immigrant cost, but they and their education and health care can be seen as either a cost or an investment. All low-income American households and many, if not most, middle-income ones with school-age children in fact present a fiscal deficit for the nation's taxpayers. This deficit is justified as not only part of building a just society, but also as training workers for the economy and investing in the future, to the benefit of all taxpayers. Moreover, to the extent that immigrants were educated in their home countries, the United States inherits that investment free of charge. Meanwhile, in the greater scheme of government spending, the immigrant burden is minor. The primary federal budget in 2002, the year of Camarota's study, for example, was $1.84 trillion. His estimated ten-billion-dollar federal fiscal hit caused by unauthorized immigration is, well, a drop in the bucket.

· **In the long run, immigrants as a group become a fiscal benefit for the United States and effectively pay back their early deficit. Education, however, is key in the performance of subgroups.**

History offers lessons. In 1909, at the height of the last great immigration wave, immigrants made up about half of all public welfare recipients. They were two-thirds in Chicago. In the country's thirty largest cities, meanwhile, more than half of all public school students were the children of immigrants. They were three-fourths in New York (Bodvarsson and Van Den Berg 2009). In other words, our cherished beliefs aside, immigrants have been a tax burden in earlier eras. Yet today their descendants are integral to the backbone of support for our governments, paying in the highest tax brackets in many cases. Perhaps Americans would pay lower taxes today had we had few or no immigrants a century ago, but not many people would make this argument.

This historical observation coincides with studies that show that as a group, the second generation of immigrants—in other words, the children born in the United States—are net fiscal contributors to all levels of government. In this arena, again, the NRC has conducted one of the most authoritative studies. It gauged federal, state, and local fiscal costs and contributions over the lifetime of immigrants and their progeny over the next three hundred years. Borrowing a standard tool used in finance, the NRC estimated what those costs and benefits are worth today. Called the "net present value," this number is calculated by discounting the interest that the gains or losses might have earned over time. The NRC study found that as a group, immigrants who came in 1996 not only will become net fiscal contributors in their lifetime, but also they will come to pay so much in taxes that they will pay off all they received in their early deficit years—with interest.

But the subgroups were more variegated. An immigrant with at least some college—whether legal or illegal—paid $105,000 more in taxes than he or she got in services in his or her lifetime. Among high school graduates, those who arrived during their teens or earlier were slightly profitable for the government. Those who arrived as adults still had a small fiscal deficit by the end of their lifetimes, but their children paid the deficit off. It is immigrant high school dropouts who are complicated. The study estimated that during his or her lifetime, a dropout received eighty-nine thousand dollars more in services than he or she paid in taxes. Descendants indeed become positive fiscal contributors, but some of that first-generation debt will not be paid back within three hundred years. These numbers are not to be taken without a caveat—benefits have changed since the study was done and many assumptions are made—but the comparative scale and the orders of magnitude are still useful. They also lead to a policy implication. The education of immigrants (whatever their legal status) is an investment and, as in earlier immigrant eras, is key to the future fiscal benefit of the nation.

Two other policy implications are raised from the overall fiscal analysis. One is that the federal government, which profits from immigration, perhaps should offer greater offsets for those state and local governments that bear a burden. The other is that a shift in the balance between skilled and unskilled immigrants—bringing in more of the former—would be a fiscal boon for American taxpayers within a few years, if not immediately.

JOBS AND WAGES: BROTHER CAN YOU SPARE A DIME?

We know the refrains. Most of us, if we don't sympathize, probably wonder at least in part if they might not be true: immigrants are stealing American jobs and undercutting our wages. And most gallingly, many of them are here illegally. Since 1980, as the current wave of immigration has gathered steam, American labor economists have been locked in a fierce debate over what really is the impact of immigrants on wages and employment. Leading one side is George Borjas of Harvard University. Leading the other are David Card of the University of California–Berkeley and increasingly a relatively young upstart, Giovanni Peri of the University of California–Davis. Curiously, all three labor economists are foreign-born: Borjas in Cuba, Card in Canada, and Peri in Italy. But while it is their differences that garner attention, what is more significant is how much they and others in the field actually agree. Their agreement grows out of widely accepted economic laws and two theoretical understandings backed by long-standing empirical research. One is that there is a difference between workers who are *substitutes* and *complements* for each other. The second is that outcomes shift between the *short term* and the *long term*.

Substitute workers compete with each other; complements do not. Native-born workers who compete with immigrant workers—who can be substituted, in other words—are the ones who are vulnerable to losing their jobs or having their wages cut or kept low. This is a basic effect of the law of supply and demand. What the public often overlooks, however, is that everyone in the native workforce who is not a substitute is complementary and *benefits*. This can be seen most simply at the microeconomic level. A surfeit of immigrant gardeners, if large enough, can undercut gardening wages and take away jobs from competing native gardeners. But by making gardening cheaper for consumers, gardening companies expand, creating more higher-paying supervisory jobs, usually for natives. The expanding gardening business also creates more complementary work and income for accountants, lawyers, garden-tool manufacturing employees, fertilizer salespeople, and so on. The positive impact of immigrants on complementary workers plays out at the macroeconomic level as well. The expanded supply of cheaper labor stimulates the economy. Some immigrants, particularly high-skilled ones, stimulate it even further by contributing to innovation. All workers thus benefit; complementary workers benefit the most.

The negative impact on substitutes, meanwhile, is mostly felt only

when there is a large, short-term shock of immigrants. The impact usually is short-term too. Economies are dynamic, not static. They absorb
some level of population growth—through births or immigration—
as part of a natural equilibrium and growth. This is partly because
new workers are also new consumers. This increases the demand for
more production, which in turn requires more workers. In the case
of a sudden increase in immigrant workers, however, the system is
briefly thrown out of whack. Capital and other factors of production,
however, usually respond through investments and innovation in the
affected sectors. This soon begins to create jobs and bid up the wages
of both the natives and the immigrants who had been competing with
each other. It is not always a smoothly adjusting system, but left to its
own devices, a new equilibrium usually returns (provided some other
factor doesn't intervene, such as a war or financial crisis, for example).

The debate is over *how much* different workers see their wages and
employment opportunities increase or decrease in the short term, and
how long that short term lasts. The consensus and the differences are
as follows:

· **Immigration has a small but positive impact on the wages of nearly
  nine of ten American workers and creates jobs.**

Almost all economists agree with this statement. The substitute workers vulnerable to today's immigration almost all fall at the two ends
of the skill scale. At one end are unskilled workers, usually defined as
lacking a high school degree. The other end is the highly skilled PhDs
in technology and engineering.[8] These two groups are vulnerable to
substitution because the *skill mix* among current immigrants is heavily
out of balance at the ends, in proportion both to other immigrants and
to the American population. In 2008, 32 percent of immigrants were
high school dropouts, compared with 12 percent of natives (Passel and
Cohn 2009). The unskilled immigrant workers were almost equal in
absolute number to the native unskilled (U.S. Department of Labor,
Bureau of Labor Statistics 2009). Among PhDs in science and engineering in 2010, meanwhile, 40 percent were foreign-born (Finn 2010).
The proportionally large numbers of immigrants at these two ends,
in other words, present a competitive challenge for the proportionally
small number of similarly educated natives.

Americans overwhelmingly, of course, fall between the two extremes.
Because the immigrants who also fall in the middle are proportionally
small compared with the number of Americans, they do not undermine

wages between the two extremes. History provides an example of this phenomenon. In the later decades of the nineteenth century, when the influx of workers was also high, the skill mix among them was similar to that of native workers. The percentage of high school dropouts was overwhelmingly high in both groups. The short-term wage impact was minimal or nil. There were shoemakers among the immigrants, for example, but not so many as to overly affect native shoemakers, particularly given that the new immigrants themselves needed shoes.

Because of the skill mix of today's immigrants, some 90 percent of American workers do not compete with immigrant workers and thus benefit from immigration. Their wages go up, though by a small amount, given that the benefit is spread over so many people. Many studies put the wage impact at between slightly more than zero and 1.0 percent in the short run and up to 3 percent or so after a decade (see Borjas 2003, 2007, 2009; Ottaviano and Peri 2005, 2006, 2008; Card and Lewis 2007; Card 2009; and Peri 2010). The size of the benefit, ironically, depends in large part on how much the other 10 percent of workers suffer. The more the negative impact on them, the more positive it is for everyone else in what is, in a sense, a transfer of wealth. If immigration restrictionists commonly overlook the benefit that immigration has on the wages of most Americans, immigration supporters (including some economists) often commit the reverse sin. In statements and studies, they maximize the benefit but dismiss the cost at the two skill ends even though you can't have it both ways.

· **Unskilled American workers probably suffer a short-term wage hit between zero and 5 percent, though exactly how much and for how long is in dispute.**

In a study on the impact of Mexican immigration between 1980 and 2000, Borjas and Harvard economist Larry Katz found a probable wage loss of −4.8 percent for unskilled native workers, defined again as high school dropouts (Borjas and Katz 2007). Focusing on Mexicans makes sense because they are by far the largest immigrant group and are overwhelmingly unskilled. In 2000, 26 percent of all unskilled workers in the country were Mexican. The study used a simulation model in which Borjas divided male workers between the ages of eighteen and sixty-four into a matrix of "skill cells" reflecting their education and years of work experience. He broke samples down among four levels of education: high school dropouts, high school graduates, some college, and college graduates. He further broke them down into eight levels of years of work experience. Borjas's models had grown in sophistication after Card and others had criticized his earlier findings, which had found even larger negative impacts.

Peri and the Italian economist Gianmarco Ottaviano, however, came up with very different results using another methodology (Ottaviano and Peri 2008). They divided the labor market into two sectors: high school graduates and dropouts in one, and college graduates and some college in the other. They did so in the belief that in the real labor market, dropouts and high school graduates are the same. Using Census data from 1990 to 2006, they concluded that the long-run impact on this bottom half of the skill market was between a negative 0.6 percent and a *positive* 0.3 percent. The difference in the range had to do with what assumptions one chooses on how substitutable immigrants and natives are. They and Borjas have had long running differences over this *elasticity of substitution,* with Borjas and others forcing Peri and Ottaviano to moderate their earlier estimates. Peri and Ottaviano's rosier results derive in large part from the same skill mix effect from the nineteenth century. Today's immigrants are made up of a high percentage of dropouts and a low percentage of high school graduates. Native workers are the reverse. The two combined groups, however, are proportionally roughly the same size. The wage impact of the immigrant workers is thus evenly distributed and diluted across the much larger native group of lesser-educated workers.

Card—whose comparisons of cities and states had long resulted in more optimistic findings than Borjas's national models using skill cells over time—largely confirmed Ottaviano and Peri's work in a separate study. He did suggest, however, that more research was needed on the types of jobs held by dropouts and high school graduates, and on how excesses of dropout labor are absorbed in high-immigrant cities (Card 2009). Borjas, on the other hand, showed that Peri's results were theoretically impossible, at least in the short term (Borjas 2009). Peri didn't challenge Borjas's use of theory. Instead, he adjusted his empirical conclusions by introducing the *business cycle* and defining *short term* and *long term.* He based these conclusions on a new study of Census surveys from 1994 to 2007 that for the first time allowed researchers to see the effects of the small 2001 downturn and the beginning of the great recession in 2007.

In what could be seen as a partial concession to Borjas, Peri said that in the short run, immigration "may" reduce native employment and wages. During a downturn in particular, he said, immigration seems to have a small negative effect on the *aggregate level* of both native employment and wages in the first one to two years. This appears to be because businesses have unused capacity during a downturn and so are slower to respond to immigration by investing. During a period of expansion, however, investment responds quickly, he said, which creates jobs. Immigration during the good times appears to have no measurable negative effect on income per worker within even the first year, his data showed. But, he added, a small number of natives still do have a harder time finding jobs (Peri 2010).[9]

As for the long run, the aggregate gains to national productivity and to the average income per worker are mostly realized within seven years, Peri concluded, and even more by ten years. The benefit that he found was small but not negligible. Pulling on simulations he had done earlier of states, Peri found that states with high levels of immigration benefited most. His findings suggested that in California, where the share of immigrants in employment increased from 25 percent in 1990 to 35 percent in 2007, the average income per worker in real terms might have increased by 2.6 percent over that period because of immigration. Texas, where the share of immigrants grew from 25 percent in 1990 to 35 percent in 2007, and New York, where it grew from 18 percent to 27 percent, saw similar gains. The numbers weren't precise, Peri said, but the patterns appeared to be consistent (Peri 2010).

As for the *distributional* effect of immigration on lesser-skilled native workers, the results were similar but slightly different. Peri found that some lesser-skilled natives—dropouts and high school graduates—were indeed crowded out from jobs during times of economic weakness in the first year or two by immigrants but not during times of expansion. In the long run there is "some evidence that immigrants lead to positive job creation, even for less-educated natives," Peri said, though this time he more cautiously didn't give a specific positive number (Peri 2010: 11). Some pro-immigrant activists have seized on the Peri studies as proof that immigrants do not have a negative impact on American workers. Peri himself is more nuanced. More importantly, his methodology of dividing the market in two sectors rather than four is sure to be poked and possibly challenged by economists as it applies to immigration. And his introduction of the business cycle stands on scant evidence, his study ending as it did just as the Great Recession was beginning. Still, it advanced the research and the debate.

· A wage loss of even 5 percent as a result of immigration is hardly shattering in global terms. But for an unskilled worker scraping by, any loss is significant.

The median wage for unskilled work is roughly twenty-five thousand dollars a year, which is close to the poverty line for a family of four. Five percent of that is twelve hundred dollars a year—a lot when you are struggling to make the rent.

· Half of the unskilled workers are earlier immigrants, reducing the number of affected Americans. These earlier immigrants may suffer the most.

Borjas, Card, Peri, and most other labor economists do agree that one group—unskilled immigrants who arrived earlier—are clearly hurt by immigrants who arrive later. This is because by 2009 unskilled immigrants had come to make up 49 percent of the unskilled workers in the country and can easily substitute for each other (U.S. Department of Labor, Bureau of Labor Statistics 2010). Ottaviano and Peri, for example, found that between 1990 and 2006, earlier immigrants suffered a wage loss of −5 percent to −8 percent as a result of later arriving immigrants (Ottaviano and Peri 2008).

They also can take jobs from each other. During the great economic expansion from 1994 to 2007, immigrants in fact had higher employment rates than natives. But immigrant fortunes began to turn even before the economy officially fell into recession in December 2007. This is because the bubble in the housing sector burst earlier, and many unskilled immigrants were employed in construction. By the first half of 2009, unemployment among immigrants had soared to 9.2 percent, surpassing the 8.3 percent among natives. Among immigrants in construction, however, the unemployment rate was 17 percent. Unskilled immigrants were further hurt in the downturn by the fact that employers, having invested little in training them, had less incentive to keep them. Higher-skilled workers may also have been moving down the skill chain and replacing them (Orrenius and Zavodny 2009).

Unauthorized immigrants had the biggest fluctuations of all. A Pew study found that in March 2005, for example, when the U.S. economy was booming, unauthorized immigrant men had a lower unemployment rate (4.5 percent) than did U.S.-born men (5.9 percent) or legal immigrant men (4.9 percent) (Pew Hispanic Center 2010).[10] But by March 2009 unemployment among the unauthorized men leapfrogged the other two groups. It was 10.4 percent, compared with 9.2 percent and 9.1 percent for U.S.-born workers and legal immigrants respectively. Such performance and the simulated economic studies support the analysis that immigrants compete most with other immigrants for jobs.

- Native-born Americans with science and engineering doctorates may receive lower wages because of immigrants, but immigrants may be creating more high-tech jobs than they fill.

Borjas found that for every 10 percent increase in the supply of doctorates caused by immigration in a given high-tech field, wages dropped 3 percent (Borjas 2006). That would seem to deter native Americans from going into those fields, and to choose instead areas such as law or business administration in which they have a language advantage. Borjas found little evidence of aggregate crowding out of natives in graduate school, however, though there might be some in particular university programs (Borjas 2007). Indeed, more recent studies find that the large presence of immigrants in high-tech fields is doing the opposite and creating a slight *crowding-in* effect. A study of H-1B visas for professionals, which includes scientists and engineers, found that the total number of jobs in science and engineering had gone up more than the number of immigrants given visas (Kerr and Lincoln 2010). This suggests that immigrants are stimulating high-tech businesses and creating more jobs than they fill, to the benefit of highly educated native-born Americans—and the nation.

NATIONAL INCOME AND GROWTH: THE BOTTOM LINE

The overall impact of immigration on the economy is, in the first instance, a summation of the labor and fiscal effects. The calculation begins with what is called the *immigration surplus*. This is the net gain for U.S. businesses, consumers, and workers caused by immigration. It is what is left over after you subtract the income earned by the immigrants themselves. This is a crucial point. Simply by consuming—or *pushing the demand curve out*—immigrants expand the size of the economy, as measured by its gross domestic product (GDP). If they consume as much as they produce, however, the economy has gotten bigger but no extra wealth was created for the rest of us. Per capita income has not gone up. Just the immigrants got richer. The rest of us benefit only to the extent that immigrants produce more than they consume through an increase in productivity. Fortunately, immigrants to the United States are doing just that. They increase productivity by bringing down the cost of labor at the two ends of the skill spectrum—how much is debated—and by expanding the pool of workers. This in turn allows business to use capital—money, land, machines, and so on—more efficiently. With more low-cost, low-skilled workers available, for example, business can either expand labor-intensive factories, such as meat processing, or divert money that might have gone into mechanization to another business, such as building airplane engines.

As consumers, we benefit from the cheap labor and resulting lower prices of goods. A study by Patricia Cortes of the University of Chicago Business School found that an increase of 10 percent in the share of low-skilled labor in a city decreases the prices of low-skilled services by approximately 2.5 percent, which is not insignificant (Cortes 2008). This is in addition to the wage benefits for the overwhelming number of Americans. The total standard of living for most of us, in other words, goes up. Many of us take these benefits for granted as just part of our daily lives, but they are not permanent—they can be lost if the low-skilled immigrants leave, in other words. Still, by all accounts, the immigration surplus at the national level is small.

The formula for calculating the immigration surplus is based on labor's share of the economy, the share of immigrants in the labor force, and the percentage change in wages caused by immigration. This last factor is the most sensitive part of the formula. It resurrects the whole fight over elasticity of wages discussed earlier. But for the sake of argument, let's use a more or less accepted standard for labor demand elasticities in general. It is that for every 1 percent increase in the supply of immigrant workers, wages drop 0.3 percent. Plugging these numbers into the formula, the immigration surplus in the American economy is just 0.1 percent of GDP.[11] For unauthorized immigrants, it is 0.03 percent (Hanson 2007, 2009). Tiny. The main reason is because immigrant labor is just a small part of the total American economy. All labor's share of GDP has run for years at around 70 percent (Pakko 2004). In 2008 immigrants made up 8.3 percent of the labor force, which if just simplistically proportional, would account for roughly 5 percent of GDP. Unauthorized immigrants account for less still (Passel and Cohn 2009).

The 0.1 percent of GDP surplus is just a rough estimate that gives a sense of the labor contribution of immigrants, legal and illegal, to national income. It is based on a static view of the economy, a snapshot at a point in time, in which labor and capital are the only two factors of production. Borjas uses wage elasticities that usually vary between 3.0 and 3.6, which at the latter level slightly increases the immigration surplus (Borjas 1999, 2003, and 2006). Card, Peri, and some others maintain that the wage elasticity is much less, but the impact is still small. Concerning unauthorized immigrants, for example, Gordon Hanson of the University of California–San Diego notes that even if their positive impact on national income were ten times larger (highly, highly unlikely), it would still be less than a third of 1 percent of GDP (Hanson 2009). Still tiny.

Now we turn to the fiscal side. Drawing on the NRC study, Hanson estimated that the short-term fiscal burden—federal, state, and local—in 1996 was −0.2 percent of GDP. A 0.1 percent, immigration surplus minus this −0.2 percent fiscal cost leaves a total change to national income of −0.1 percent of GDP (Hanson 2007). This would mean that, in the short run, immigration slightly hurts the economy more than it helps. Not much credence should be given to the precision of these numbers, however. Since the NRC fiscal study was done, the number of immigrants has gone up, as have enforcement costs. On the other hand, government services overall have been cut, and the New Jersey–California average is probably generous compared with spending by most states. The fiscal needle, in other words, may have moved up or down since the NRC study, though probably not by much.

What may be more sensitive is the labor side of the final tally. An implication of some of the labor calculations by Card and Peri is that they might be enough to turn the total impact on the economy to positive. No poll has been taken, but one wouldn't be surprised if the majority of labor economists believe just that, if only out of wishful thinking. But whether positive or negative, all the estimations of the bottom line are still so close to zero and so filled with assumptions that they fall within rounding errors. The safest thing to say, in other words, is that the short-term impact of immigration, both legal and illegal, on national income is *essentially a wash*.

But that's short term. Long term is another matter. Immigrants clearly have contributed to American economic growth. They have brought skills, energy, and economies of scale created by their sheer numbers, all of which has been central in making the United States into the economic (and military) superpower it is today. They push native-born Americans (often grudgingly) to be more competitive, work harder, and move up the job ladder. And they become net fiscal contributors—so much so that they pay back the deficit from their early years in the country and more. But the total long-term impact is difficult to actually measure. Labor market models are very limited in studying the short term, and not built at all for the long term—say, for more than ten years. In trying to isolate the impact of immigration on wages and employment, most studies are based on a closed market economy and "all other things being equal," when in real life hardly anything remains equal. By contrast, trade economists like to build multisector models of an open economy. These models focus on long-term effects. What is needed is a new type of sophisticated general equilibrium model of the economy that differentiates between short- and long-term adjustments caused by immigration (Bodvarsson and Van Den Berg 2009).[12] And even then, human behavior is affected by more than just economic rules.

We do know, nonetheless, that the key driver to long-term economic growth is technological progress. This takes us back to the role of productivity. In an increasingly globalized and competitive world, the most innovative companies and countries are the ones that perform best. It is no mistake that Australia, Canada, and the European Union try to recruit high-skilled immigrants for permanent settlement, while China and India, two of the main sources of those migrants, try to attract their descendants back. They all do so precisely because they see the contributions that immigrants have made to U.S. technological leadership and economic growth. One measure of that contribution is patents. The United States issues far more patents than any country in the world; immigrants are responsible for 24 percent of them (Kerr and Lincoln 2010; Gauthier-Loiselle and Hunt 2010).[13]

At Intel, the world's largest maker of semiconductors, 40 percent of the patents are for work done by Chinese or Indian immigrants (Council on Foreign Relations 2009). Immigrants create patents at twice the rate of native-born Americans. It's not that they are smarter or more talented than Americans. It is that they disproportionately hold degrees in science and engineering (Gauthier-Loiselle and Hunt 2010). In the 2000 U.S. Census, immigrants made up 24 percent of the nation's science and engineering workers with a bachelor's degree, and 47 percent of those with a doctorate. The percentages are surely higher today (Kerr and Lincoln 2010). The pathway for immigrants to these jobs is through American universities, where the immigrants come to study. In 2006 immigrants and foreign students received 40 percent of science and engineering PhDs and 65 percent of computer science doctorates at U.S. schools. The data imply that a one-percentage point rise in the share of immigrant college graduates in the population increases patents per capita by 6 percent (Gauthier-Loiselle and Hunt 2010).

Of all the U.S. engineering and technology companies started between 1995 and 2005, meanwhile, 25 percent had at least one immigrant founder. These companies were responsible for fifty-two billion dollars in sales in 2005 and employed 450,000 people. Another 27 percent of the companies founded during those years had a foreign-born chief executive or chief technology officer (Wadwha 2007). Recent studies have shown that admitting more highly skilled workers would promote still more entrepreneurship, innovation, and increased productivity (Lee and Miller 2000; Mankiw 2008).

But what about low-skilled immigrants? They have general economic value, but what may be more important is a crucial need for them in certain sectors. The proportion of high school dropouts among native Americans plummeted from 52 percent in 1960 to 8.7 percent in 2000. Immigrants, especially unauthorized ones, stepped into the breach for needed unskilled manual and service work. They have been particularly crucial to the agriculture, construction, and leisure and hospitality industries, parts of which would collapse without them. In 2008 unauthorized immigrants alone made up 19 percent of building, groundkeeping, and maintenance workers; 17 percent of construction workers; 12 percent of food preparation workers and servers; 10 percent of production workers; and 7 percent of transportation and material moving workers. Within these broad categories, immigrants make up 40 percent of the nation's brick masons, 37 percent of our drywall installers, 28 percent of dishwashers, 27 percent of maids and housekeepers, and 21 percent of parking lot attendants (Passel and Cohn 2009).

Farming is particularly reliant on immigrants. Three-fourths of all the hired farm workers (and almost all of the ones working with fresh fruits and vegetables) are legal or illegal immigrants (Kandel 2008). The stakes in immigration policy are crucial not just for farm owners, but also for their suppliers and whole communities in a sector of the economy that was vibrant even through the major recession that began in 2008. American farms produce more than 9 percent of our exports and almost all the food on our tables each day. All that would wither without immigrants. Can these industries adjust by paying higher wages to attract native workers? Yes, but a closer look at what is happening on the farm suggests what the costs and limits of that might be.

It is unclear what wage level would attract more Americans to farm work, but certainly it would have to be much higher than the average $7.52 an hour paid to migrant workers and $8.53 an hour paid to settled farm workers in 2006. These relatively low salaries are for jobs that the Labor Department ranks as some of the most difficult and dangerous in America (U.S. Department of Agriculture 2008). The resulting higher price for food would be borne by American consumers. Mechanization is raised as an alternative, but mechanization is already extensive, especially for harvesting grains. U.S. farm production grew 150 percent between 1950 and 2006, while farm employment dropped from ten million to three million because of technological innovation (U.S. Department of Agriculture 2008). Not much more can be gained from mechanization.

Two million of today's farm workers are paid or unpaid family members, while the rest are hard-to-get seasonal workers who mostly pick fresh fruits and vegetables. This requires sensitive work by hand to maintain quality. Farmers began picking tomatoes by machine in the 1960s, the last time immigrant workers were kicked out when a formal temporary worker program with Mexico called Bracero was ended. Consumers rejected the resulting hard tomatoes for all but canning. Meanwhile, farm-operating costs are already so high that food imports are growing and American farmers are investing abroad. Significant raises in farm wages and costs would likely be a pyrrhic victory.

Understanding the economic contributions made by skilled and unskilled workers thus leads to several policy implications. One concerns temporary worker programs. Instead of labor needs, the nation's system for permanent residency visas since 1965 has been driven mostly by allowing in the relatives of people already in the country. This needs adjusting to allow in more temporary and permanent immigrant workers. Existing temporary work programs are small, complicated, and often not in line with labor demands. The challenge for policy makers is to find an optimal level and skill mix of legal immigration that fuels business productivity, responds to consumer demands, stokes innovation, and doesn't cost native American workers too much in the short term. It also must help replace illegal immigration. A tall order.

One proposal gaining currency is for the creation of an independent commission that would set work visa levels based on a technical reading of labor demand and unemployment.[14] An alternative is for the commission to use an auction system in which businesses bid for visas based on their actual demand (Peri 2010). To avoid the susceptibility of temporary workers to labor abuses, the consensus appears widespread to make the visas portable, so that workers can press for raises or leave for another employer. For impacted unskilled native workers, measures other than immigration policy might be more effective to meet their needs. These include job training, health-care subsidies, expanded unemployment benefits, liberalized earned income tax credits, and the like. Is this a redistribution of wealth? Of course. But it pales against the redistribution that would be caused by imposing restrictions on immigration. Restrictions make 90 percent of the country's workers sacrifice gains in wealth so as to mostly benefit the bottom 10 percent.

. . .

This chapter ends on one last economic turn of the screw. In a globalized world, immigration not only improves American competitiveness; it also expands global productivity and wealth—to the benefit of all nations. Economists have only begun to focus on how to use immigration as a tool to lift lesser-developed countries out of poverty. Theoretically, the benefits—and costs—of migration flows are similar to those of trade and money. The freer the flow of labor, the greater the maximizing of global production and wealth for all will be.[15] But complicating matters are social, cultural, and political considerations. Every country jealously guards its sovereign prerogatives over immigration—over who it will let in, and how many. They do so no matter what the economists say.

NOTES

The author wishes to thank Martina Viarengo di Castagneto and Lant Pritchett for their helpful comments, Melinda Kuritzky for her diligent research, and Annmarie Sasdi for early contributions.

1. Both legal and unauthorized immigrants actually commit violent and other non-immigration-related crimes at rates far lower than native-born Americans. See, for example, Rumbaut and Ewing 2007.

2. A great failure is that no comprehensive fiscal study has been done by an independent government agency. Academic economists, meanwhile, seem to steer clear of the detailed accounting needed. That leaves the field mostly to advocates with a point of view to promote. This is one reason why the NRC study remains so valuable, as old as it is.

3. Stephen C. Goss, letter to the Honorable Richard J. Durbin, June 5, 2007.

4. Stephen C. Goss, chief actuary of the Social Security Administration, e-mail communication to the author, August 25, 2010.

5. Goss, letter to Durbin, p. 3.

6. Ibid.

7. Goss, e-mail.

8. Education is used as a proxy for skill because it is based on readily available annual and decennial census studies and thus easily measurable.

9. This may coincide with studies in Europe, which have found that during periods of high immigration, it takes longer for workers receiving unemployment benefits to find new jobs. This extension in unemployment time marginally drives up the unemployment rate in the short term. But over the long term, most European studies have found that immigrants created more jobs than they occupy, lowering unemployment (Okkerse 2008).

10. The Pew Hispanic Center looked at just men because unauthorized women stay home to take care of children at a much higher rate than natives or other immigrants.

11. The actual formula is $-0.5 \times$ labor's share of GDP $\times$ wage elasticity $\times$ the square of immigrants' share in the labor force.

12. The Cato Institute, a libertarian think tank, in 2009 began to adapt general equilibrium trade models to immigration, but as of this writing, the models had still not been subjected to widespread academic review.

13. Research and development expenditures and the number of publications authored in peer-reviewed journals are two other measures of innovation. Patents, however, are more widely used as a measure because they are more internationally comparable and consistent over time.

14. See, for example, "Harnessing the Advantages of Immigration for a Twenty-first Century Economy: A Standing Commission on Labor Markets, Economic Competitiveness, and Immigration," a report by Demetrios Papademetriou, Doris Meissner, Marc R. Rosenblum, and Madeleine Sumption, issued by the Migration Policy Institute in 2009.

15. A World Bank study estimates that just increasing migration between developing and high-income countries by 3 percent by the year 2025 would increase the world's real income by 0.6 percent, or 356 billion dollars in 2025 (World Bank 2006). The Bank and other studies conclude that labor-market restrictions are imposing a much larger burden on the global economy than trade restrictions.

REFERENCES

Bodvarsson, Örn B., and Hendrik Van Den Berg. 2009. *The Economics of Immigration: Theory and Policy.* New York: Springer.

Borjas, George. 2009a. "The Analytics of the Wage Effect of Immigration." National Bureau of Economic Research (NBER) Working Paper No. 14796.

———. 2009b. "Immigration in High-Skill Labor Markets: The Impact of Foreign Students on the Earnings of Doctorates." In *Science and Engineering Careers in the United States.* Edited by Richard B. Freeman and Daniel L. Goroff. Pp. 131–62. Chicago: University of Chicago Press.

———. 2007. "Do Foreign Students Crowd out Native Students from Graduate Programs?" In *Science and the University.* Edited by Ronald G. Ehrenberg and Paula E. Stephan. Pp. 134–137. Madison: University of Wisconsin Press.

———. 2006. "Native Internal Migration and the Labor Market Impact of Immigration." *Journal of Human Resources* 41, no. 2: 221–58.

————. 2005. "The Labor-Market Impact of High-Skill Immigration." *American Economic Review* 95, no. 2: 56–60.

————. 2003. "The Labor Demand Curve *Is* Downward Sloping: Reexamining the Impact of Immigration on the Labor Market." *Quarterly Journal of Economics* (November): 1335–74.

————. 1999a. "The Economic Analysis of Immigration." In *Handbook of Labor Economics*. Volume 3. Edited by Orley Ashenfelter and David Card. Pp. 1697–1760. Amsterdam: Elsevier Science.

————. 1999b. *Heaven's Door: Immigration Policy and the American Economy*. Princeton, N.J.: Princeton University Press.

Borjas, George, Richard B. Freeman, and Lawrence F. Katz. 1997. "How Much Do Immigration and Trade Affect Labor Market Outcomes?" *Brookings Papers on Economic Activity* 1: 1–90.

Borjas, George, Jeffrey Grogger, and Gordon H. Hanson. 2010. "Immigration and the Economic Status of African-American Men." *Economica* 77 (April): 255–82.

————. 2008. "Imperfect Substitution between Immigrants and Natives: A Reappraisal." NBER Working Paper Series No. 13887.

Borjas, George, and Lawrence F. Katz. 2007. "The Evolution of the Mexican-born Workforce in the United States." In *Mexican Immigration to the United States*. Edited by George Borjas. Pp. 13–56. Chicago: University of Chicago Press.

Camarota, Steven A. 2004. "The High Cost of Cheap Labor: Illegal Immigration and the Federal Budget." Center for Immigration Studies: Washington, D.C.

Camarota, Steven A., and Karen Jensenius. 2009a. "A Huge Pool of Potential Workers: Unemployment, Underemployment, and Non-work among Native-born Americans." Center for Immigration Studies: Washington, D.C.

————. 2009b. "Jobs Americans Won't Do? A Detailed Look at Immigrant Employment by Occupation." Center for Immigration Studies: Washington, D.C.

Capps, Randy, et al. 2007. "A Profile of Immigrants in Arkansas." The Winthrop Rockefeller Foundation and the Urban Institute. Washington, D.C.

Card, David. 2009. "Immigration and Inequality." *American Economic Review* 99, no. 2: 1–21.

————. 2005. "Is the New Immigration Really So Bad?" *Economic Journal* 115, no. 507: 300–323.

————. 2001. "Immigrant Inflows, Native Outflows, and the Local Labor Market Impacts of Higher Immigration." *Journal of Labor Economics* 19: 22–64.

Card, David, and Ethan Lewis. 2007. "The Diffusion of Mexican Immigrants during the 1990s: Explanations and Impacts." In *Mexican Immigrants to the United States*. Edited by George J. Borjas. Pp. 193–228. Chicago: University of Chicago Press.

Congress of the United States, Congressional Budget Office (CBO). 2010. "The Role of Immigrants in the U.S. Labor Market: An Update." Pub. No. 4159, July.

————. 2008. "Key Issues in Analyzing Major Health Insurance Proposals." Available online at www.cbo.gov/doc.cfm?index=9924.

————. 2007a. "Cost Estimate: Senate Amendment 1150 to S. 1348, the Comprehensive Immigration Reform Act of 2007." June 4.

————. 2007b. "The Impact of Unauthorized Immigrants on the Budgets of State and Local Governments." Available online at www.cbo.gov/doc .cfm?index=8711.

Cortes, Patricia. 2008. "The Effect of Low-skilled Immigration on U.S. Prices: Evidence from CPI Data." *Journal of Political Economy* 116, no. 3: 381–422.

Cunningham, Peter J. 2006. "What Accounts for Differences in the Use of Hospital Emergency Departments across U.S. Communities?" *Health Affairs* 25, no. 5: w324–w336.

Decker, Christopher, Jerry Deichert, and Lourdes Gouveia. 2008. *Nebraska's Immigrant Population: Economic and Fiscal Impacts.* OLLAS Special Report No. 5. Omaha: Office of Latino/Latin American Studies (OLLAS), University of Nebraska at Omaha.

Feinlab, Joel, and David Warner. 2005. "The Impact of Immigration on Social Security and the National Economy." Social Security Advisory Board. Issue Brief No 1. Available online at www.ssab.gov/Documents/IMMIG_Issue _Brief_Final_Version_000.pdf

Finn, Michael G. 2010. "Stay Rates of Foreign Doctorate Recipients from U.S. Universities, 2007." Oak Ridge Institute for Science and Education (ORISE). Oak Ridge, Tenn.

Gauthier-Loiselle, Marjolaine, and Jennifer Hunt. 2010. "How Much Does Immigration Boost Innovation?" *American Economic Journal: Macroeconomics* (April): 31–56.

Goldman, Dana P., James P. Smith, and Neeraj Sood. 2006. "Immigrants and the Cost of Medical Care." *Health Affairs* 25, no. 6: 1700–11.

Goss, Stephen C. 2007. Letter to the Honorable Richard J. Durbin. June 5. Provided to author by Social Security Administration Office of the Chief Actuary: Washington, D.C.

Hanson, Gordon H. 2009. "The Economics and Policy of Illegal Immigration in the United States." Migration Policy Institute: Washington, D.C.

————. 2007. "The Economic Logic of Illegal Immigration."Council Special Report No. 26. Council on Foreign Relations.

Hunt, Jennifer, and Marjolaine Gauthier-Loiselle. 2010. "How Much Does Immigration Boost Innovation?" *American Economic Journal: Macroeconomics* (April): 31–56.

Kandel, William. 2008. "Profile of Hired Farmworkers: A 2008 Update." United States Department of Agriculture (USDA) Economic Research Report No. 60.

Kerr, William R., and William F. Lincoln. 2010. "The Supply Side of Innovation: H-1B Visa Reforms and U.S. Ethnic Invention." NBER Working Paper No. 15768.

Lee, Ronald, and Timothy Miller. 2000. "Immigration, Social Security, and Broader Fiscal Impacts." *American Economic Review* 90, no. 2: 350–54.

Mankiw, N. Greg. 2008. "What If the Candidates Pandered to Economists?" *New York Times.* July 13.

National Research Council (NRC). 1997. *The New Americans: Economic, Demographic, and Fiscal Effects of Immigration.* Edited by James P. Smith and Barry Edmonston. Washington, D.C: NRC.

Okkerse, Liesbet. 2008. "How to Measure Labour Market Effects of Immigration: A Review." *Journal of Economic Surveys* 22, no. 1: 1–30.

Orrenius, Pia M., and Madeline Zavodny. 2009. "Tied to the Business Cycle: How Immigrants Fare in Good and Bad Economic Times." Migration Policy Institute, November. Washington, D.C.

Ottaviano, Gianmarco, and Giovanni Peri. 2008. "Immigration and National Wages: Clarifying the Theory and the Empirics." NBER Working Paper No. 14188.

———. 2006. "The Economic Value of Cultural Diversity: Evidence from U.S. Cities." *Journal of Economic Geography* 6, no. 1: 9–44.

Pakko, Michael R. 2004. "Labor's Share." National Economic Trends. The Federal Reserve Bank of St. Louis, August.

Passel, Jeffrey S., and D'Vera Cohn. 2010. "U.S. Unauthorized Immigration Flows Are Down Sharply since Mid-decade." Pew Hispanic Center. Washington, D.C. September 1.

———. 2009. "A Portrait of Unauthorized Immigrants in the United States." Pew Hispanic Center. Washington, D.C.

Peri, Giovanni. 2010. "The Impact of Immigrants in Recession and Economic Expansion." Migration Policy Institute. Washington, D.C.

———. 2009. "The Effect of Immigration on Productivity: Evidence from U.S. States." NBER Working Paper No. 15507.

Peri, Giovanni, and Chad Sparber. 2009. "Task Specialization, Immigration, and Wages." *American Economic Journal: Applied Economics* 1, no. 3: 135–69.

Pew Hispanic Center. 2010. "Statistical Portrait of the Foreign-born in the United States." Available online at http://pewhispanic.org/factsheets/factsheet.php?FactsheetID=59.

Pew Hispanic Center. 2010. "Statistical Portrait of Hispanics in the United States, 2008," Table 24. Available online at http://pewhispanic.org/factsheets/factsheet.php?FactsheetID=70.

Rumbaut, Rubén, and Walter Ewing. 2007. "The Myth of Immigrant Criminality and the Paradox of Assimilation." American Immigration Law Foundation. Washington, D.C. Spring.

Stimpson, Jim P., Fernando A. Wilson, and Karl Eschbach. 2010. "Trends in Health Care Spending for Immigrants in the United States." *Health Affairs* 29, no. 3: 544–50.

Strayhorn, Carole Keeton. 2006. "Undocumented Immigrants in Texas: A Financial Analysis of the Impact to the State Budget and Economy." Office of the Comptroller of Texas. Available online atwww.cpa.state.tx.us/special rpt/undocumented/undocumented.pdf.

United States Department of Agriculture 2008. "Amber Waves." Economic Research Service. Volume 6, Issue 2. Washington, D.C.

United States Department of Homeland Security (DHS). 2009. *Yearbook of Immigration Statistics*. Washington, D.C.: Department of Homeland Security. Available online at: www.dhs.gov/files/statistics/publications/yearbook .shtm.

United States Department of Justice. 2010. "State Criminal Alien Assistance Program." Bureau of Justice Assistance. Available online at www.ojp.usdoj .gov/BJA/grant/scaap.html.

United States Department of Labor, Bureau of Labor Statistics. 2010. "Economic News Release: Table 3. Employment Status of the Foreign-born and Native-born Populations 25 Years and over by Educational Attainment, Race, and Hispanic or Latino Ethnicity, 2008–09 Annual Averages." Bureau of Labor Statistics. March 19. Available online at www.bls.gov/news.release/ forbrn.to3.htm.

United States Social Security Administration. 2009. *The 2009 Annual Report of the Board of Trustees of the Federal Old-Age and Survivors Insurance and Federal Disability Insurance Trust Funds*. Committee on Ways and Means. Washington, D.C.: U.S. Government Printing Office.

Wadhwa, Vivek, Anna Lee Saxenian, Ben Rissing, and Gary Gereffi. 2007. "America's New Immigrant Entrepreneurs: Part I." Duke Science, Technology & Innovation Paper No. 23. 4 January 2007.

World Bank. 2006. *Global Economic Prospects 2006: Economic Implications of Remittances and Migration*. Washington, D.C.: World Bank.

Zuñiga et al. 2005. "Mexico-United States Migration: Health Issues." UCLA Center for Health Policy Research, October. Accessed at: http://www.health policy.ucla.edu/pubs/publication.

6

Ten Top Myths and Fallacies Regarding Immigration

BARRY R. CHISWICK

Most Americans have strong feelings about immigration and immigrants—sometimes pro, sometimes con, and often contradictory. Part of the difficulty of coming to terms with a national immigration policy, however, is that much discussion in the press and by politicians, as well as among the populace, is dominated by myths and fallacies. A clarification of these myths and fallacies will not completely resolve the debate over immigration policy, but it will narrow the range of the discourse, thereby facilitating arriving at sensible, effective policies. In 1970 about 4.7 percent or one of every twenty persons living in the United States was foreign-born. In 2009 the proportion is about 13 percent, or one of every eight people living in the United States. What are the characteristics and impact of immigrants? Do immigrant characteristics matter? Since 2001, about a million people each year have received permanent resident status in the United States. Is an annual intake of a million immigrants too few or too many? With apologies to David Letterman, I would like to offer my list of top ten myths and fallacies regarding immigration and immigrants in the United States today.

1. "Immigrants are needed to do jobs natives will not do."

This is undoubtedly the most common of all the myths and fallacies regarding immigration (Chiswick 2006). It is often said that native workers will not do the three "D" jobs—the dirty, dangerous, and difficult jobs. Natives will not do construction work, mow lawns, or clear and wash restaurant dishes. These jobs are performed disproportionately by immigrants in California, where they comprise about a third of the population. Yet it is patently untrue that American natives will not do these jobs. In Washington State and in West Virginia, where few immigrants live, the same jobs are performed by American workers. I have it on good authority that houses are built and repaired, lawns are mowed, restaurant tables are cleared, and dishes washed in these areas.[1]

The United States has experienced in recent decades a very large increase in low-skilled immigration, and immigrants with little schooling and little or no English language proficiency are to be expected to be found in the lowest-skilled jobs, tending to drive down wages in these jobs. In the absence of low-skilled immigrants, native-born low-skilled workers would be able to obtain higher wages in the labor market (Hamermesh and Bean 1998). Native-born labor would be forthcoming to take on these jobs in response to the higher wages. But the jobs would probably be done differently. In addition to—or because of—offering higher wages, employers would also have an incentive to make these jobs less "D"-intensive—that is, less dirty, dangerous, and physically difficult. With higher labor costs for low-skilled workers, employers would have an incentive to switch to production techniques that use less low-skilled labor, more physical capital (machinery), and more higher-skilled workers.

I am often asked, if not for the large number of low-skilled (legal and undocumented) immigrant workers where I live, how would my grass be mowed? In the absence of very low-wage labor, I would adopt some or all of various techniques for adjusting, including mowing the lawn every other week instead of weekly in the summer and replacing all or part of the lawn with groundcover. Grass seed companies would have an incentive to develop and sell new strains of grass that grow more slowly and require less frequent watering and fertilizer treatments. My lawn care company would purchase more efficient lawn mowers that require less human effort. Higher wages would attract more native-born workers back to lawn care, including teenagers and adults with lower levels of schooling. The higher cost of lawn care might even induce me or my spouse to mow our own lawn!

For some goods and services, imports or outsourcing would replace domestic production. That is, instead of importing low-skilled workers to do certain jobs, the jobs would be performed abroad and the product imported. This applies not only to manufactured goods but also to agricultural products. Tomatoes, for example, can either be grown and picked in the United States by low-skilled Mexican-born workers or grown and picked in Mexico and imported directly into the United States. The point is that higher wages for low-skilled workers would encourage alternatives (substitutes) in both consumption (by families) and production (by business enterprises). Higher wages for low-skilled native-born workers will also mean that more of them will be in the labor force, fewer of them will be in poverty, and the recent trend toward increased income inequality could be reversed. The fear that goods and services currently being provided by low-skilled immigrant workers will no longer be available is completely without foundation.

2. "There is no effect of immigration on the earnings of native-born workers."

This myth and fallacy, which is now widespread, may actually be a consequence of misguided research by some economists and sociologists. The statistical analyses, often using advanced statistical techniques, looked at the wages of workers in different areas (such as states, cities, or industries in the United States) and related these wages to the number or proportion of immigrants in the area or industry (Borjas 1990). In some analyses the focus was on relating the wages of low-skilled native-born workers to the extent to which low-skilled immigrant workers were employed. The concept of native wages and immigrant workers would vary across studies, but the fundamental methodology was the same. The overall finding was of no consistent relationship between native wages and the prevalence of immigrant workers. The conclusion was drawn that immigration has little or no effect on native wages.[2]

This conclusion, however, cannot be drawn from this methodology (Chiswick 1991 and 1992). To do so requires that each area or industry be considered a "closed economy," with no interstate, intercity, or interindustry mobility of labor or capital, except for the entry of the immigrant workers themselves. Because we know that capital and native labor move freely across states, cities, and industries, we need to consider their response to anything—like low-skilled immigration—that drives down the earnings of low-skilled native-born and foreign-born workers, while raising the return to high-skilled workers and to capital in the impacted area. The result would be an exodus from the impacted area of low-skilled native-born workers, tending to ameliorate the decline in their wages, and an inflow of high-skilled workers and capital to take advantage of their higher returns, tending to dampen the increase in their compensation (Filer 1992). This process would continue until the wages of workers of a given skill level and the returns to capital are again approximately equalized across regions and industries.

The finding of no relation in these cross-sectional studies does not mean that immigration does not affect native wages, but rather that the wage effects of immigration are distributed across the entire country. If labor and capital markets function well and factors of production are highly mobile, as they are in the United States, this dissipation of wage effects occur quickly, especially if the immigration is anticipated. The fact that the immigrants themselves are disproportionately concentrated in relatively few areas or industries should not lead us to expect that the wages of low-skilled workers there would be persistently lower than elsewhere. Far from demonstrating that immigrants have no effects on the earnings of natives, these studies merely confirm the efficiency of labor, capital, and product markets in the United States.

3. "Immigrants pay more in taxes than they receive in benefits."

The validity of this statement depends, in part, on which immigrants are under discussion.[3] Given the progressive tax structure in the United States, primarily through federal and state income taxes, high-income individuals pay proportionately more in taxes than do those with lower incomes, whether they are foreign-born or native-born. This tendency has increased with the expansion of the earned income refundable tax credit for low-income families. The broad range of public benefits paid for by the tax system includes cash transfer programs targeted toward the poor, noncash benefits (such as food stamps), subsidized school breakfast and lunch programs, public (subsidized) housing, publicly provided health care (including Medicaid and free medical care at public hospitals), and public schooling. These public benefit programs are specifically intended to raise the living standards of the low-income population and, with public schooling a major exception, the receipt is dependent on having a low income.

As a result, high-income immigrants are likely to pay more in taxes than they receive in public benefits. Low-income immigrants, however, especially if they are legal immigrants accompanied by family members (a spouse and minor children), are likely to pay less in taxes than they receive in public benefits. Thus the validity of the statement depends on the income level (and hence the skill level), legal status, and family structure of the immigrant worker, as well as the range of taxes and benefits under consideration.

4. "Sealing the border will solve the illegal migrant problem."

There are several fallacies in this claim. One is that currently only about half of the illegal immigrants living in the United States crossed the border without inspection, the popular image of illegal migrants. The other half of them are "visa abusers" who entered the United States with a fraudulent visa or who violated a condition of a valid visa. Among those who entered with a valid visitor, student, temporary worker, or other nonimmigrant visa, the most frequent violations occur by overstaying the time limit or by working in violation of the terms of the visa.

An EWI (someone who "entered without inspection") or a visa abuser are two alternative ways of being in an illegal status in the U.S. labor market. By raising the price of using one mechanism, for example, by raising the cost of being an EWI, the incentive to use the other increases. Increasing border enforcement provides a stronger incentive for individuals who wish to be in the United States illegally, but who cannot penetrate the border, to become visa abusers. Very high levels of border enforcement provide another perverse incentive. Illegal aliens who successfully penetrate the border would face a high cost of reentry if they should ever leave the United States. This discourages them from going back to their home country, whether for a short-term visit or in response to poor U.S. job opportunities in an economic downswing. Instead, it encourages them to feel locked into the U.S. labor market and limits their economic opportunities accordingly.

Moreover, there is no way of perfectly sealing the border. The border with Mexico is two thousand miles long, and the border with Canada is even longer. The cost of constructing fences and walls along even just the Mexican border, and of then effectively policing these barriers, would be prohibitive. The Border Patrol would have to counter the fence-cutting tools and the ladders used to scale the walls and fences. Perfect enforcement at the border is impossible. This is not to say that border enforcement is without merit. Border enforcement serves as a first line of defense against illegal migration, but its deterrent effect is very limited if an illegal migrant receives de facto amnesty once he or she successfully penetrates the border. "Internal" enforcement—that is, enforcement away from the land crossings, seaports, and airports—is essential for a comprehensive enforcement strategy.

Because most illegal migrants come to the United States for jobs, and those who come for other reasons typically seek jobs once they are in the United States, "work site" enforcement is an important component of internal enforcement. The 1986 Immigration Reform and Control Act for the first time made it illegal for an employer to knowingly hire a person not authorized to work in the United States. This feature of the 1986 legislation has been poorly enforced by both Democratic and Republican administrations. The growth in the illegal migrant population to its present estimated size of twelve million is attributable primarily to the lack of enforcement of employer sanctions.

Illegal migration can be controlled by the joint application of both border and interior enforcement. *Controlled* as distinct from *ended*. Just as we cannot end other illegal activities, so too we will probably never be able to completely end illegal immigration. As with other violations of U.S. law, however, we can seek an optimal level and strategy for enforcement for immigration law.

5. "Temporary workers (guest workers and undocumented migrants) will go home on their own."

Wishful thinking characterizes much of the discussion regarding temporary or undocumented migrant workers. Many workers come with the intention of their stay being temporary and do return home. However, the European experience with guest worker programs (from the 1960s until 1973) and the U.S. experience with the Bracero program (1942 to 1962) demonstrate that once low-skilled workers from less-developed countries experience the high wages, educational opportunities for their children, and free and open society in the advanced liberal democracies, many do not want to leave; or if they have left the United States, they want to return or encourage others to try to migrate. Instead of leaving, they often try to bring to the host country their family members—in particular, their spouses, children, and siblings. The World War I song "How Are You Going to Keep Them Down on the Farm Once They've Seen Paree?" applies as well to those from less developed countries (LDCs) working or living "temporarily" in the high-income, developed, liberal democracies.[4]

6. "If low-skilled immigration was a benefit to the United States in 1910, it must be a benefit to the United States in 2010."

The fallacy in this argument is that there have been major technological and political changes that make the United States of 2010 very different from that of a century ago. Hindsight about past immigration experiences is not sufficient by itself to determine whether today's low-skilled immigration is a benefit to the United States. An important characteristic of the late nineteenth and early twentieth centuries was the change in industrial structure from artisan-based production to factory-based manufacturing. The new machinery and the new methods of production resulted in lower costs for existing goods as well as the introduction of new goods. It also resulted in an increased demand for low-skilled and even unskilled workers who replaced skilled artisans. In response to this "de-skilling" of the labor force, many artisans left the manufacturing cities of the East Coast for western frontiers, where the old skills were still in demand (Ferrie 2011). Others sent their children to the expanding land-grant colleges to enter the labor force as high-skilled workers. In the big manufacturing cities, low-skilled immigrants were in high demand to fill these new production jobs and were easily able to find work.

We are now in the midst of another major change in technology, but it is one in which the premium is on high-skilled workers. In our current science- and engineering-based information age, the new technology creates a high demand for workers with technical skills in computer science, biotechnology, engineering, and high-level management as well as in advanced medical fields. Demand has fallen in general for workers who lack these skills, but the decline has been especially dramatic for those at the very low end of the educational ladder. The long-term decline in demand for low-skilled workers has accelerated in the current recession, but the trends of the past few decades are expected to continue unabated after the recovery. In contrast to the economic situation in 1910, the large low-skilled immigration that the United States has experienced in recent decades has arisen not because of high demand for low-skilled workers, but despite a marked decline in that demand.

In addition to these changes in technology, the twentieth century also saw dramatic political changes with regard to public policy toward the poor. A century ago assistance for the poor was not a major public policy concern. If economic hard times fell on a family, even if through no fault of their own, this was considered to be unfortunate but not a governmental concern. Support might come from other family members, church groups, or civic organizations, but government intervention was rare and the poor were expected to fend for themselves. Many immigrants would return to their origin country during an economic downturn, as has even been the case in the current recession.

Fortunately, attitudes have changed. Public policy is now concerned with income inequality, especially at the low end of the income distribution. Detailed data on poverty are reported not just for informational purposes but as guides to antipoverty policies. A myriad of cash programs and in-kind programs (for food, shelter, and medical care) are available to help those in economic distress, whether this is a short-term or a long-term proposition. In many respects the public concern for helping those in poverty through the governmental tax and transfer system has had the effect of reducing the role of private mechanisms, whether through the family, the church, or civic organizations. This decline has intensified the poor's reliance on the government for assistance.

Both the change in technology that has reduced the demand for low-skilled labor and the change in policies toward the low-income population have important implications for differences between the low-skilled immigrants of 1910 and those of 2010. Today's low-skilled workers have more difficulty finding opportunities for upward mobility and are much less attractive for the U.S. economy than their earlier counterparts were a hundred years ago.

7. "Immigrants do not want to and do not need to learn English."

The two points in this proposition are usually separated and uttered by different groups, with different political agendas. Yet both are false. Most immigrants to the United States *do* want to learn English, today as in the past (see Carola Suárez-Orozco's and Mary C. Waters's chapters in this book). There are strong economic incentives for becoming proficient in English. Employment prospects and earnings are greater for those who are proficient in English, and this effect is greater for those with higher levels of other skills, including schooling. The impressive increase in earnings with duration in the United States among immigrants is in large part due to their increase in English-language proficiency the longer they live in the United States (Chiswick and Miller 2007). There are also many noneconomic benefits for immigrants from becoming proficient in English. These include greater access to and participation in the civic, cultural, social, and political life of the country, including passing the English language test for becoming a citizen (Chiswick and Miller 2009).

Certain factors, however, make it more difficult for some individuals or immigrant groups to become proficient in spoken or written English (Chiswick and Miller 2007). Older immigrants have greater difficulty than their younger counterparts in acquiring English proficiency, presumably associated with the aging human brain's diminishing ability to absorb and retain new language skills. More important, however, learning English (or any language) depends largely on exposure, practice, and repetition. The ease with which an immigrant or an immigrant group can avoid using English is a crucial determinant of the ability to function in English (Chiswick and Miller 2007).

In many parts of the country the English-language acquisition of Spanish-speaking immigrants is slowed by the pervasive presence of Spanish—newspapers, TV, radio, and even signage are all available in Spanish. In such areas one can work and shop in a Spanish-language enclave without suffering serious adverse consequences. For most other languages, however, there would be little exposure or opportunity to use the origin language in the United States. Hence, whether they want to or not, speakers of these other languages acquire greater English-language proficiency sooner than do Spanish-speaking immigrants. Regardless of the English-language proficiency of immigrant parents, however, the United States–born children of immigrants are invariably proficient in English. Among adults in the second generation, English is the main language spoken in nearly every home, and by the second or third generation the ancestral language is usually lost (Chiswick and Miller 2007).

8. "Family-based visas promote fairness; employment-based visas are elitist (if not racist)."

It has become commonplace in the United States to view family ties as the most appropriate mechanism for allocating visas among the increasingly greater number who want to immigrate to the United States than there are visas available. It is highly ironic that in no other sphere of public life do we ask—or are we even permitted to ask—the question "to whom are you related" (nepotism) rather than the question "what are your qualifications" (meritocracy). In 2007, for example, about

65 percent of the one million permanent resident visas were issued to the spouses, children, parents, and siblings of U.S. citizens or permanent resident aliens (U.S. Department of Homeland Security 2008). Only 16 percent of visas were allocated to workers (and their spouse and minor children) primarily on the basis of the worker's skill upon application by a U.S. employer who can demonstrate that there are no qualified citizens or resident aliens available at prevailing wages who can perform the job. A small number of visas in 2007 were issued on the basis of refugee status (13 percent), through a "diversity visa" lottery (4 percent), and on other criteria (2 percent).

The view that it would be racist to allocate visas on the bases of the applicant's skills stems from the false notion that such visas go primarily to whites of European origin. With the abolition of the virtual ban on South Asian and East Asian immigration in the 1965 legislation, it was the employment and investor visas that served as the mechanism for many Asians to gain entry into the United States. More recently, increased immigration from Africa has also come about through the employment visas. The employment visas provide immigration opportunities for skilled workers who do not have family members already established in the United States. They have therefore expanded the racial and ethnic diversity of the immigrant stream, and hence of the American population.

9. "Charging large fees or auctioning visas is discriminatory."

Since the United States apparently does not want to return to the "open door" policy regarding immigration that largely prevailed in the nineteenth and early twentieth centuries (see point 6, earlier in this chapter), nor does it want a "closed door" ban on immigration, a mechanism is needed to ration the limited supply of immigrant visas among the much larger number of those seeking a visa (the demand). Thus far a non-price-rationing mechanism has been used, based primarily on relationship to a U.S. citizen or resident alien and secondarily on the applicant's ability to find a sponsoring employer.

Because U.S. wages are often far greater than the wages they can receive in their home country, those immigrants fortunate enough to obtain a visa usually find that living and working in the United States is like winning a lottery—their wealth has increased greatly. The windfall that this implies can be very large. Selling or auctioning legal visas would permit the native-born U.S. population to capture some of this economic rent and partially compensate for any adverse consequences of increased immigration. If Americans could receive a greater benefit from immigration through this mechanism, public support for an increase in the number of visas issued annually might be more broadly based than it is today.

There would be several concerns regarding requiring the payment of the large fee at the time of immigration (Chiswick 1981). One is that because of capital market constraints, many immigrants could not pay the fee "up front" from their own resources and could not borrow the funds from conventional and legal lending institutions. Another concern is the uncertainty as to how successful they would be in the U.S. labor market, perhaps discouraging applicants who are risk averse. A large upfront fee would also discourage those who plan on staying temporarily, or who are concerned that for family or other reasons they might want to return home. A possible solution to each of these concerns is linking the payment of the visa fee to a surcharge on the federal income tax. This would relax the capital market constraint, provide insurance against wage uncertainty, and make the fee a function of the immigrants' duration in the United States. To avoid abuse, such a program might be limited to those with more than a minimal level of skill.

10. "Immigration: Are you for it or against it?"

I am frequently asked this question, and a one-word answer—for or against—is usually expected. But this is the wrong way to pose the immigration question. What are the objectives of an immigration policy—family reunification, refugee relief, economic benefit to the current U.S. population? And what are the relative weights to be given to each of these objectives? Another question: Who gains and who loses from alternative immigration policies? Are there mechanisms through which the gainers (including the immigrants themselves) can compensate others, especially those who lose? How can we enforce immigration law both at the border and away from the border (workplace enforcement) while minimizing the adverse effects on those with a legal right to work in this country and on employers who obey the law?

A rational immigration policy can be developed for the United States that is consistent with our economic interests, humanitarian concerns (regarding both families and refugees), and civil liberty objectives, but to do so requires an understanding of the myths and fallacies that have dominated the immigration discourse for far too long. Immigration as a whole has been beneficial to the United States, and there is every reason to believe that a well-designed immigration policy can continue to be beneficial. Such a policy includes legal mechanisms for permanent and temporary migration and the enforcement of immigration policy at the border and in the interior, especially work site enforcement. An optimal immigration policy would not be an "open door" nor would it be a "closed door." Thus a mechanism is needed to ration the finite number of visas among the greater number of potential applicants each year.

An immigration policy for the twenty-first century must consider the nature of the American economy, the skills that are in high demand, and the types of workers who will contribute most to maintaining U.S. economic leadership in a global economy. It must also consider the myriad of tax policies and transfer programs that redistribute income and wealth in the United States. Family-based visas benefit the visa recipient and his or her family but are likely to have a smaller overall favorable impact (and perhaps a negative impact) on the U.S. economy, the tax and transfer balance, and the U.S. populace as a whole, compared with a visa policy that focuses on the scientific, technical, managerial, and entrepreneurial skill that immigrants can bring to the United States. With an increase in the favorable impact of immigrants, the American public would be more inclined to increase the number of visas that are made available annually.

The short answer to the question as to whether I am for or against immigration is: Yes!

NOTES

An earlier version of this chapter was presented at the Conference on Covering Immigration at Harvard University in October 2008 and at the Honorary Doctorate Seminar of the School of Economics and Management at Lund University in May 2009. Comments received at both presentations are appreciated. The views expressed in this chapter are those of the author and are not to be attributed to either seminar or the author's affiliations.

1. As this chapter was being written, an article appeared in the *International Wall Street Journal* (Jordan 2009) about native-born Americans seeking jobs in slaughter houses that they had previously avoided.

2. George Borjas (1990: 88) uses this technique and puts in italics for emphasis that it demonstrates there is no effect of immigration on native wages.

3. Julian Simon (1989), for example, does the computation for all immigrants and concludes that they pay more in taxes than they consume in public benefits. His methodology is open to criticism as it also implies that natives pay

more in taxes than they receive in public benefits. He considers all taxes paid, but only some public expenditures. He does not consider differences in impact by level of income or schooling.

4. The liberal democracies in North America and Europe are at a disadvantage compared with authoritarian states (for example, those in the Persian Gulf), when it comes to enforcement of the temporary status for guest workers.

REFERENCES

Borjas, George J. 1990. *Friends or Strangers: The Impact of Immigrants on the U.S. Economy*. New York: Basic Books.

Chiswick, Barry R. 2006. "The Worker Next Door." *New York Times*. June 3, A23.

———. 1992. "Review of *Immigration, Trade, and the Labor Market* by Abowd and Freeman." *Journal of Economic Literature* 30, no. 1 (March): 212–13.

———. 1991. "Review of *Friends or Strangers* by Borjas." *Journal of Economic Literature* 29, no. 2 (June): 627–29.

———. 1981. "Guidelines for the Reform of Immigration Policy." In *Essays in Contemporary Economic Problems 1981–82*. Edited by William Fellner. Pp. 309–47. Washington, D.C.: American Enterprise Institute.

Chiswick, Barry R., and Paul W. Miller. 2009. "Citizenship in the United States: The Roles of Immigrant Characteristics and Country of Origin." *Research in Labor Economics* 29: 91–130.

———. 2007. *The Economics of Language: International Analyses*. London: Routledge.

Ferrie, Joseph. 2011. "A Historical Perspective on High-skilled Immigrants to the U.S., 1820–1920." In *High-skilled Immigration in a Globalized Labor Market*. Edited by Barry R. Chiswick. Pp. 15–49. Washington, D.C.: American Enterprise Institute.

Filer, Randell. 1992. "The Impact of Immigrant Arrivals on Local Labor Market Equilibria for Native Workers." In *Immigration and the Work Force: Economic Consequences for the United States and Source Areas*. Edited by George J. Borjas and Richard Freeman. Pp. 245–70. Chicago: University of Chicago Press.

Hamermesh, Daniel S., and Frank D. Bean, eds. 1998. *Help or Hindrance? The Economic Implications of Immigration for African Americans*. New York: Russell Sage Foundation.

Jordan, Miriam. 2009. "In U.S. Immigrants and Locals Compete for Once Scorned Jobs." *International Wall Street Journal*, May 26, 18–19.

Simon, Julian. 1989. *The Economic Consequences of Immigration*. Cambridge, Mass.: Basil Blackwell.

United States Department of Homeland Security. 2008. *Immigration Statistics of the United States, 2007*. Washington, D.C.: U.S. Government Printing Office.

A Son of Immigrants on Covering Immigration

GEORGE DE LAMA

In many ways, as my colleagues have captured so well with the depth and sophistication of their observations throughout this book, the quality of our best immigration coverage has improved considerably in the thirty years since I began my career as a kid reporter at the *Chicago Tribune*. For my first year and a half, I was the only Latino on the staff, pretty incredible for an immigrant city like Chicago. Coverage of Hispanics was viewed as something exotic, a local version of foreign correspondence about strange people from strange lands, living in dangerous, segregated areas of the city that most *Tribune* readers avoided.

I was born and raised in the city, and I knew those attitudes well. My father was an immigrant waiter who never finished high school. He used to get bigger tips from the people he served at a hotel restaurant downtown when they would ask him to do like Bill Dana, that guy that Ed Sullivan had made famous on his TV show. My dad would grit his teeth into what looked like a tight smile—but really he was sneering— and say: "My naaiing eees Jose Jimenez." I saw my father do it once when I was a little kid visiting him at work, and I still remember the instant repugnance I felt. Not at my father but at the well-to-do people around the table, hysterically laughing at his thick Cuban accent. He hated it too, of course. But as he explained to me later when I asked him why he had done it, he was just trying to do whatever he needed to do to take care of his family.

Forget those people, he said. *They're just stupid people and they don't matter.* But I never did forget. My father is gone now, but the memory still wrenches my stomach and sets my teeth on edge. That's part of the immigrant experience too. For my father, to be sure. But also for me, like other children of the foreign-born, cementing forever that I would always have one foot in each culture, never belonging entirely to either. The only Latino characters I ever saw on TV back then were Ricky Ricardo and Jose Jimenez, national laughingstocks, caricatures that Americans laughed at for talking like my parents did. On the flip side, I'll never forget the first time I saw anyone remotely like us portrayed in a movie. It was, of all people, Alan Arkin, playing a Puerto Rican building superintendent and part-time waiter, the father of two small boys in the Bronx, in a long-forgotten movie called *Popi.* I was mesmerized. I had never seen anything like it. Here was Arkin, a Jewish guy from New York, convincingly playing the role of a Latino man, very much like my father and my uncle. The magic in the movie was that Arkin played a universal role, a father in tough circumstances, far from his home, struggling mightily to do right by his sons in an often hostile world. I must have been about eleven or twelve years old when my father took me to see that movie, and the experience was a powerful one.

I recount all of this here because even in our 24/7 celebrity culture, where we are constantly bombarded by images, how people are portrayed in the media is still important. It is important to the public perception about people outside the mainstream of society. And it is important to those marginalized people's own self-image. Naturally enough, I've often looked at immigration through my parents' life story and my own experience. Like Patrick J. McDonnell, whose experience is recounted in Interlude I, I've spent a lot of time challenging myself to make sure that my work, as a reporter and later as an editor, did not reflect this bias, even as it was informed by this perspective. As it turned out, that sense of not quite belonging to either world served me pretty well in preparing to become a journalist. The experience of growing up in a three-generation immigrant home, where Spanish was the dominant language, in an inner-city neighborhood largely hostile to people like us, naturally led me to become a most interested observer of everything happening around me. I learned at an early age to walk around with my antenna up and pay attention.

. . .

In a 2006 issue of *Nieman Reports* dedicated to the coverage of immigration, Hector Tobar of the *Los Angeles Times* evoked that experience when he wrote about news coverage that focuses on cultural conflict and heightens "the otherness" of immigrants. "Entering immigrant America on behalf of an English-language newspaper is, by definition, a cross-cultural experience," he wrote.[1] There is a lot of terrific journalism being committed out there, but unfortunately, too often in covering this cross-cultural story, too many things get lost in translation. I reluctantly have to agree with Roberto Suro, who wrote the book's introduction, that too much of the media coverage focuses on the polarized conflict, on the illegal aspects of immigration and the crisis atmosphere that often surrounds so much of the debate in Washington, D.C., and around the country.

As a people, Americans have a short attention span, and we get bored easily. When there is no crisis, we tend to move on. We in the media reflect this, and we feed it. But this ill serves our readers and viewers and listeners, and in the process, our society. This is not the path to preserve the credibility and long-term health of our own news organizations, either. Unfortunately, the trend is being exacerbated by many of the changes we are seeing in the fragmentation of the news media and the growing popularity of advocacy journalism, where people increasingly turn to their favorite news organizations for coverage that validates the views they already hold, on immigration or politics or any number of other subjects.

This is magnified by the modern megaphones of anti-immigrant advocacy groups and their online bloggers, ratings-hungry cable television personalities, and unabashedly pro-immigrant Spanish-language media, who do their own readers and viewers no service when they take up sides in the game and neglect their duty to thoughtfully cover all the opposing facts and viewpoints in this debate. Neither do traditional news organizations when they turn to a misplaced emphasis on employing emotion and "attitude" to create a "buzz" and attract demographically desirable audiences, depth and substance be damned.

Everyone is shouting, and no one is heard.

Throw in the currently fashionable fascination with shorter stories, more briefs and in-depth reports reduced to *charticles*—even of immensely complicated issues—and it can serve to further distort complex realities and poorly inform the public. We've made a lot of progress as a nation in our attitudes toward immigrants since my folks came to Chicago as young newlyweds in the mid-1950s. Americans are more tolerant of the notion of diversity since those days. Yet for many people, immigration is perceived primarily as a threat—a cultural threat, an economic threat, and since 9/11, a security threat. That was certainly clear to me in my final years at the *Chicago Tribune* when I had to deal with readers who spewed vitriol on this topic like no other.

As journalists we have to ask ourselves, what roles do we play in stoking controversy when we should be providing context? Making things worse in the long term, the self-evident need for greater diversity in coverage and in the staffs of our newsrooms is slipping as a priority in these troubled economic times. The sense of urgency we've felt about bringing new faces in through the front door of our profession seems to have faded amid the panicked perception that our house is burning. To cite just one example, at the Tribune Company, where I worked for many years, one of the first steps the new ownership took was to eliminate the word *diversity* from the official list of company values. A trivial thing, some might say. But the message was unmistakable. The aspirational notion of diversity, the journalistic and business promise it holds, is just not that important to the company. They made this clear right away. Perhaps not surprisingly, no one in the senior management ranks of the company is a minority. There are only two minorities on the mastheads of its five biggest newspapers put together. But to be fair, that doesn't make the Tribune Company that much different from most of the biggest media companies in the United States today.

. . .

You don't need to be a minority reporter to do great work on immigration, of course, as evidenced by the distinguished coverage produced by so many of my colleagues throughout this book. Although there can be cultural advantages for minority journalists covering their own communities, great reporters of any background can cover anything, and they should. Still, I was struck by McDonnell's observation that he hasn't had too many editors with direct knowledge of or exposure to immigrants. We need to do much better in this area as an industry. It would help us immensely in providing our readers and viewers and listeners with the most compelling, relevant, richly textured coverage they would not otherwise find anywhere.

At the end of the day, that is the point.

In the United States coverage of immigration is in the highest traditions of our profession. More than a century ago, the photojournalist

Jacob Riis documented the lives of poor immigrants on the Lower East Side of Manhattan in his seminal book, *How the Other Half Lives*. In the process he helped change American journalism. I first saw that book in high school, with its powerful photography and impassioned investigative reporting. I remember thinking: *That's what I'd like to do with my life. I'd like to tell people stories and take them to places they haven't seen. I'd like to help make a difference.*

All these years later, after having reported, edited, and read so many stories on immigration, I wonder sometimes whether we have.

NOTES

1. Hector Tobar, "Attempting to Bridge the Divide," *Nieman Reports* 60, no. 3 (Fall 2006): 19.

Immigration and
the Second Generation

In Part Three of the book Ginger Thompson of the *New York Times;*
Carola Suárez-Orozco of New York University's Steinhardt School of
Culture, Education, and Human Development; Tyche Hendricks of the
KQED Public Radio San Francisco and the University of California–
Berkeley Graduate School of Journalism; Vivian Louie of the Harvard
Graduate School of Education; and Mary C. Waters of Harvard's
Department of Sociology turn their attention to what will define the
long-term consequences of the massive immigration wave of the past
generation: the integration and well-being of the children of immigrants. They focus on the needs of immigrant families, the experiences
of children in schools, and their transition to the labor market. Below
are some of the exchanges generated on immigration and the second
generation at the Nieman Foundation for Journalism conference.

. . .

Audience question: Many folks are focusing on the economic role
   of immigrants and that's sort of how we think about immigration and how policymakers are thinking about how we craft an
   immigration reform and so forth, what levels of skill do we want,
   and how many immigrants and so forth; but there are also folks
   who are saying that's sort of immaterial. What we should mostly
   focus on is how thoroughly we integrate immigrants and that we

have a number of immigrants that we can absorb, that we put the resources into bringing them fully into American society and polity. What do you folks think should be the balance there?

Panelist Carola Suárez-Orozco: I think we need to be providing systematic information to immigrant children and to parents, certainly in the education and workplace realms. They come here to be successful in our society, right? They want to join the society. The kids clearly want to join the society. You're right, there's no doubt that they want to become Americanized. If you spend any time with adolescents, that's what they want more than anything. What we need to be doing is getting them systemic information about how to play the game in the new society. It's not about "you need to become like us." It is about how to obtain access. The frame isn't how do you become more American? It's how do you find a job, how do you get information about getting to college? It's about how you frame it. It's not about how you become more like us, but how do you get information that every middle-class kid has access to, right? Their parents are paying tutors $150 an hour to get that access.

Panelist Barry R. Chiswick: We have an immigration policy. We don't have an absorption policy; it's laissez-faire. Some other countries do have more explicit absorption policies, and I think that is one of the failings in the United States. If we are admitting legal immigrants, we should make greater efforts to facilitate their economic integration, including greater access to English-language training programs, which is really, after immigrating to the United States, the second best investment that immigrants can make.

Panelist Eduardo Porter: If I could just address the issue of absorption—that sounds like there's an underlying assumption that there is something to absorb into, some kind of fixed entity, cultural construct that you absorb into. In the United States this has been changing with every cohort of immigrants. So absorb into what? Well, I would posit that they are absorbing into a new kind of United States that has lots of Hispanics in it and where the Virgin of Guadalupe is more important than she was thirty years ago. Even though I do see the value of taking on specific characteristics of the United States—like learning English, for instance—I would dispute that there is this kind of like exterior thing that one comes in and absorbs into.

Panelist Miriam Jordan: But I think also the point was that there are countries like Israel that have absorption ministries that take it upon themselves to educate, integrate through language, do job training and other things for new arrivals in a way that we don't. I mean, we have a shortage of English classes out there.

Panelist Jess Benhabib: It's probably very important to integrate the children of immigrants and to provide them with appropriate schooling and language training. That is probably something we are sometimes even putting impediments toward rather than encouraging.

. . .

Audience question: I am a French reporter, and I am a Nieman fellow this year. You keep speaking of immigrants as one single group without making any difference regarding their origins. So what I would like to know, if you look at the second or the third generation, what do the numbers say about how do they economically do regarding each other?

Panelist Barry R. Chiswick: Well, in terms of my own work, I focus on skill differences; but I think skill differences—the skill packages that immigrants bring—is primary. I also look at country of origin, but what we find is that the children of low-skilled immigrants also tend to be low-skilled—not as low-skilled as their parents—it sort of narrows; but the children of low-skilled immigrants do get less schooling than the children of high-skilled immigrants, and there is this persistence across generations.

Panelist Jess Benhabib: I was puzzled because this is a very important topic. I just read the experts on this—Mary Waters's discussion and Barry Chiswick's negative assimilation work—which is very interesting. So I couldn't make heads or tails as to which view is right and how well the children of immigrants integrate, but it is an open question.

Panelist Barry R. Chiswick: Can I just make one point on the issue of language? There's a lot of talk about Mexican immigrants, in particular, and how they are not interested in learning English, and their children don't learn English—it is just not true. Their children may be bilingual; but their children do learn English and actually, by the third generation, the descendants of Mexican immigrants have pretty much abandoned Spanish. Certainly by the fourth generation there's no Spanish.

Convener Marcelo M. Suárez-Orozco: May I offer a reflection? We can drive to Lawrence, Massachusetts, an old mill town full of the descendants of Syrian, Lebanese, and Irish immigrants from 150 years ago. The [Hispanic] kids in these schools are hermetically isolated from mainstream peers. They go to school where 90 percent of the children in the Lawrence schools now are Dominican, Puerto Rican, or Central American. That's the issue. They live days, lives where they don't have any meaningful contact with the mainstream society.

7

The Education Transformation

Why the Media Missed One of the Biggest Stories
in America

GINGER THOMPSON

At the end of 2007 the *New York Times* assigned a group of reporters
to write a series of stories about immigration's impact on America. The
stories, published over seven weeks beginning in March 2009, explored
the ways that record waves of immigrants had transformed workplaces,
neighborhoods, and families. One story focused on public schools. Five
decades after *Brown v. Board of Education,* there are no "whites only"
signs hanging on school bathrooms, but that doesn't mean there are no
barriers. It only means that they are harder to identify. This is the story
behind the story that attempted to do so.

. . .

The dirty little secret about reporting is that it's often like chasing an
ambulance. I had spent months and traveled hundreds of miles looking for the right place to set a story about immigration's impact on
American schools, when I came across a brief item deep in the metro
section of the *Washington Post* about a crisis that was playing out in
Prince William County, Virginia. The *Post* reported that hundreds of
foreign-born students were disappearing from the county's schools after
officials there had implemented one of the nation's toughest crackdowns
against illegal immigration.

    The measure authorized police to check the status of anyone they
suspected of living in the United States illegally. Immigrant families,
worried about becoming the targets of harassment, began leaving in

droves. The first concrete signs of the exodus were seen in schools. I called district administrators that very afternoon. I told them in broad terms the goals of my story. Over the past decade immigration had fueled the most robust growth in public schools since the baby boom. The growth had severely strained the capacity of districts already short on resources needed to serve students with special needs, and put classrooms on the front lines of the nation's fights over how to assimilate immigrants and their children.

What I needed was a place to bring that story to life, I explained to county officials. And Prince William, a sprawling exurb of shopping malls and chain restaurants located some thirty-five miles south of the nation's capital, seemed a perfect microcosm of the national dilemma. Schools, officials told me, had been shielded from the turmoil. Even with budget cuts, per pupil spending was among the highest for public schools in the Washington, D.C., metropolitan area. Almost every school in the district had special instruction for students who were not proficient in English. Test scores suggested a majority of those students were thriving. And although the political fights over illegal immigration had divided Prince William into two angry camps, teachers said that hostility stopped at the school house door.

That's the story the county wanted the *New York Times* to tell. They proposed that I spend as much time as I wanted at Cecil D. Hylton High School so that I could see the county's achievements for myself. Hylton had one of the most ethnically diverse student populations in the district—about 30 percent white, 30 percent black, 30 percent Hispanic, and 10 percent Asian. In 2001 it established a kind of magnet program offering courses in international affairs, and it has one of the largest Model United Nations organizations on the East Coast. The school's principal, Carolyn Custard, had just been named one of the three best principals in the country. When talking about the award, she praised her staff and students for treating one another like one big happy family.

That's certainly what things looked like when I first walked Hylton's hallways. Black kids were hanging out with white kids, who were hanging out with Hispanic kids and Asian kids. Then I spent a school day with Amalia Raymundo, a seventeen-year-old sophomore, who had just arrived in Prince William Country from a rural village in the Guatemalan mountains. Seeing Hylton through her eyes allowed me to discover some students were still being left out.

WOODBRIDGE, Va.—Walking the halls of Cecil D. Hylton High School outside Washington, it is hard to detect any trace of the divisions that once seemed fixtures in American society.

Two girls, a Muslim in a headscarf and a strawberry blonde in tight jeans, stroll arm in arm. A Hispanic boy wearing a Barack Obama T-shirt gives a high-five to a black student with glasses and an Afro. The lanky homecoming queen, part Filipino and part Honduran, runs past on her way to band practice. The student body president, a son of Laotian refugees, hangs fliers about a bake sale.

But as old divisions vanish, waves of immigration have fueled new ones between those who speak English and those who are learning how.

Walk with immigrant students, and the rest of Hylton feels a world apart. By design, they attend classes almost exclusively with one another. They take separate field trips. And they organize separate clubs.

"I am thankful to my teachers because the little bit of English I am able to speak, I speak because of them," Amalia Raymundo, from Guatemala, said during a break between classes. But, she added, "I feel they hold me back by isolating me."

Her best friend, Jhosselin Guevara, also from Guatemala, joined in. "Maybe the teachers are trying to protect us," she said. "There are people who do not want us here at all."[1]

Like thousands of other school districts across the country, Hylton responded to the unprecedented waves of immigrant students with a modern-day version of segregation. This version—often conducted with the best of intentions—separates students who are not proficient in English so they can get the extra attention they need to earn their diplomas without interrupting the flow of the mainstream. The degrees of separation vary from school to school. But at Hylton educators had established a kind of school within a school for students who are not proficient in English. The program was known as English for Speakers of Other Languages (ESOL). Its students attended most classes together, including science, history, and math. They went on separate field trips. They established separate clubs. And their parents were invited to separate parent-teacher association meetings.

This new version of segregation was not some throwback to the days when separate but equal was the law of the land. In fact, educators reject the use of the word *segregation* when describing instruction models that remove students from the mainstream. Instead, they compare their work to teaching a child to swim in the shallow end of a pool before allowing him or her to jump into the deep end. But watching ESOL up close for an extended period of time made clear it's not all that it's billed to be. Hylton claims, for example, that ESOL students get the same education as their English-speaking peers. My reporting there showed they do not. Hylton says that ESOL students are better served in separate classrooms where they can get the extra help they need. Administrators boast about reports showing that in recent years ESOL students performed as well or better than their English-speaking peers on state standardized tests. In the age of No Child Left Behind, however, good test scores serve schools more than students. Since the implementation of the 2001 law, those scores determine whether schools will receive government funding and whether teachers get to keep their jobs. But they do not determine whether students are prepared to compete for opportunities beyond high school.

ESOL served Hylton well in other ways. The program helped keep the peace among the majority of the faculty who did not want to deal with the burdens of having special-needs students in their classrooms. And with anti-immigrant attitudes raging all around the school, ESOL allowed administrators to keep foreign-born newcomers out of sight and out of mind of those parents who might complain that English-language learners (ELLs) were a drain on precious resources. But the calm in the hallways belied resentments simmering among students who barely knew one another. In interviews, students readily labeled one another "stupid" or "racist," or fell back on other easy stereotypes. The tensions erupted at times into walkouts and cafeteria fights, including one in which immigrant students tore an American flag off the wall and black students responded by shouting, "Go back to your own country!"

Many of these tensions are as old as public schools themselves. What's different today is that with so many immigrants entering the country illegally, schools are more frequently charged with preparing students to become productive members of a society that seems increasingly hostile to them. I saw the sense of helplessness in teachers' eyes as they watched immigrant students overcome all the hurdles of high school only to get detained and deported after graduation. I saw illegal immigrants with excellent grades drop out to take minimum-wage jobs because they knew they would not be able to qualify for financial aid to go to college.

Not once did I see an easy answer. As a former Latin America correspondent, I went into Prince William County thinking that penetrating schools in a solidly middle-class suburb would be a cinch compared with the seedy border towns where I had spent so much of my career. I ended the assignment awed by the magnitude of the task schools face, exhausted by the amount of time and energy required to get people to speak candidly about such a hot-button issue, and conflicted about whether American schools were leveling playing fields or perpetuating long-standing power relationships.

> It was crunch time at Hylton High: ten minutes until the bell, two weeks before state standardized tests, and a classroom full of blank stares suggesting that [the teacher,] Ms. [Ginette] Cain, still had a lot of history to cover to get her students ready.
>
> The question hanging in the air: "What is the name for a time of paranoia in the United States that was sparked by the Bolshevik Revolution?"
>
> "What's that?" Delmy Gomez, a junior from El Salvador, said with a grimace that caused her classmates to burst into laughter.
>
> The question might have stumped plenty of high school students. But for Ms. Cain's pupils, it might as well have been nuclear physics.
>
> Freda Conteh had missed long stretches of school in war-torn Sierra Leone. Noemi Caballero, from Mexico, filled notebooks with short stories and poetry in Spanish, but struggled to compose simple sentences in English.
>
> Nuwan Gamage, from Sri Lanka, was distracted by working two jobs to support himself because he found it difficult to live with his mother and her American husband after spending most of his life apart from her. And Edvin Estrada, a Guatemalan, worried about a brother in the Marines, headed off for duty in some undisclosed hot spot.
>
> Few of these students had heard of the Pilgrims, much less the history of Thanksgiving. Idioms like "easy as pie" and "melting pot" were lost on them. They knew little of the American Revolution, much less the Bolshevik.
>
> "American students come to school with a lot of cultural knowledge that other teachers assume they don't have to explain because their kids get it from growing up in this country, watching television or surfing the Internet," Ms. Cain said. "I can't assume any of that."[2]

Education experts have said it takes at least two years for a student learning English to acquire enough of the language to hold real conversations, and between five to seven years for them to establish the range of proficiency needed to write essays, comprehend a novel, and articulate scientific processes or math calculations at the same level as their native English-speaking counterparts. English-language learners who arrive in this country old enough to go to high school present even bigger challenges. Unlike the immigrant students in elementary schools, a larger number of high school immigrants are foreign-born and have a harder time straddling two cultures. It's harder for them to overcome the setbacks of having grown up in countries with crippled schools. As a result, they generally require special attention from the day they start school until the day they graduate. Few ever make it to the point where they can attend classes in the mainstream.

Hylton argued that separate can be equal. Its ESOL program, established by a petite, bespectacled spark plug of a teacher named Ginette Cain, offered students the same kinds of classes as those in the mainstream. ESOL students had to pass the same standardized tests. But after months of rotating between ESOL and regular classes, I learned significant differences existed between them. ESOL students spent twice the amount of class time as regular students on core subjects, which means they had very little opportunities to take the kinds of electives that make for a well-rounded education. ESOL classes were light on lectures and heavy on drills, games, and worksheets intended to help them memorize facts about topics as varied as European monarchies, rock formations, and the workings of the human heart. Regular freshmen English classes finished Shakespeare's *Romeo and Juliet* in a month, while immigrant students pored only over selected sections for an entire semester. Most mainstream Earth science students took tests with essay questions on the phases of the water cycle; the English-language learners had the option to draw posters, like one by a Bolivian-born boy who depicted himself as a water molecule rising from an ice cube, drifting into a cloud, and raining over his homeland.

The immigrant students were given less homework and rarely got failing grades if they demonstrated good-faith efforts. They were given more credit for showing what they know in class participation than on written assignments. On state standardized tests, they were offered accommodations unavailable to other students. Teachers, for example, were allowed to read test questions to them. In some cases the students were permitted to respond orally while teachers record their answers. In Cain's ninety-minute history review classes, which touched on topics from the reign of Marie Antoinette to the Iraq war, getting ready for tests often seemed the sole objective. Cain routinely interrupted discussions to emphasize potential questions. "Write this down," she told a class one day. "There's always a question about Huguenots." Significant historical episodes are often reduced to little more than sound bites. "You don't really need to know anything more about the Battle of Britain, except that it was an air strike," Cain told one class. "If you see a question about the Battle of Britain on the test, look for an answer that refers to air strikes."

In 2008, 98 percent of Hylton's ESOL students passed Virginia's writing exam; by comparison, 97 percent of the general population passed. In math 91 percent of ESOL students passed the exam, the same percentage as regular students. And 89 percent of the English-language learners passed the history exam, compared with 91 percent of the others. Cain's students have performed so well on state tests that she was once accused of cheating. An audit concluded the accusations were unfounded. But, since then, lots of other questions have arisen. Months after I first began reporting at Hylton, teachers and administrators who had initially sung ESOL's praises began opening up to me about their reservations about the program.

> Custard, the principal, gushed with pride about how well Hylton's ESOL students perform on standardized tests. But in the same interview, the African American native of North Carolina who graduated from her hometown's first integrated high school, said she couldn't help wondering whether Hylton's ESOL program unintentionally relegated immigrant students to second-class status.
>
> Brenda Byrd, a tall, broad-shouldered, African-American assistant principal who patrolled the halls with the bearing of a drill sergeant, broke down into tears during one interview when she talked about her own inner conflicts over immigration. A product of a segregated education, she told me about the many times she had defended immigrant students from local police officers who wrongly accused the youths as gang-bangers. But she also admitted her own flashes of prejudice after an undocumented Mexican driver ran over and killed a nephew she had raised as a son.
>
> Amy Wiler, another assistant principal, was an outspoken critic of the school's ESOL program, charging that it was rife with abuses by teachers who advocated sheltering immigrant students, even after proficiency exams showed they were ready to exit the program, and by students who misused ESOL as a way to take an easier path through high school.
>
> "If you ask whether our program is successful at getting our students to pass tests, the data would indicate that it is," she said. "But if you ask whether we are helping our students to assimilate, there's no data to answer that question.
>
> "My fear," she added, "is that if we take a look at where our ESOL students are ten years from now, we're going to be disappointed."[3]

I couldn't find any research that served as a crystal ball. Most of the education experts I interviewed agreed that immigrant students who received at least some instruction in their native language tended to perform better in school than those who did not. They said the same was generally true for students who received some kind of sheltered instruction—which segregated them for at least some period of time—compared with those who were immersed into the mainstream without any special services. But that's where the consensus ended. Ultimately I did not quote a single academic by name. That doesn't mean, however, I didn't rely heavily on them.

I did. Their research became a kind of skeleton for my story, helping turn a jumble of anecdotes from a single school into a representative accounting of the challenges faced by almost all schools. Among the first people I spoke to was Richard Fry at the Pew Hispanic Center, who had done some of the most detailed demographic research on the characteristics of America's immigrant population, with special emphasis on students. A June 2007 report by Fry—"How Far Behind in Math and Reading Are English Language Learners?"—found that the students learning English lagged behind whites, blacks, and Hispanics by almost every academic measure. In many states, the report said, performance gaps between ELLs and whites on math and reading tests exceeded 50 percent.

I also went to New York to speak with Carola and Marcelo Suárez-Orozco, who had just finished a landmark book about the challenges faced by immigrant students, called, *Learning in a New Land: Immigrant Students in American Society.*[4] "This is the perfect storm," Mr. Suárez-Orozco told me during an interview. "What we're seeing is the profound misalignment between three powerful forces of change: an angry echo from communities experiencing the biggest waves of foreigners in history; a broken immigration system that has delivered twelve million people without papers, including two million children; and a broken education system unable to fulfill its responsibilities to give all children a shot at the new jobs of the twenty-first century."

In the frantic weeks leading up to the publication of my story in the *New York Times,* Jack Levy, the former director of the National Clearinghouse for English Language Acquisition, and Deborah Short at the Center for Applied Linguistics became unofficial advisers, graciously agreeing to review large blocks of copy for accuracy, sometimes in the very early hours of the morning. My road map was Laurie Olsen's *Made in America: Immigrant Students in Our Public Schools.* Olsen, former director of an immigrant advocacy organization, embedded herself in a typical American high school, which she called Madison, to do what I was trying to do, but on a much larger scale. What she experienced at Madison sounded a lot like what I had seen at Hylton. "Most of the educators at Madison believe in integration, fairness, and equal opportunity," Olsen wrote. "They mostly say they enjoy and appreciate living in a diverse community. But the way they perceive the world is that students are all equally positioned and free to participate in school and that matters of achievement are the result of the individual choices students make. What they collude in not seeing is the active process of exclusion and sorting that goes on in the school's program and practice, a sorting that consigns students by skin color, class, and English fluency into positions of very unequal access to resources, opportunities, and education. The reality is that few immigrants get the preparation they need academically or the language development required for academic success," she went on. "The reality is they are largely precluded from access to the curriculum that their English-fluent and U.S.-born schoolmates receive."[5]

Madison's immigrant students were grappling with some of the same identity issues as the students I'd met at Hylton. "People ask me, why can't you be both Vietnamese and American?" one Madison student told Olsen. "It just doesn't work because you run into too many contradictions. After a while you realize you can't be both, because you start crossing yourself and contradicting yourself and then it's like math, when two things contradict each other, they cancel each other out and then you're nothing. You are stuck as nothing if you try to be both. So I chose to be Vietnamese. I'm not sure I really could have been American anyway."[6]

Silence and separation at Hylton fueled an us-versus-them dynamic. The president of Hylton's parent-teacher-student organization recalled her daughter complaining about an immigrant student wearing a T-shirt that said, "They Can't Deport Us All." A Peruvian mother remembered her son coming home and asking, "Are we legal?"

When asked why they did not have any friends among the immigrant students, some mainstream students responded by mentioning a worker who did not finish a job their parents had paid for, or a line of pregnant women at the clinic where their mother works, or a gang member who stole a friend's books.

"I identify with the people I hang around with," said an editor of the student newspaper, who is not named because she spoke without her parents' permission. "My friends' parents are not cashiers or people who wash dishes."

When Ms. Cain's students are asked why they have not made friends outside their group, they often tell stories about a customer who cursed at them while they were working at McDonald's, or an employer who cheated their father of his wages, or a student who told them to stop speaking Spanish on the school bus.

Romina Benitez Aguero said that a neighbor greeted her cheerfully on the street, but that the woman's daughters—both Hylton students—snubbed her.

And Francisco Espinal, from Honduras, said a teacher once shouted at him for running in the halls. "This is not your country," he recalled the teacher saying. "You are in America now."[7]

The most compelling moments in my own reporting came from students, particularly those who had nothing to do with ESOL. While Prince William's immigration debate made headlines across the country, there was not a single story about it in the Hylton High School *Watchdog*. "I don't want to sound racist," explained Lorraine Archibald, coeditor of the student newspaper. "But people are afraid of the Spanish kids. Whenever they look at a girl it seems like they're thinking something obscene." Madina Beg, the other coeditor, said, "People look at ESOL kids bad because they come here from places like El Salvador, and have all these rights, and they don't even speak English."[8] Ironically, both Lorraine and Madina were children of immigrants. Madina's parents immigrated from Afghanistan. Lorraine's father was born in Peru. Still, the girls did not identify themselves as immigrants at all. Neither did the officers of Hylton's Model United Nations.

Mareeha Niaz, a senior of Pakistani decent, was representative of that irony. Her background was not all that different than a typical ESOL student. Her parents had come to the United States and accepted low-skilled jobs—one was stocking shelves at Target and the other was a cashier at Blockbuster—so that they could give their children better opportunities for advancement. Mareeha arrived in the United States at the age of five. She learned English in a couple of years. She's been in the top of her class ever since. She almost never ran into ESOL students, she said. When she did, she didn't feel any empathy for them. "I may have some ESOL students in PE," she said. "But I don't feel comfortable inviting them to play with my group because I don't really know them." I asked Mareeha and other Model UN members whether they had ever considered inviting ESOL students to provide firsthand perspectives on some of the issues the group studied, like migration, poverty, and war. The room went silent. Then Jasmil Perez, whose parents are Puerto Ricans, shook her head, and said, "I would have never thought ESOL students could contribute in that way."[9]

ESOL students expressed the same disdain for the regular kids. Yet everything about the hooded sweatshirts and baggy pants they wore, the American slang they sometimes slipped into their conversations, and the rap and rock they listened to on their iPods seemed an unspoken, though equally blatant, plea for approval. Audelia Espinal of Honduras embodied those feelings. She dressed in T-shirts with either the Honduran flag or map, wearing them to school at least a couple of times a week. But she also flirted with the idea of joining the Key Club and trying out for the field hockey team. "What's hard sometimes is that I'm Honduran, and I'm also a part of this country," she said. "In high school, you have to choose."[10]

For most ESOL students, choices seemed out of their control. In two and a half years in this country, Darwin Lobos of El Salvador had settled into the routines of an average American teenager, going to school by day and flipping burgers at night. Darwin, nineteen, was older than most students, and so Ms. Cain had enrolled him in summer school—at the county's expense—to help him onto a fast track. Two weeks after finishing summer school, at dawn on a Sunday morning, immigration agents descended on the home where Darwin was living, rousted everyone out of bed at gunpoint, gave Darwin time to dress, drove him to a detention center in nearby Arlington County, and deported him twenty days later. Seated behind a thick-glass prison partition before his deportation, Darwin was still having trouble comprehending what had happened to him. "Everything I wanted to do with my life is ruined," he said, staring through bloodshot eyes. "So many people come here, and do bad things, and nothing happens to them. All I did was go to school and to work. Why won't they let me have my dream?"[11]

Jorge Rosales of Mexico came close to dropping out of high school because the bank had foreclosed on his family's house, and he thought they could use the extra money. His father called his bluff and took Jorge to work with him at a construction site. Jorge was back in high school the next day, saying he wanted to do something "better" with his life. He aced his senior year, winning a place on the principal's honor roll. But after graduation, Jorge, who was living in the country illegally, could not get financial aid. That meant he could not afford college. A couple of months after he graduated, I met Jorge for tacos in a hole-in-the-wall outside Alexandria. He was so sleepy he could barely keep his eyes open. Jorge told me he woke up at four every morning and went to work with his Dad. What about your dreams of doing something better, I asked him. "That was a dream," he said. "I'm living in the real world."[12]

Then there was Amalia, who had come to the United States with dreams of becoming a doctor and now thinks often about dropping out of school because the longer she stayed in, the more she felt her options narrowing. "When I came to this country, I had my bags packed with dreams," said Amalia, who came with plans to become a doctor and now believes she will wind up as a maid, like her mother. "Now I see my dreams are limited."[13]

NOTES

1. Ginger Thompson, "Where Education and Assimilation Collide," *New York Times*, March 15, 2009.

2. Ibid.

3. Ibid.

4. Carola and Marcelo Suárez-Orozco, *Learning in a New Land: Immigrant Students in American Society* (Cambridge: Harvard University Press, 2008).

5. Laurie Olsen, *Made in America, Immigrant Students in Our Public Schools* (New York: The New Press, 1997), 10–11.

6. Ibid., 54.

7. Thompson, "Where Education and Assimilation Collide."

8. Ibid.

9. Ibid.

10. Ibid.

11. Ibid.

12. Ibid.

13. Ibid.

8

Moving Stories

Academic Trajectories of Newcomer Immigrant Students

CAROLA SUÁREZ-OROZCO

A powerful narrative of the struggles of immigration—particularly when focused on immigrant children and youth—rarely fails to move the reader. Individual stories or case studies are thus a device often shared by journalists and social scientists alike. But beyond this, what do journalists and social scientists writing about immigration share, and more important, how and why do our paths diverge? As a consumer of news stories, I am often moved by the journalists' accounts I read. But as a social scientist, I am also, admittedly, envious of the apparent ease and supersonic speed with which the information seems to be gathered without the interminable via crucis of grant writing, human subjects committee approvals, and ordeal of obtaining formal permissions to enter institutional settings before ever talking to the first participant (not to mention the exhaustive ritualistic literature reviews in one's own discipline as well as others when one does interdisciplinary work).

Gifted journalists have an admirable capacity to enter a space, talk to a few key informants ("sources" in their lingo), and capture often with remarkable accuracy and vivid detail the contours that we social scientists spent long years systematically establishing. Academics must offer at the altar of the peer-review process our most precious gift— the unbroken chain of evidence that is the critical ingredient for credibility, theory building, and sound conceptual innovation. While journalists are distinctly more agile and responsive to the pulse of current events, social scientists must take the long road. Some of us gather evidence across time and in different contexts, allowing us to explain how life stories change over the course of time as young people grow and their contexts and circumstances alter. In my view both perspectives, each with its own arsenals of methodologies, provide the public information, metaphors, and analytical frameworks that shed light on the ever-evolving immigrant experience.

Using the tools of my trade (cultural developmental psychology), I provide in this chapter a chain of evidence—a rationale for the study, a theoretical framework, references to the foundational work of previous researchers, a condensed methodological description and results section (given space constraints with references to the original study), along with a discussion and some policy recommendations. I do this in the spirit of sharing with my colleagues in journalism the architectural blueprint most often used in the scholarly study of immigration. Yet within the scholarly tradition, I should note that three features set apart my work from most other scholarship on the topic. First, my work is interdisciplinary in its scope, as I use tools from the field of research psychology as well as anthropology; second, it is longitudinal in nature (the data are gathered over a period of five years and another four years of analysis); and third, it is comparative in that I focus on several immigrant groups in more than a single context. As do my journalist colleagues on a daily basis, I use representative "moving stories" (in my case derived from seventy-five in-depth case studies that were systematically gathered and analyzed as part of a larger study) to both illustrate and bring to life key themes that emerge from the data. This research provides a longitudinal lens that complements my journalist colleagues' daily contributions to the field of writing immigration.

THE RATIONALE FOR STUDYING NEWCOMER IMMIGRANT EARLY ADOLESCENTS

While immigrant youths arrive with dreams to make it in America, all too many struggle to succeed in the educational system, performing poorly on a variety of academic indicators, including achievement tests, grades, dropout rates, and college attendance (Gándara and Contreras 2009; Orfield 2002). In particular, newcomer students who arrive sometime during their secondary education must surmount "formidable barrier[s]" (Hood 2003: 9) in adjusting to their new land (C. Suárez-

Orozco, M. Suárez-Orozco, and Todorova 2008), developing academic English skills (Carhill, Suárez-Orozco, and Páez 2008), and fulfilling graduation requirements (Ruíz-de-Velasco, Fix, and Clewell 2001)—all of which must be accomplished in a high-stakes testing environment that is not designed with their educational obstacles in mind (Hood 2003; Menken 2008). Moreover, the parents of these students are often ill-equipped to help them navigate a complex, foreign, and sometimes hostile educational system (Gándara and Contreras 2009; Olsen 1997; C. Suárez-Orozco, M. Suárez-Orozco, and Todorova 2008). Consequently, for many immigrants length of residence in the United States is associated with declining academic aspirations (Hernández and Charney 1998; Portes and Rumbaut 2001).

Such academic declines are particularly troubling when we consider the number of immigrant-origin youths in the American educational system. Indeed, 22 percent of youth growing up in the United States have immigrant parents, and it is projected that by 2040 over a third will be growing up in immigrant households (Hernández, Denton, and Macartney 2007). Newcomer immigrant students undergo myriad stresses of migration (García-Coll and Magnuson 1997; C. Suárez-Orozco and M. Suárez-Orozco 2001) while adapting to a new schooling environment, placing them particularly at educational risk. Of these newcomer students, approximately half arrive sometime during their secondary education (Ruíz-de-Velasco, Fix, and Clewell 2001), a time identified as being one of heightened developmental vulnerability (Eccles and Roeser 2003). The middle and high schools they encounter are often ill-equipped to address the needs of these early adolescent newcomers, leaving them "overlooked and under-served" (Ruíz-de-Velasco, Fix, and Clewell 2001: 1). In a knowledge-intensive economy in which the stakes of school failure are greater than ever before (Bloom 2004), deepening our understanding of the processes that contribute to trajectories of academic success and failure has clear social implications.

Despite the cumulative stresses of migration, limited familial capital, and less than optimal school contexts, not all newcomer youths fall prey to school failure and disengagement. Some appear to retain their initial optimism over time, while others fall prey to structural obstacles that lead to varying patterns of upward and downward assimilation (Portes and Rumbaut 2001). Still others demonstrate fluctuating levels of achievement during the course of their education.

CONTEXTS OF DEVELOPMENT

An Ecological Perspective

Immigrant youth do not grow up in a vacuum. Their academic trajectories are determined not only by their own efforts, but also by the contexts in which they develop (Bronfenbrenner and Morris 1998). In particular, the most proximal school and home ecologies influence the development of immigrant families, while macro systems of significant importance include both the societies that they leave (Portes and Rumbaut 2001) and their reception in their new land (Bean and Stevens 2003; Deaux 2006; Portes and Rumbaut 2001). Circumstances leading up to the immigration—such as political upheaval, undocumented status, or long family separations—have implications for the well-being and adaptation of the family (Portes and Rumbaut 2001; C. Suárez-Orozco, M. Suárez-Orozco, and Todorova 2008). Similarly, significant variations in the opportunity structure of the new land are linked to widely different trajectories, resulting in what Alejandro Portes and Min Zhou (1993) have termed "segmented assimilation." Variations in school, family, and individual characteristics are linked to widely different trajectories.

School Contexts

Immigrant youth typically find themselves in racially and ethnically segregated schools, which has been closely linked with reduced access to educational resources and negative school outcomes (Orfield and Lee 2006). Immigrant students, specifically those of Latino origin, also face an added burden of attending linguistically isolated schools that place them at particular academic risk (Orfield and Lee 2006). These dimensions of significant segregation are associated with a variety of negative school characteristics, including limited school district resources (Orfield and Lee 2006), low teacher expectancies (Weinstein 2002), poor achievement test outcomes (Gándara and Contreras 2009), high dropout rates (Orfield and Lee 2006), and limited information about access to college (Gándara and Contreras 2009; Orfield and Lee 2006). These school contexts are also associated with negative school climates (Noguera 2003) as well as school violence (Conoley and Goldstein 1997). Such schools do not offer an optimal, developmentally appropriate student fit (Eccles et al. 1993), undermining students' capacities to concentrate, their sense of security, and hence their ability to learn. These school contexts have implications for the education new-comers receive and their trajectories of academic adaptation over time (C. Suárez-Orozco, M. Suárez-Orozco, and Todorova 2008).

Family Characteristics

A host of reduced familial resources has been strongly linked to academic attainment (Perreira, Harris, and Lee 2006; Stanton-Salazar and Dornbusch 1995).

Parental education. There are well-established relationships between parental education and academic performance on such outcomes as grades, dropout rates, and achievement tests (Bourdieu and Passeron 1977; Madaus and Clarke 1998). In particular, the mother's education plays a significant role in shaping children's development and academic outcomes (O'Connor and McCartney 2007). More educated parents are better equipped to guide their children in studying, accessing, and making meaning of educational information. Research has established the link between parental education and academic outcomes among immigrant populations (Portes and Rumbaut 2001; C. Suárez-Orozco, M. Suárez-Orozco, and Todorova 2008). Educated immigrant parents are more likely to seek information about the educational system in the new land, while parents with limited education are often intimidated and misunderstood by school authorities, and are unable to help their children navigate the complicated college pathway system (C. Suárez-Orozco, M. Suárez-Orozco, and Todorova 2008).

Parental employment. Parental employment is one of the most robust indicators of family resources related to child development (Hauser and Warren 1997; Sirin and Rogers-Sirin 2005). Parents who are active in the workforce are better able to provide the resources and support needed for their children (Perreira, Harris, and Lee 2006). While maternal employment has "an ambiguous effect on child development" (Perreira, Harris, and Lee 2006: 4), paternal employment is consistently linked to better educational outcomes (Perreira, Harris, and Lee 2006; Sirin and Rogers-Sirin 2005).

Household structure. Children growing up in homes with two parents tend to have better developmental and academic outcomes than their peers living in single-parent households (Thompson, Hanson, and

McLanahan 1994). Two-parent homes are more likely to have access to greater resources, time, and attention to invest in children's well-being than single parents (Gibson-Davis 2008; Thompson, Hanson, and McLanahan 1994). Many newcomer immigrant youths may grow up in nontraditional, complex households that may include parents remaining in the homeland as well as multiple generations of caretakers (Hernandez, Denton, and Macartney 2007; Suárez-Orozco, Todorova, and Louie 2002). Families with more than one adult in the home may be better equipped to deploy resources to promote better educational outcomes than those with only one adult by diffusing the stressors of childcare in a foreign country and allowing for the provision of financial resources and supervision (Portes and Rumbaut 2001).

Family separations. The family structure is often disrupted over the course of the migratory journey. During immigration parents are frequently separated from their children as they search for adequate housing in the host country (Hondagneu-Sotelo 1994; Suárez-Orozco, Todorova, and Louie 2002). When one or both parents are first to migrate, children are often left in the care of extended family members and subsequently undergo two sets of separations: first from their parents, then from their caretakers to whom they may have become attached. Complications may arise at both junctures as well as when the children are ultimately reunited with their parents (Suárez-Orozco, Todorova, and Louie 2002). Each of these three points of high stress—separation from parents, separation from extended-family caretakers, and reunification with parents—can give rise to a host of emotional problems and social challenges that may affect academic performance (Arnold 1991; Sciarra 1999; C. Suárez-Orozco, M. Suárez-Orozco, and Todorova 2008).

Individual Characteristics

Several individual-level factors may be expected to lead to different trajectories of performance.

Academic English proficiency. The majority of newcomer immigrants face the challenge of mastering English while concurrently adjusting to a new school and gaining academic skills (Ruiz-de-Velasco, Fix, and Clewell 2001). English-language proficiency (ELP) affects students' abilities to detect social nuances in the school setting and is also highly predictive of academic success (Muñoz-Sandoval et al. 1998).

The ability to perform well on multiple-choice tests, to extract meaning from written text, and to argue a point both orally and in writing are essential skills for high levels of academic attainment. While oral proficiency can be developed within a couple of years, the level of language skills necessary to be competitive with native-born peers in the classroom takes, on average, five to seven years to acquire under optimal conditions (Cummins 1991). English-language fluency is a significant predictor of positive academic adjustment in studies of first- and second-generation immigrant students (Portes and Rumbaut 2001) as well as newcomer students (C. Suárez-Orozco, M. Suárez-Orozco, and Todorova 2008).

Academic engagement. "The degree to which students are 'connected' to what is going on in their classes" (Steinberg, Brown, and Dornbusch 1996: 131) has been shown to contribute to academic performance (Fredricks, Blumenfeld, and Paris 2004; National Research Council 2004; Steinberg, Brown, and Dornbusch 1996). "Academic engagement" has been used in a variety of ways in the literature and encompasses cognitive, behavioral, and emotional dimensions (Fredricks, Blumenfeld, and Paris 2004; Marks 2000). The behavioral dimensions of engagement—including students' participation and efforts around academic tasks of attending school, paying attention and behaving in class, completing homework, and turning in assignments on time—are particularly linked to performance. Immigrant youth tend to arrive with high levels of optimism and drive (C. Suárez-Orozco and M.M. Suárez-Orozco 1995; Kao and Tienda 1995). As they encounter the frustrations of navigating a new land and acquiring a second language, while often attending less-than-optimal urban schools, academic engagement may be difficult to sustain, however.

Psychological distress. In nonimmigrant adolescent populations, self-reported psychological distress has been linked to lower levels of academic performance (Blechman, McEnroe, and Carella 1986; Ripple and Luthar 2000). Data examining the well-being of immigrant-origin youth populations across generations and ages reveal mixed results according to country of origin, developmental group, cohort, and age of arrival, as well as developmental outcome (Rumbaut 2004; Takeuchi et al. 2007). There is a fairly consistent "immigrant paradox" regarding engagement in risk behaviors; greater length of residency is linked to higher levels of engagement in substance abuse in particular (Vega et al. 1998). The results are less consistent regarding psychological health, however (Alegría et al. 2007; Rumbaut 2004; Takeuchi et al. 2007); not surprisingly, the greatest risk for affective disorder is found among youths of refugee origin who have undergone trauma (Lustig et al. 2004). This can also be the case for unauthorized youth who experience traumatic crossings and may be in constant erosive fear of apprehension (Capps et al. 2007). Lengthy separations followed by complicated reunifications can also result in initial family turmoil and reported depressive symptoms (Suárez-Orozco, Todorova, and Louie 2002). Last, the initial losses and disorientation upon arrival to a new land may lead many newcomers to at least initial symptoms of anxiety and depression (Grinberg and Grinberg 1990).

Gender. Scholars have noted a gender gap in the academic performance of immigrants and minorities, with girls outperforming boys (García-Coll, Szalacha, and Palacios 2005; Suárez-Orozco and Qin-Hilliard 2004). A number of factors have been identified as contributing to this phenomenon. Boys of color face lower expectations, as well as more stigmatization and blatant discrimination, than girls and are thus at greater risk for academic disengagement (Crul and Doomernik 2003; López 2003). In addition, immigrant girls often have more responsibilities at home than their brothers, who tend to be allowed more freedom to engage in the local street culture (Valenzuela 1999; Waters 1999). At school boys tend to have fewer meaningful relationships with their teachers and perceive their school environments to be less supportive than do their female classmates (Suárez-Orozco and Qin-Hilliard 2004; Way and Chu 2004).

School transitions. High rates of school mobility place students at significant disadvantage for school performance (Mehana and Reynolds 2004; Seidman et al. 1996). Immigrant families are a particularly mobile population as they have yet to fully establish stable ties to work and communities; thus their children are likely to be less stable in their school attendance across the years of their education, placing them at great academic risk (Rumberger and Larsen 1998).

OVERVIEW OF THE STUDY

Immigration to the United States presents both opportunities and challenges that interact with a range of individual and contextual factors to produce different pathways of academic achievement. Our understanding of such factors, however, has been constrained in part by the limitations of previous studies. Most scholars have employed cross-sectional approaches comparing two or more generations of cohorts (Portes and Rumbaut 2001; Steinberg et al. 1996; C. Suárez-Orozco and M.M. Suárez-Orozco 1995), rather than addressing trajectories of change over time within the same cohort (Fuligni 2001). Moreover, studies that include second- and third-generation immigrants have been less able to capture the initial adjustment patterns and unique experiences of recently arrived immigrant students (Fuligni and Pederson 2002; García-Coll, Szalacha, and Palacios 2005; Portes and Rumbaut 2001). This study seeks to address these limitations through a longitudinal study of recent immigrant youth.

Ecological (Bronfenbrenner and Morris 1998) and segmented-assimilation (Portes and Zhou 1993) theories informed the conceptual framing of this study. Latent-growth modeling was used to describe trajectories of performance over time. Multinomial logistic regression was used to delineate associations between indicators of family capital, school characteristics, and individual characteristics to academic trajectories. We deepened our understanding of academic trajectories of performance by using a complementary mixed-methods strategy (Bergmann 2008), implementing multiple case studies to uncover unanticipated causal links, which quantitative data do not reveal, and to shed light on the developmental and interactional processes at play (Yin 2003). This mixed-methods approach allowed us to triangulate our findings and deepened our understanding of the ecological challenges newcomer adolescent youth encounter as they enter American schools.

The data reported here were derived from the Longitudinal Immigration Student Adaptation (LISA) study (C. Suárez-Orozco, M. Suárez-Orozco, and Todorova 2008), a five-year longitudinal study that used interdisciplinary and comparative approaches, mixed methods, and triangulated data to document patterns of adaptation among 407 recently arrived immigrant youth from Central America, China, the Dominican Republic, Haiti, and Mexico.[1] Students were recruited from seven school districts in Boston and San Francisco areas with high densities of newcomer immigrant students.[2] Students were interviewed annually, and parents were interviewed at the beginning and then again five years later at the end of the study. In the third year of the study we selected seventy-five students evenly distributed by country of origin (fifteen participants in each) who represented a range of academic engagement profiles for case-study research. These students were selected based on an examination of school records and ethnographic observations by the research assistants, with an eye to capturing a range of patterns of school engagement and performance across country-of-origin groups analyses of the case studies. Representative cases are presented here to illustrate the findings.[3]

FINDINGS OF THE STUDY

The aims of this study were to identify the varying academic trajectories of recently arrived immigrant students and then describe family, school, and individual contextual factors associated with membership to the different trajectories. Latent class-growth modeling revealed five distinct trajectories of performance for the newcomer students (see C. Suárez-Orozco, M. Suárez-Orozco, and Todorova 2008 for details). We examined the contributing role of several family capital factors, school characteristics, and individual characteristics using multinomial logistic regression analyses (see Suárez-Orozco et al. 2010 for details).

These analyses established factors that distinguished trajectories, including: having two adults in the household, school segregation and school poverty, student's perceptions of school violence, academic English proficiency, reported psychological symptoms, gender, and being over-age for grade. A multiple case study approach (Yin 2003) triangulated and validated many of these quantitative findings. This approach "capture[d] the complexity of the experiences" (Foster and Kalil 2007: 831) across school and home contexts, allowing us to make cross-case conclusions, and revealed patterns that did not emerge simply from the descriptive data nor from the multinomial regressions.

Mixed-method Insights into Trajectories of Performance

Approximately a quarter of the participants did remarkably well academically. These *high achievers* started out as high performers and maintained high achievement through the course of the five years of the study. *High achievers* demonstrated predictable advantages in family capital and family structure associated with academic achievement (Bourdieu and Passeron 1977; Madaus and Clarke 1998; Sirin and Rogers-Sirin 2005). Relative to the other groups, *high achievers* attended schools that were the least segregated and had the fewest students qualifying for free lunch. They had the strongest English-language skills and were the most engaged in their studies. In the representative case of Li, we see the convergence of good fortune and hard work:

> Li, the son of a university professor, attends a highly competitive exam school. His parents take an active role in his day-to-day academic work, securing him a wide range of tutoring and extra-curricular supports. His Chinese immigrant parents "always push me. Although I don't like it at the moment, it's good for my future." Li is engaged in many activities at school and outside school, and he spends about three hours every day on homework. He is one of the few students in our sample for whom proficiency in English is equivalent to that of his native language and for whom English is not a barrier to academic pursuits. As a result of Li's persistence and determination, by the end of the study, he was accepted to one of the most prestigious universities in the country.
>
> Li has had at his disposal optimal resources for academic success: highly educated and successful parents who know the university system well, and ample economic resources that have given him access unavailable to families that are less well-off. These resources, coupled with Li's intelligence and drive for success, place him at a considerable advantage over other immigrant youths. A pragmatic, driven attitude, a willingness to work hard toward a clear goal, and knowledge of how to maneuver the system has helped Li achieve his extraordinary success. In describing the "steps of going to college," Li has an exhaustive list: "hard classes, good grades, good SAT, sports team, music, publication, volunteer, awards, funny essay, recommendations, and internship. I have done all of these."

The academic performance of nearly two-thirds of the sample declined over the course of the study. Approximately a quarter of the participants were *slow decliners,* demonstrating a waning in performance of approximately a half of a grade over five years. The analyses of our multiple case studies data set allowed us to code for unanticipated patterns, which revealed that in many cases a premature transition into a demanding academic setting led to a downward trend in grades. Often we would see a newcomer student put in a Herculean effort in a fairly sheltered setting, one that was not particularly demanding academically, and achieve high grades in that setting. After two or three years students would then be transferred into a more demanding academic setting. However, they did not necessarily have the requisite academic English skills in place and received little in the way of social or academic supports while making that transition. This academic context would lead to a drop in grades as well as a highly stressful academic voyage. Some young people swam against these strong currents, eventually getting to the other side, but others had trouble sustaining the energies it took to do so (C. Suárez-Orozco, M. Suárez-Orozco, and Todorova 2008).

In the illustrative case study of Lotus, we see how her grades are compromised by social isolation, along with her transfer to an exam school before her academic English skills were strong enough for her to keep up with native-born peers.

> Twelve-year-old Lotus immigrated from China with her younger brother to come and live with a seventy-year-old critical and demanding grandmother and father, who works long hours, leaving her mother and younger sister behind in China. Lotus's family holds traditional gender role expectations. She explains: "They don't have any expectations for me. . . . If I were a boy, my family would care more about me [and] pay for my college tuition. . . . But since I am a girl, they expect me to work for my tuition fee." Nonetheless, Lotus throws herself into her class work and though she is painfully shy and rarely says anything in class, she manages to get straight A's. Because she is so successful, she transitions into an exam high school, where most of her peers are middle- and upper-middle-class native English speakers. In this program her grade point average slips by half a grade point. Her inability to maintain her goal of straight A's, despite intense hard work on her part, leads to painful self-doubt and self-deprecation taking an emotional toll. Lotus reports that she often feels anxious, shy, sad, has stomach aches, has trouble concentrating, and feels that she is not as good as others.
>
> Lotus faces huge disadvantages in terms of her poverty, immigration history, and home circumstances. She is further disadvantaged by her limited social skills and support as well as her limited English fluency. These factors contribute to her feeling constant pressure and to her difficulties adapting to her new homeland. Despite a myriad of obstacles, she does remarkably well in school. Although her grades slip over time, this seems largely attributable to the combination of her English-language skills with the stricter grading standards in the new school.

More alarming was the grade and a half drop that *precipitous decliners* (who comprised 27.8 percent of the sample) experienced. The multinomial logistic regressions indicate that these students struggled with multiple school and background impediments. They attended low-quality schools and had poor English-language proficiency. In addition, *precipitous decliners* were the most likely of all the groups to report psychological symptoms both at the beginning and end of the study— clearly these issues took their toll. The case studies revealed that many of these students had difficult premigratory histories (hardship abroad and long separations from parents) and arrived to complicated circumstances (difficult reunifications, less-than-optimal neighborhoods and schools) in their new land. Students who were initially engaged in their school work had difficulty maintaining this engagement for long in far-from-optimal and often hostile school environments (C. Suárez-Orozco, M. Suárez-Orozco, and Todorova 2008). Few had adult support or academic models, though they sometimes had active social lives with peers. Although the majority of *precipitous decliners* arrived with great hopes and dreams, they could not sustain them in the face of cumulative adversity.

As we see in the illustrative case study of Marieli, a complicated reunification, psychological challenges, unsupportive school environments, an unsupportive context of reception, and the uncertainties of undocumented status lead to a precipitous drop in school engagement.

Traumatic loss and separations are recurring themes for Marieli. When she was four, her father was assassinated in front of his wife and children. Her mother reluctantly left Guatemala for the United States to support the family. Seven years passed before the mother could marshal the resources to send for her children. During that time the grandmother, who raised the children in the mother's absence, died, and the mother hired another caretaker to substitute for her. Marieli arrived in the United States at age eleven without documentation to join a mother she barely knew along with a new stepfather and stepsister; the reunification has been complicated and fraught with ambivalence.

Ironically, considering the brutality Marieli witnessed in Guatemala, she finds that one of the worst things about her new land is the violence: "In Guatemala, there was less danger, more freedom." Marieli's neighborhood is a hub of gang activity. She laments being *"enserrada"* (locked in): "You can't go anywhere or leave your house because something might happen to you," she complains. Her negative perceptions of America increase over time as she has witnessed and experienced discrimination aimed at people who lack residency papers and cannot speak English. She also reports high levels of ethnic tension and violence at school: "A lot of things can happen to you in school," she says. "A group of kids can still beat you down. There are only five security [guards] and they can't cover the whole school. Last week, there was a fight and a female teacher stepped in to separate them and they hit her. Cut her face. Lots of blood."

Though Marieli starts high school with straight A's and dreams of a soccer scholarship to college, because of the difficulties at home, the preoccupations with violence, and the dawning realization that her documentation status stands in the way of college opportunities, she begins to experience plummeting grades. As it dawns on her that her undocumented status will hold her back, Marieli gives up on her dreams of college. The more familiar she becomes with the school system and U.S. society, the more she sees that her lack of documentation is a significant barrier, the more she pulls back in righteous anger; working hard in school no longer seems worth the effort.

Another 14.4 percent of our participants—the *low performers*—started out with low performance and declined further over time. Low-achieving students tended to arrive in their new land with a series of significant challenges. The quantitative data showed that these students had families with the least resources. Their English skills were weak, and they admitted to the least academic engagement, which distinguished them from all of the other trajectories. Their low engagement was not surprising given that school segregation and poverty, indicators of poor-quality schools, also separated them from all of the other performance trajectories. The multiple case-study analyses added further insights into the role of interrupted schooling, lengthy family separations, undocumented status, and barren social worlds in the poor academic performance of these youths. The *low achievers* simply never found their academic bearings and found the lure of work both economically more viable and a salve to their egos. In the illustrative case study of León, we see how a multitude of negative circumstances leads to compromised academic opportunities.

León's mother ventured to the United States as a single mother with her son and daughter to provide better opportunities for her children. Because of her long hours, limited education, and scant knowledge of English, she cannot help her children with their schooling. Their mother would like to be more involved at their school but feels uncomfortable expressing her opinions to the teachers "because I don't know the right words to use." She wants her children to do well and worries constantly about their well-being, constantly telling them to "stay out of gangs and to do well in school." Her worries are well founded as her son attends a school in a city classified within the twenty-five most violent in the nation.

León admits that he was never much of a student while in Mexico, saying that he thinks he is not "all that smart." When he first arrived, he applied himself but quickly became discouraged by the frustrations of learning English. He entered a failing middle school and soon transitioned into a chaotic high school. He quickly established a pattern of behavior in school reported by a math teacher: "He is absent almost every day. However, when he is in class, he pays attention and completes assignments."

As time goes by, León finds the lure of paid work increasingly attractive, locating a job at an upscale restaurant, where a change into a uniform, good manners, and warm style work well with customers. The contrast between his confidence at his job and his inadequacy in the classroom is striking. His mother appreciates that he is contributing to the family income, and he likes making discretionary purchases. Although he continues to retain vague ambitions about attending college—"if I can"—he checks off his obstacles: his inability to write well in English, his poor school record and study habits, the likelihood that he may not graduate, his lack of knowledge about getting into college, and his inability to pay for college. In addition, he is worried about his undocumented status; at college, he says cringing, "they ask for a lot of papers."

The remaining 11 percent of the students—the *improvers*—started out quite low, but over the course of time they overcame their initial "transplant shock" and reached nearly the same levels of achievement as the *high achievers*. With these participants the quantitative data revealed that they tended to be more engaged and attend less problematic schools than their counterparts, who precipitously declined or who achieved poorly. The multiple case studies, however, provided evidence that there were other distinguishing patterns among these newcomers. Many had sustained some sort of premigratory trauma. They had undergone long family separations and problematic initial family reunifications. To their advantage, they tended to settle into schools that provided a healthy fit with their developmental needs (Eccles et al. 1993). Over time, many found mentors and community supports that guided them in their journeys in their new land and that arguably contributed to their academic engagement (C. Suárez-Orozco, M. Suárez-Orozco, and Todorova 2008). In Ramon's representative case study, we see how knowing the right people played a transformational role.

> Fearing for his life, Ramon's father, a union organizer during turbulent years in El Salvador, had crossed the border. His family joined him three years later with temporary asylum status when Ramon was nine. Ramon had undergone several traumatic events besides the fears for the life of his father; someone had attempted to assassinate his older brother, and he and his mother had had a serious car accident. These repeated traumas and the disorientation of migration take their toll on Ramon, leaving him anxious and cautious. Ramon's mother frames her motivation for migration as seeking both safety and educational opportunities for her children. "My goal is to get ahead, principally for my children so they do something good for mankind." Still, she regrets the decline in their quality of life.
>
> Ramon's mother enrolled him in a dual-immersion language program, where all subjects are taught 50 percent in English and 50 percent in Spanish. Ramon had received a limited education before arriving in the United States, having attended a small village school, and he is ill prepared for the high-quality and demanding curriculum at this school. In our classroom observations, it seems that Ramon is barely on his teachers' radar screens. As his academic foundation is shaky, Ramon finds it hard to keep up with the privileged middle-class children who are his peers. His parents have little education and read and write haltingly in their native Spanish and not at all in English, and therefore cannot help him with a snowballing homework load.
>
> With little outside support, the quality of Ramon's work pales next to

that of his peers. His grades reflect his teachers' perceptions that he is doing poor work. By the end of his third year in the United States and his second year in the dual-immersion program, Ramon's teachers recommend that he be held back for a year to "catch up." This recommendation devastates Ramon and his mother. She seeks the counsel of the asylum interpreter, community leaders, and the college professor mother of the boy for whom she babysits. They find someone in the community to provide daily after-school homework help—the kind of support routinely available to middle-class students from parents or paid tutors. Both interventions prove transformational. Ramon makes excellent progress in summer school, and his teacher tells the principal that he is prepared for the next school year. A bilingual graduate student in education volunteers an hour every day after school to help with math tutoring and oversees the completion of nightly homework. By the end of fifth grade, Ramon has pulled up his grades to steady B's with a sprinkling of A's, and he maintains this average into the following year, when our study comes to an end.

Overall, students with the most school, familial, and individual resources tended to perform better academically over time. The *high achievers* often demonstrated a constellation of advantages: they started out as high performers and maintained high achievement throughout the five years of the study. On the other hand, the *low performers* started out with low performance and declined further over time, unable to engage in school given the myriad of risk factors. The *precipitous decliners* started out doing better in school than their low-achieving peers, but after struggling with multiple school and background impediments, they appeared unable to sustain the effort over the course of time. *Improvers,* on the other hand, faced initial challenges but had enough environmental supports that over time allowed them to overcome their initial "transplant shock."

How Are These Findings Consistent and Inconsistent with Nonimmigrant Populations?

In some ways these patterns of findings are consistent with findings among nonimmigrant students.

- Families with limited resources often enter our poorest school systems, which have the very least to offer the students most in need of support. Thus the poor performance of low performers and precipitous decliners can in part be attributed to the particularly poor quality of the schools they attended, which did little to foster engagement in their students and possibly motivated transfers to other schools, augmenting their academic risk (Eccles et al. 1993; Orfield and Lee 2006).

- The pattern of slow decliners is typical of this age group as they make transitions through middle and high schools; the academic demands of high school are greater than those of middle school, the distractions of puberty increase, and the social supports from adults tend to lessen (Alspaugh 1998). Our findings also show how premature transitions into new academic settings without sufficient supports place newcomers at risk of declining performance despite great efforts on their part.

- Consistent with previous findings in other populations, girls demonstrated better educational outcomes than boys both initially and over time (Conchas and Noguera 2004; García-Coll, Szalacha, and Palacios 2005; Portes and Rumbaut 2001; Smith 2002; Suárez-Orozco and Qin-Hilliard 2004). Girls were more likely to report interpersonal relationships in school that bolstered their engagement and persistence in the face of academic frustration (López 2003; Suárez-Orozco and Qin-Hilliard 2004; Qin-Hilliard 2003).

- School engagement was related to higher academic performance (Fredricks, Blumenfeld, and Paris 2004; Greenwood, Horton, and Utley 2002), as has been found in other school populations. The effort required to do well in school—regular attendance, completing homework assignments, being able to express and understand the language—were related to high academic performance over time.

- As with other populations, students who reported greater psychological distress were at greater risk for academic decline (Blechman, McEnroe, and Carella 1986; Ripple and Luthar 2000).

Other risk factors were more unique to the immigrant experience.

Family separations. The issue of parental separations as a result of migration is an issue very specific to the immigrant youth experience. For a variety of reasons—the high cost of migration, the difficulty establishing stable work and living conditions in the new land, and inefficient (at best) or draconian (at worst) immigration policies—a majority of immigrant children experienced separations from their parents of a prolonged nature, lasting anywhere from six months to nearly their entire childhood as part of the migratory process. Our analysis of parental separations revealed complicated relationships between various dimensions of the separation experience and resulting academic trajectories. The presence of a maternal separation in the child's immigration history is negatively associated with academic trajectory: students who have experienced separation from their mothers were more likely to be *precipitous decliners* or *slow decliners* than *higher performers*. This was also the case for separations from the father. Furthermore, the longer the separation from the father, the greater the negative effect on academic trajectories.

School changes. In addition to their immigrant transition, we found that early adolescent newcomers must cope with what has been established to be extremely disruptive to academic performance: school changes. Participants changed schools two or three times in the course of the five years; thus multiple school transitions proved to be a norm and placed them at risk for academic decline (Mehana and Reynolds 2004).

Second language acquisition. It has been well established that four to seven years of *optimal academic instruction* are generally required for students to develop academic second language skills comparative to native English speakers (Cummins 1991; Hakuta, Butler, and Witt 2000). Unfortunately, instead, many newcomers enter highly segregated, high poverty, linguistically isolated schools (Orfield and Lee 2006) that provide far-from-optimal conditions. Thus struggles in language are well presented in the LISA data: only 7 percent of the sample had developed academic English skills comparable to those of their native-born English-speaking peers after an average of seven years in the United States (Carhill, Suárez-Orozco, and Páez 2008; C. Suárez-Orozco, M. Suárez-Orozco, and Todorova 2008).

The case studies revealed that in many cases newcomer immigrant children have almost no meaningful contact with English-speaking peers. Indeed, more than a third of the immigrant students in the LISA study reported that they had little opportunity to interact with peers who were not from their country of origin, which no doubt contributed to their linguistically isolated state (C. Suárez-Orozco, M. Suárez-Orozco, and Todorova 2008). When English learners are not able to participate and compete in mainstream classrooms, they often read more slowly than native speakers, do not understand double entendres, and simply are not exposed to the same words and cultural information of native-born middle-class peers. Their academic language skills may also prevent them from being easily engaged in academic contexts and from performing well on "objective" assessments that are designed for native English speakers. It is not surprising that children with limited English proficiency were likely to evidence lower trajectories of performance.

Unauthorized status. Because this was a longitudinal study and it was important to us not to compromise our participants' trust, we never directly asked about citizenship status as part of our data collection. Thus this was not a variable available to us for our quantitative analyses. Over the course of the study, however, many of our participants confided to us their worries about their precarious unauthorized status. Particularly for the *low* and *precipitous achievers,* the case studies revealed that the students' sense of being unable to participate in this society and their hopelessness about their ability to continue on to college and work at anything but the lowest echelons of the service and underground economies contributed to their academic disengagement in palpable ways.

Chinese exceptionalism. Students with the most familial, school, and individual resources tended to perform better academically over time than the students who had less advantage. As a group, the Chinese students in our sample had more overall constellations of resources than all the other country-of-origin groups. This in part explains the notable finding that approximately half of all *high achievers* in this study were Chinese immigrant students. Consistent with findings of others, it is important to note, however, that some of the Chinese youths with constricted family resources attending poor-quality schools demonstrated comparable patterns of low achievement and decline as their counterparts from other country-of-origin groups facing similar stratifying forces (Lee 1996; Lew 2006; Louie 2004). Nonetheless, the Chinese participants demonstrated a consistent academic advantage.

Ruben Rumbaut and Wayne Cornelius (1995) have noted the differing "sending context" of certain groups, which gives them a premigratory advantage and predispose them to do better when they arrive in the United States. The effects of these premigration advantages have been noted in previous reviews of research (Li 2004; Louie 2004; Tseng, Chao, and Padmawidjaja 2007) and are seen in our sample of Chinese students as well (see table 1). The Chinese families in

TABLE I. DESCRIPTIVE STATISTICS BY COUNTRY OF ORIGIN

	Total Sample (N=309)	Central America [n=57]	China [n=72]	Dominican Republic [n=60]	Haiti [n=50]	Mexico [n=70]
Family Characteristics						
Separation from mother	53.40%	80.36%	25.00%	73.33%	61.22%	38.57%
Separation from father~*	45.95%	58.93%	36.11%	35.00%	57.14%	47.14%
Length of separation from mother (years)	1.10	1.92	0.45	1.54	1.39	0.54
	(1.20)	(1.15)	(.86)	(1.20)	(1.30)	(0.80)
Length of separation from father (years)~*	1.10	1.55	0.69	0.99	1.52	0.96
	(1.31)	(1.39)	(1.10)	(1.32)	(1.40)	(1.19)
High school graduate mother	32.87%	18.87%	49.25%	48.28%	9.52%	28.99%
Working parent	65.05%	66.04%	83.58%	42.37%	65.00%	65.71%
School Characteristics						
Percentage low-income students in school*	49.22	43.00	36.97	64.22	47.28	55.887
	(23.54)	(22.21)	(26.70)	(8.49)	(20.43)	(23.33)
School segregation rate***	78.77	84.48	58.97	91.14	75.11	87.11
	(23.22)	(16.96)	(29.38)	(10.95)	(18.24)	(17.78)
Average perceived school violence**	22.03	22.24	19.30	22.30	22.73	23.85
	(4.72)	(4.43)	(4.02)	(5.03)	(3.92)	(4.81)

Individual Characteristics

Average academic engagement***	21.00	20.72	21.78	21.23	21.29	20.04
	(3.42)	(2.92)	(4.05)	(3.52)	(3.56)	(2.73)
Average academic English proficiency***	70.67	63.84	79.93	68.43	73.89	67.35
	(19.12)	(15.24)	(27.99)	(14.56)	(10.76)	(15.57)
Psychological symptoms*	19.11	19.48	15.51	19.48	22.26	19.81
	(7.86)	(8.43)	(6.98)	(8.43)	(7.79)	(7.13)
Three or more school transitions	37.1%	39.3%	36.1%	23.3%	24.5%	57.1%
Gender (percentage female)**	56.68%	62.50%	61.11%	61.67%	53.06%	45.71%
Cumulative GPA year 1	3.53	3.54	3.72	3.65	3.31	3.42
(Range 1–5)	(0.89)	(0.89)	(0.92)	(0.80)	(0.96)	(0.84)
Cumulative GPA year 5	2.99	2.93	3.62	2.74	2.63	2.88
(Range 1–5)	(1.12)	(.92)	(1.13)	(1.14)	(.94)	(1.13)

~* $p < 0.10$.

* $p < 0.05$.

** $p < 0.01$.

*** $p < 0.001$.

NOTE: For continuous data, we report least square means and establish significance with ANOVA. For categorical variables, we report percentage and establish significance with chi squares. Length of separation variables are coded as follows: 0 = no separation, 1 = less than two years, 2 = two to four years, 3 = five years or longer.

our sample tended to arrive with more resources than students from the other groups, and their parents had higher levels of education upon entry and better jobs once they settled in the United States. This is the nature of the Boston-area Chinese newcomer population; had we collected our Chinese data in New York or San Francisco, where there are more diverse Chinese-origin immigrants (including some that are quite disadvantaged), we might have had less pronounced group country-of-origin differences. The Chinese newcomers in our sample were less likely to endure lengthy and complicated family separations during the migration process (Suárez-Orozco, Todorova, and Louie 2002), were less likely to be undocumented, and less likely to attend the most troubled schools.

The Chinese newcomers in our sample were also more likely to find their way to integrated schools, where they came in contact with American children from mainstream households who could act as strong linguistic models. Chinese immigrants, who are expected by many of their teachers to embody the cultural myth of the "model minority" (Lee 1996), generally encountered more positive teacher expectations (Weinstein 2002) than did their Mexican, Dominican, Haitian, and Central American counterparts (C. Suárez-Orozco, M. Suárez-Orozco, and Todorova 2008).

In addition, the qualitative data revealed that the Chinese immigrant families understood the culture of testing, as this is the main route to enter highly coveted schools in China. Chinese parents arrived in the United States with an understanding that all schools are not equal and that the high-school-to-college maze is essentially a game that needs to be skillfully and strategically played. This active pursuit of the direct benefits of education is instilled in Chinese children from a very young age (Li 2004). More acculturated Chinese-origin immigrants and second-generation Chinese who have high levels of educational capital become brokers, imparting the skills and cultural understanding needed to succeed in school to new arrivals.

Unexpectedly, our data showed that the Chinese participants were on average two years over-age for their grades, which may have provided them a cognitive developmental advantage over their peers. Last, Chinese students in this sample, especially girls, reported spending more time on academic tasks and homework and greater levels of turning their work in on time (Qin, Way, and Pandey 2008; C. Suárez-Orozco, M. Suárez-Orozco, and Todorova 2008). Given these cumulative advantages, it is not surprising that Chinese-origin youth in this sample did better academically than all the other groups who did not possess this same constellation of capital. As suggested by others, this underscores the importance of looking across groups, as we did in this study, to distinguish whether advantages displayed by the particular groups are in fact cultural or are attributable to other contextual factors (Sue and Okazaki 1990).

Policy Implications

This data illuminated the cumulative challenges newcomer immigrant youth encounter as well as the ways in which their educational environments currently often fail to meet their socioemotional and educational needs. Understanding various family, school, and individual variables that contribute to varying patterns of academic trajectories for newcomer youth is an essential first step. Working to develop and implement policies to bridge the gap between newcomers' developmental challenges and their educational environments is the crucial next step to helping our nation's newest students achieve their potential.

As a country, we have no coherent strategy to ease the transition of newcomer immigrant youth to schools (especially secondary schools), college, or the labor market (C. Suárez-Orozco and M. Suárez-Orozco 2009). This "nonpolicy" approach to policy has failed too many of our newest Americans and robs the U.S. economy and society of the future contributions of a growing share of citizens. Countries that better align their immigration objectives with the objectives of labor markets, language and education, citizenship, and social cohesion are managing the integration of their immigrants in ways that are more rational, productive, and humanitarian. The United States should take on a national conversation to both normalize the overheated immigration debate and to build the consensus required to align our immigration objectives to our economic objectives, our need for social cohesion, and our cultural values as a country of immigrants.

Regularizing the status of the eleven million individuals (Passel and Cohn 2010) who are de facto if not de jure members of our society must be another priority. Most of these unauthorized immigrants—especially those with children—are not going back to their countries of birth. Policies currently in place have created a permanent underclass of marginalized, largely low-educated and low-skilled individuals, surviving in the shadows of society and facing overwhelming economic and social burdens. The status quo undermines the rule of law, basic

American values, and the promise of American mobility. It is especially troubling that millions of children and youth, American in spirit but alas not in law, are unable to pursue formal education to the limit of their talents and ambition. The bipartisan Development, Relief, and Education for Alien Minors (DREAM) Act would be one step forward in improving the educational prospects of undocumented students. The act would make undocumented students eligible for in-state tuition benefits, state and federal financial aid, and eventually create a path to legal permanent residence. These benefits would generally be available to undocumented youths who were brought to the United States as minors, have continuously lived in the United States since childhood, attended and graduated from a U.S. high school, and have no criminal record along with demonstrated good moral character. In addition to college access, students would benefit from the increased likelihood of financial productivity and improved job prospects that come with a college degree (Gonzalez 2009).

Many recent immigrant students face the unique challenge of learning English while immersed in the general academic curriculum, all while acclimating to a school culture. English proficiency proved to contribute greatly to students' achievement over time. While levels of English proficiency at arrival vary greatly within and across immigrant groups, for most newcomer immigrants the task of learning academic English at a competent level takes considerable time (Collier 1995; Cummins 1991; Hakuta, Butler, and Witt 2000).

Current high-stakes testing accountability systems add a further level of complexity to the academic experience of English-language learners (ELLs), creating unintended consequences that appear to outweigh what few benefits standardized tests may have (Menken 2008). The strong emphasis on high-stakes tests of No Child Left Behind is making the educational context of ELLs extremely challenging. To meet the required "adequate yearly progress," ELLs' curriculum and daily instruction are increasingly focused on English-language skills rather than academic content knowledge. As a result, many ELLs are tested well before their skills are adequately developed. For a valid and just assessment for these students, we urge educational policymakers to reconsider the accountability system that has an overreliance on standardized tests. Certainly, assessments are necessary to measure students' progress, but linguistically and culturally valid strategies, as well as portfolio assessments, should be implemented for ELLs.

The results of this study underscore the negative effects of poor school contexts. Rather than presenting impediments, schools should strive to serve as "sites of possibility" (Weis and Fine 2004), facilitating the transition of recent immigrants. A variety of academic interventions could serve to close the academic gap, including thorough assessments of previous academic and literacy histories, providing academic and homework supports, designing programs that provide explicit information about college access and pathway knowledge, and engaging parents in the learning community (C. Suárez-Orozco, M. Suárez-Orozco, and Todorova 2008).

High levels of racial segregation within the schools has been linked to a variety of forms of inequitable distribution of resources (Orfield and Lee 2006). Education for today's global era requires higher-order skills than ever before to ensure cognitive, behavioral, and ethical engagement with the world (Suárez-Orozco and Qin-Hilliard 2004). For youth to develop the ethics, skills, and competencies needed to identify, analyze, and solve problems from multiple perspectives, schools must nurture students who are curious and cognitively flexible, who can tolerate ambiguity, and who can synthesize knowledge within and across disciplines (M. Suárez-Orozco and Qin 2004). In addition, these schools must provide a number of supplemental resources to educationally at-risk immigrant-origin students to ease their educational transition and ameliorate their outcomes in the new land's educational system.

At a minimum, schools need to be safe spaces where students can feel safe and concentrate on the task of learning. The climate in the schools that many recent immigrant students attend is challenging even to the most dedicated and focused of students. A number of policy and practice interventions that focus on proactive, rather than reactive, solutions have shown promising results. Such programs include school-wide violence prevention programs (Hahn et al. 2007), conflict resolution programs (Bucher and Manning 2003), and psychoeducational curricula designed to increase pro-social behaviors (Kilian, Fish, and Maniago 2006).

. . .

The effects of immigration are not confined to a mere change of geography. Political upheaval, ethnic or religious persecution, and traumas before migration add additional burdens for some youths beyond the usual dislocations and adjustment of immigration. Separations from parents for lengthy periods of time occur in a majority of migratory journeys. Past research has shown that separations from parents during immigration is associated with increased depressive symptomatology and that family reunifications are also often complicated and may take significant adjustment time for the family members (Suárez-Orozco, Todorova, and Louie 2002). The repercussions of these upheavals were evidenced by the higher levels of reported psychological symptoms among *precipitous decliners*. In recognition of the unique constellation of risks that burden some immigrant youths and their families, mental health and community support services should be made available to at-risk students.

Social relationships and daily interactions with schoolmates, teachers, and counselors along with the flow of informational capital (Pereira, Chapman, and Stein 2006; Pianta 1999; Ryan, Stiller, and Lynch 1994) play a significant role in shaping academic outcomes for youth with limited opportunities (Stanton-Salazar and Dornbusch 1995). For newcomers, positive relationships with family, community, and school members create a sense of well-being in school. Formal and informal relationships with supportive adults and mentors can help newcomers by providing crucial information about the educational system as well as explicit academic tutoring, homework assistance, and college pathway scaffolding. Programs developed with the needs of this target population in mind can play an important role in easing their transition to their new land (Roffman, Suárez-Orozco, and Rhodes 2003; C. Suárez-Orozco, M. Suárez-Orozco, and Todorova 2008).

NOTES

1. By the end of the five-year study there were 309 participants in the study. The multinomial regressions were conducted on the 287 participants for whom we had complete data.

2. We do not claim that this sample is representative of the entire immigrant population in the United States, as it was not randomly generated all across the country. As participants were recruited from public schools, it would not be inclusive of middle- and upper-status families who send their children to private or parochial schools. We are confident, however, that this sample is representative of immigrant youth from these five sending regions attending public schools in the Boston and San Francisco areas.

3. For more details on the specific case studies presented in this chapter, as well as several other case studies for each trajectory of performance, see C. Suárez-Orozco, M. Suárez-Orozco, and Todorova 2008.

REFERENCES

Alegría, M., N. Mulvaney-Day, M. Torres, A. Polo, Z. Cao, and G. Canino. 2007. "Prevalence of Psychiatric Disorders across Latino Subgroups in the United States." *American Journal of Public Health* 97, no. 1: 68–75.

Alspaugh, John W. 1998. "Achievement Loss Associated with the Transition to Middle School and High School." *Journal of Educational Research* 92, no. 1: 20–25.

Arnold, Elaine. 1991. "Issues of Reunification of Migrant West Indian Children in the United Kingdom." In *Caribbean Families: Diversity among Ethnic Groups*. Edited by J. L. Roopnarine and J. Brown. Pp. 243–58. Greenwich, Conn.: Ablex.

Bean, Frank, and Gillian Stevens. 2003. *America's Newcomers and the Dynamics of Diversity*. New York: Russell Sage Foundation.

Bergmann, Maxwell. 2008. *Advances in Mixed Methods Research: Theories and Applications*. London: Sage Publications.

Blechman, E. A., M. J. McEnroe, and E. T. Carella. 1986. "Childhood Competence and Depression." *Journal of Abnormal Psychology* 43: 292–99.

Bloom, David E. 2004. "Globalization and Education: An Economic Perspective." In *Globalization: Culture and Education in the New Millennium*. Edited by Marcelo Suárez-Orozco and Desirée Qin-Hilliard. Pp. 56–77. Berkeley: University of California Press.

Bourdieu, Pierre, and James Passeron. 1977. *Reproduction in Education, Society and Culture*. Beverly Hills, Calif.: Sage.

Bronfenbrenner, Urie, and Pamela Morris. 1998. "The Ecology of Developmental Processes." In *Handbook of Child Psychology*. Edited by W. Damon and R. M. Lerner. Pp. 993–1028. New York: Wiley.

Bucher Katherine T., and M. Lee Manning. 2003. "Challenges and Suggestions for Safe Schools." *Clearing House* 76, no. 3: 160–64.

Capps, Randy, Rosa Maria Castañeda, Ajay Chaudry, and Robert Santos. 2007. *The Impact of Immigration Raids on America's Children*. Washington, D.C.: Urban Institute.

Carhill, Avary, Carola Suárez-Orozco, and Mariela Páez. 2008. "Explaining English Language Proficiency among Adolescent Immigrant Students." *American Educational Research Journal* no. 4: 1155–79.

Collier, Virginia P. 1992. "A Synthesis of Studies Examining Long-term Language-minority Student Data on Academic Achievement." *Bilingual Research Journal* 16, nos. 1 and 1: 187–212.

Conchas, Gilberto, and Pedro Noguera. 2004. "Adolescent Boys: Exploring Diverse Cultures of Boyhood." In *Adolescent Boys in Context*. Edited by N. Way and J. Chu. New York: New York University Press.

Conoley, Jane C., and Arnold P. Goldstein, eds. 1997. *School Violence Intervention: A Practical Handbook*. New York: Guilford Press.

Crul, Maurice, and Jan Doomernik. 2003. "The Turkish and Moroccan Second Generation in the Netherlands: Divergent Trends between and Polarization within the Two Groups." *International Migration Review* 37, no. 4: 1039–64.

Cummins, Jim. 1991. "Language Development and Academic Learning." In *Language, Culture, and Cognition*. Edited by L.M. Malavé and G. Duquette. Pp. 161–75. Clevedon, U.K.: Multilingual Matters.

Deaux, Kay. 2006. *To Be an Immigrant*. New York: Russell Sage Foundation.

Eccles, Jacquelynne S., C. Midgley, C.M. Buchanan, A. Wigfield, D. Reuman, and D. MacIver. 1993. "Development during Adolescence: The Impact of Stage/Environment Fit." *American Psychologist* 48, no. 2: 90–101.

Eccles, Jacquelynne S., and Robert Roeser. 2003. "Schools as Developmental Contexts." In *Blackwell Handbook of Adolescence*. Edited by G.R. Adams and M.D. Berzonsky. Pp. 129–48. Malden, Mass.: Blackwell Publishing.

Foster, E. Michael, and Ariel Kalil. 2007. "Developmental Psychology and Public Policy: Progress and Prospects." *Developmental Psychology* 41, no. 6: 827–32.

Fredricks, Jennifer A., Phyllis C. Blumenfeld, and Alyson H. Paris. 2004. "School Engagement: Potential of the Concept, State of the Evidence." *Review of Educational Research* 74, no. 1: 54–109.

Fuligni, Andrew. 2001. "Family Obligations and the Achievement Motivation of Adolescents from Latin American, Asian, and European Backgrounds." In *Family Obligations and Assistance During Adolescence: Contextual Variations (New Directions in Child and Adolescent Development)*. Edited by Andrew J. Fuligni. Pp. 61–76. San Francisco, Calif.: Jossey Bass.

Fuligni, Andrew, and S. Pederson. 2002. "Family Obligation and the Transition to Young Adulthood." *Developmental Psychology* 38, no. 5: 856–68.

Gándara, Patricia, and Frances Contreras. 2009. *The Latino Educational Crisis: The Consequences of Failed Policies*. Cambridge: Harvard University Press.

García-Coll, Cynthia, and Katherine Magnuson. 1997. "The Psychological Experience of Immigration: A Developmental Perspective." In *Immigration and the Family*. Edited by A. Booth, A.C. Crouter, and N. Landale. Pp. 91–132. Mahwah, N.J.: Lawrence Erlbaum.

García-Coll, Cynthia, Laura Szalacha, and Natalia Palacios. 2005. "Children of Dominican, Portuguese, and Cambodian Immigrant Families: Academic Pathways during Middle Childhood." In *Developmental Pathways through Middle Childhood: Rethinking Contexts and Diversity As Resources*. Edited by Catherine Cooper, Cynthia García-Coll, W. Todd Bartko, Helen Davis, and Cekina Chatman. Pp. 207–33. Mahwah, N.J.: Erlbaum Associates.

Gibson-Davis, C.M. 2008. "Family Structure Effects on Maternal and Paternal Parenting in Low-income Families." *Journal of Marriage and Family* 70: 452–65.

Gonzalez, Roberto. 2009. *Untapped Talent and Unrealized Dreams: The Rich Potential of Undocumented Students*. New York: The College Board.

Greenwood, C.R., B.T. Horton, and C.A. Utley. 2002. "Academic Engagement: Current Perspectives in Research and Practice." *School Psychology Review* 31, no. 3: 1–31.

Grinberg, Leon, and Rebecca Grinberg. 1990. *Psychoanalytic Perspectives on Migration and Exile*. New Haven, Conn.: Yale University Press.

Hahn, R., D. Fuqua-Whitley, H. Wethington, J. Lowry, A. Crosby, M. Fullilove, and others. 2007. "Effectiveness of Universal School-based Programs to Prevent Violent and Aggressive Behavior." *American Journal of Preventive Medicine* 33, no. 2S: 114–29.

Hakuta, Kenji, Yuko Goto Butler, and Daria Witt. 2000. "How Long Does It Take English Learners to Attain Proficiency?" *University of California Linguistic Minority Research Institute Policy Report 2000–1.*

Hammersley, M. 1996. "The Relationship between Qualitative and Quantitative Research: Paradigm Loyalty versus Methodological Eclecticism." In *Handbook of Research Methods for Psychology and the Social Sciences.* Edited by J.T.E. Richardson. Leicester, U.K.: BPS Books.

Hauser, R.M, and J.R. Warren. 1997. "Socioeconomic Indexes for Occupations: A Review, Update, and Critique." In *Sociological Methodology.* Edited by A.E. Raftery. Pp. 177–298. Cambridge: Basil Blackwell.

Hernández, Donald, and E. Charney, eds. 1998. *From Generation to Generation: The Health and Well-being of Children of Immigrant Families.* Washington, D.C.: National Academy Press.

Hernández, Donald, Nancy A. Denton, and S.E. Macartney. 2007. "Children in Immigrant Families—The U.S. and 50 States: National Origins, Language, and Early Education." *Research Brief Series Publication No. 2007–11.* Albany: Child Trends Center for Social and Demographic Analysis at State University of New York.

Hondagneu-Sotelo, P. 1994. *Gendered Transitions: Mexican Experiences of Immigration.* Berkeley: University of California.

Hood, Lucy. 2003. *Immigrant Students, Urban High Schools: The Challenge Continues.* New York: Carnegie Corporation of New York.

Kao, Grace, and Marta Tienda. 1995. "Optimism and Achievement: The Educational Performance of Immigrant Youth." *Social Science Quarterly* 76, no. 1: 1–19.

Kilian, J.M., M.C. Fish, and E.B. Maniago. 2006. "Making Schools Safe: A System-Wide School Intervention to Increase Student Prosocial Behaviors and Enhance School Climate." *Journal of Applied School Psychology* 23, no. 1: 1–30.

Lee, Stacey. 1996. *Unraveling the "Model Minority" Stereotype: Listening to Asian American Youth.* New York: Teachers College Press.

Lew, Jamie. 2006. *Asian Americans in Class: Charting the Achievement Gap among Korean American Youths.* New York: Teachers College Press.

Li, J. 2004. "'I Learn and I Grow Big': Chinese Preschoolers' Purposes for Learning." *International Journal of Behavioral Development* 28, no. 2: 116–28.

López, Nancy. 2003. *Hopeful Girls, Troubled Boys: Race and Gender Disparity in Urban Education.* New York: Routledge.

Louie, Vivian S. 2004. *Compelled to Excel: Immigration, Education, and Opportunity among Chinese Americans.* Palo Alto, Calif.: Stanford University Press.

Lustig, Stuart L., Maryam Kia-Keating, Wanda G. Knight, Paul Geltman, Heidi Ellis, J. David. Kinzie, and others. 2004. "Review of Child and Adolescent Refugee Mental Health." *Journal of American Academy of Child and Adolescent Psychiatry* 43, no. 1: 24–36.

Madaus, G., and M. Clarke. 1998. "The Adverse Impact of High Stakes Testing on Minority Students: Evidence from 100 Years of Test Data." Paper presented at the High Stakes K–12 Testing Conference. New York.

Marks, H.M. 2000. "Student Engagement in Instructional Activity: Patterns in the Elementary, Middle, and High School Years." *American Educational Research Journal* 37, no. 1: 153–84.

Mehana, M., and A.J. Reynolds. 2004. "School Mobility and Achievement: A Meta-analysis." *Children and Youth Services Review* 26, no. 1: 93–119.

Menken, Kate. 2008. *English Language Learners Left Behind: Standardized Testing as Language Policy*. Clevedon, U.K.: Multilingual Matters

Muñoz-Sandoval, A.F., J. Cummins, C.G. Alvarado, and M.L. Ruef. 1998. *Bilingual Verbal Ability Tests: Comprehensive Manual*. Itasca, Ill.: Riverside Publishing.

National Research Council. 2004. *Engaging Schools: Fostering High School Students' Motivation to Learn*. Washington, D.C.: National Academy Press.

Noguera, Pedro. 2003. *City Schools and the American Dream: Reclaiming the Promise of Public Education*. New York: Teacher's College Press.

O'Connor, Erin, and Katherine McCartney. 2007. "Examining Teacher–Child Relationships and Achievement As Part of an Ecological Model of Development." *American Educational Research Journal* 44, no. 2: 340–69.

Olsen, Laurie. 1997. *Made in America: Immigrant Students in Public Schools*. New York: The New Press.

Orfield, Gary. 2002. Commentary. In *Latinos: Remaking America*. Edited by M. M. Suárez-Orozco and M. M. Paez. Pp. 389–97. Berkeley: University of California Press.

Orfield, Gary, and Chungmei Lee. 2006. *Racial Transformation and the Changing Nature of Segregation*. Cambridge: Civil Rights Project at Harvard University.

Passel, Jeffrey S., and D'Vera Cohn. 2010. *Unauthorized Immigrant Population: National and State Trends*. Washington, D.C.: Pew Hispanic Center. Available online at http://pewhispanic.org/reports/report.php?ReportID=133.

Perreira, Krista M., M.V. Chapman, and G.L. Stein. 2006. "Becoming an American Parent: Overcoming Challenges and Finding Strength in a New Immigrant Latino Community." *Journal of Family Issues* 27, no. 10: 1383–414.

Perreira, Krista M., Kathleen M. Harris, and Dohoon Lee. 2006. "Making It in America: High School Completion by Immigrant and Native Youth." *Demography* 43, no. 3: 1–26.

Pianta, Robert C. 1999. *Enhancing Relationships between Children and Teachers*. Washington, D.C.: American Psychological Association.

Portes, Alejandro, and Ruben G. Rumbaut. 2001. *Legacies: The Story of the Second Generation*. Berkeley: University of California Press.

Portes, Alejandro, and Min Zhou. 1993. "The New Second Generation: Segmented Assimilation and Its Variants." *Annals of the American Academy of Political and Social Science* 530, no. 1: 74–96.

Qin, Desirée, Niobe Way, and P. Pandy. 2008. "The Other Side of the Model Minority Story: The Familial and Peer Challenges Faced by Chinese American Adolescents." *Youth and Society* 39: 480–506.

Qin-Hilliard, Desirée. 2003. "Gendered Expectations and Gendered Experiences: Immigrant Student Adaptations in Schools." *New Directions for Youth Development: Theory, Practice, and Research* (Winter): 91–110.

Rhodes, Jean E. 2002. *Stand by Me: The Risks and Rewards of Youth Mentoring Relationships.* Cambridge: Harvard University Press.

Ripple, C.H., and S. Luthar. 2000. "Academic-risk among Inner City Adolescents: The Role of Personal Attributes." *Journal of School Psychology* 38, no. 3: 277–98.

Roeser, Robert W., and Jacquelynne S. Eccles. 1998. "Adolescents' Perceptions of Middle School: Relation to Longitudinal Changes in Academic and Psychological Adjustment." *Journal of Research on Adolescence* 8, no. 1: 123–58.

Roffman, Jeanne, Carola Suárez-Orozco, and Jean Rhodes. 2003. "Facilitating Positive Development in Immigrant Youth: The Role of Mentors and Community Organizations." In *Positive Youth Development: Creating a Positive Tomorrow.* Edited by D. Perkins, L.M. Borden, J.G. Keith, and F.A. Villaruel. Brockton, Mass.: Klewer Press.

Ruíz-de-Velasco, Jorge, Michael Fix, and Beatriz C. Clewell. 2001. *Overlooked and Underserved: Immigrant Students in U.S. Secondary Schools.* Washington, D.C.: Urban Institute.

Rumbaut, Ruben. 2004. "Ages, Stages, and Generational Cohorts: Decomposing the Immigrant First and Second Generations in the United States." *International Migration Review* 38: 1160–206.

Rumbaut, Ruben, and Wayne Cornelius. 1995. *California's Immigrant Children: Theory, Research, and Implications for Policy.* La Jolla, Calif.: Center for U.S.-Mexican Studies.

Rumberger, Russell W., and Kay A. Larsen. 1998. "Student Mobility and the Increased Risk of High School Dropout." *American Journal of Education* 107, no. 1: 1–35.

Ryan, R.M., J. Stiller, and J.H. Lynch. 1994. "Representations of Relationships to Teachers, Parents, and Friends As Predictors of Academic Motivation and Self-esteem." *Journal of Early Adolescence* 14, no. 2: 226–49.

Sciarra, D.T. 1999. "Intrafamilial Separations in the Immigrant Family: Implications for Cross-cultural Counseling." *Journal of Multicultural Counseling and Development* 27, no. 18: 30–41.

Seidman, Edward, John L. Aber, LaRue Allen, and S. French. 1996. "The Impact of the Transition to High School on the Self-System and Perceived Social Context of Poor Urban Youth." *American Journal of Community Psychology* 24, no. 4: 489–516.

Sirin, Selcuk R., and Lauren Rogers-Sirin. 2005. "Components of School Engagement among African American Adolescents." *Applied Developmental Science* 9, no. 10: 5–13.

Smith, Robert C. 2002. "Gender, Ethnicity, and Race in School and Work Outcomes of Second-Generation Mexican Americans." In Suárez-Orozco and Páez, *Latinos: Remaking America.* Berkeley: University of California Press.

Stanton-Salazar, Ricardo D., and Sanford Dornbusch. 1995. "Social Capital and the Reproduction of Inequality: Information Networks Among

Mexican-Origin High School Students." *Sociology of Education* 68, no. 2: 116–35.

Steinberg, Lawrence. 1996. *Beyond the Classroom*. New York: Simon and Schuster.

Suárez-Orozco, Carola. 2004. "Formulating Identity in a Globalized World." In *Globalization: Culture and Education in the New Millennium*. Edited by M. Suárez-Orozco and Desirée Qin-Hilliard. Pp. 173–202. Berkeley: University of California Press and the Ross Institute.

Suárez-Orozco, Carola, Francisco X. Gaytán, Hee Jin Bang, E. O'Connor, J. Pakes, and Jean Rhodes. 2010. "Academic Trajectories of Newcomer Immigrant Youth." *Developmental Psychology* 42, no. 3: 602–18.

Suárez-Orozco, Carola, Allyson Pimentel, and Margary Martin. 2009. "The Significance of Relationships: Academic Engagement and Achievement among Newcomer Immigrant Youth." *Teachers College Record* 111, no. 3: 5–6. Available online at http://www.tcrecord.org.

Suárez-Orozco, Carola, and Desirée Qin-Hillard. 2004. "The Cultural Psychology of Academic Engagement: Immigrant Boys' Experiences in U.S. Schools." In *Adolescent Boys: Exploring Diverse Cultures of Boyhood*. Edited by N. Way and J. Chu. New York: New York University Press.

Suárez-Orozco, Carola, and Marcelo Suárez-Orozco. 2009. "Educating Latino Immigrant Students in the Twenty-first Century: Principles for the Obama Administration." *Harvard Educational Review* 79: 327–40.

———. 2001. *Children of Immigration*. Cambridge: Harvard University Press.

———. 1995. *Transformations: Immigration, Family Life, and Achievement Motivation among Latino Adolescents*. Stanford, Calif.: Stanford University Press.

Suárez-Orozco, Carola, Marcelo Suárez-Orozco, and Irina Todorova. 2008. *Learning a New Land: Immigrant Students in American Society*. Cambridge: Harvard University Press.

Suárez-Orozco, Carola, Irina Todorova, and Josephine Louie. 2002. "Making up for Lost Time: The Experience of Separation and Reunification among Immigrant Families." *Family Process* 41, no. 4: 625–43.

Suárez-Orozco, Carola, I. Todorova, and Desirée Qin. 2006. "The Well-being of Immigrant Adolescents: A Longitudinal Perspective on Risk and Protective Factors." In *The Crisis in Youth Mental Health: Critical Issues and Effective Program*. Volume 2. Edited by H. E. Fitzgerald and Z. R. and K. Freeark. Pp. 53–84. Thousand Oaks, Calif.: Sage Press.

Suárez-Orozco, Marcelo, and Desirée Qin. 2004. *Globalization: Culture and Education in the New Millennium*. Berkeley: University of California Press.

Sue, Stanley, and Sumie Okazaki. 1990. "Asian American Educational Achievements." *American Psychologist* 45, no. 8: 913–20.

Takeuchi, David T., Seunghye Hong, Krista Gile, and Margarita Alegria. 2007. "Developmental Contexts and Mental Disorders among Asian Americans." *Research in Human Development* 4, nos. 1–2: 49–69.

Thomson, E., T. L. Hanson, and S. McLanahan. 1994. "Family Structure and Child Well-being: Economic Resources vs. Parental Behaviors." *Social Forces* 73: 221–42.

Tseng, Vivian, Ruth K. Chao, and I. Padmawidjaja. 2007. "Asian Americans Educational Experiences." In *Handbook of Asian American Psychology. Racial and Ethnic Minority Psychology (REMP) Series.* 2nd edition. Edited by F. Leong, A. Inman, A. Ebreo, L. Yang, L. Kinoshita, and M. Fu. Pp. 102–23. Thousand Oaks, Calif.: Sage Publications.

Valenzuela, Abel. 1999. "Gender Roles and Settlement Activities among Children and Their Immigrant Families." *American Behavioral Scientist* 42, no. 4: 720–42.

Vega, W. A., E. Alderete, B. Kolody, and S. Aguilar-Gaxiola. 1998. "Illicit Drug Use among Mexicans and Mexican Americans in California: The Effects of Gender and Acculturation." *Addiction* 93, no. 12: 1839–50.

Waters, Mary. 1999. *Black Identities: West Indian Dreams and American Realities.* Cambridge: Harvard University Press.

Way, Niobe, and Judy Chu. 2004. *Adolescent Boys in Context.* New York: New York University Press.

Weinstein, Rhona S. 2002. *Reaching Higher: The Power of Expectations in Schooling.* Cambridge: Harvard University Press.

Weis, Lois, and Michelle Fine. 2004. *Working Method and Social Justice.* New York: Routledge.

Yin, Robert K. 2003. *Case Study Research: Design and Methods.* 3rd edition. Thousand Oaks, Calif.: Sage.

9

Who Will Report the Next Chapter of America's Immigration Story?

TYCHE HENDRICKS

At a San Francisco union hall, Ahmed Yahya Mushreh and his fellow janitors huddled around a table, planning a gathering to honor the memory of a young Yemeni immigrant who had died almost thirty years before, fighting for the cause of California farmworkers. The martyred activist, Nagi Daifullah, was a leader in the United Farm Workers (UFW) grape strike and became a legend among Yemeni immigrants, particularly the janitors of SEIU Local 87, many of whom had ties to the vineyards of the San Joaquin Valley. Mushreh, age sixty-five, picked grapes as a young man, still carried his UFW card, and remembered Daifullah. "He was very courageous," he said. "Telling us, 'This is democracy. . . . You fight for your rights. This is the United States.'" Janitors, like farmworkers, are often isolated, said Monadel Herzallah, an SEIU organizer, but the union has helped them feel more connected: "Being part of a union has helped the Yemenis . . . feel part of American society, part of the people that contribute to the economy with taxes and hard work."[1]

. . .

Thirty-two ingredients. That's what goes into Marco Guzmán's *mole* recipe, taught to him by his Mexican-born mother and passed down from her mother before that. Pumpkin seeds, onion, tomatillo, cinnamon, cumin, raisins, chocolate, and five kinds of dried chile peppers. The ingredients were assembled in bowls and pans all over Guzmán's

cramped San Francisco apartment kitchen. With the blender whir-
ring, the thirty-year-old corporate information-technology consultant
was preparing to compete in the "Mole to Die For" contest, timed to
coincide with Día de los Muertos. He didn't butcher his own chicken
or grind the ingredients on a stone *metate* as his grandmother had
taught his mother to do. But for Guzmán, who sported an earring and
a hipster sensibility, the event was not only a test of his culinary prow-
ess, it was a chance to reconnect with his Mexican roots: "My mother
(would) call us to come and watch while she cooked. She'd say, '*Pon
atención*, because one day this *mole* will make you famous.'"[2]

. . .

Two days after Cyclone Nargis slammed into Burma's south coast in
2008, Mabel Tun, a nurse at the Veterans Affairs Hospital in Palo Alto,
was working the phones nonstop. When she wasn't trying to reach her
family in Rangoon, she was dialing her Burmese friends in the San
Francisco Bay Area. "We're all worried because we've heard that a
lot of people are dying, but we cannot get through," said Tun, who
sought political asylum in the United States in 1994. "I don't know
what to do." Though she felt helpless, thousands of miles from her parents, Tun busied herself activating a network of fellow Burmese exiles
across the country. Together they shared news, organized prayer services, collected funds for cyclone relief, and mobilized political pressure on their country's repressive regime. For long-standing dissidents
like Tun and for recent refugees still struggling to adjust to America,
the cyclone heightened both their continuing bond to their homeland
and their painful distance from it.[3]

. . .

Stories like these, which I reported for the *San Francisco Chronicle,*
offer a window into the varied ways that immigrants and the children
of immigrants remain connected to their roots while at the same time
engaging fully in the life of the United States. Ideally such stories—
be they substantial portraits or quick sketches—help form bridges
that link readers across differences of culture and custom. They can
also allow people from wide-ranging backgrounds to see themselves
reflected in the newspaper. The United States is experiencing a period
of high immigration, and California has been grappling more intensely
with the resulting demographic changes than just about any other state.
Political leaders and citizens must wrestle with questions of how soci-

ety integrates newcomers and in turn how it is shaped by them. These are issues and concerns that the rest of the country is also facing: not just how immigrants fare but how well their children do.

Journalists can provide their audiences with an understanding of the history, causes, and context for immigration. They can raise questions about the social impacts of immigration and the consequences of the country's success or failure to integrate immigrants. Journalists can also tell the human stories that allow audiences to understand others in the community as individuals—conveying the texture of their daily lives and their particular struggles and triumphs. Keith Woods, the dean of faculty at the Poynter Institute who has long taught journalists about reporting on race and ethnicity, once told me that his watchwords for compelling and insightful coverage of diversity were: voice, context, and complexity. I scratched those three words on a Post-it, which I still have taped to my computer monitor.

As a reporter at the San Francisco Chronicle, I looked at multiple facets of immigration—from questions of politics and policy, to border crossing and legal status, to the economic and civic role of immigrants. I was the paper's lead demographics reporter. Over the course of eight years I focused especially on the Latino community, though, as the Chronicle's reporting staff dwindled, I was also called on to cover a broader range of stories related to various immigrant communities and to the dynamics of race and diversity. I wrote explanatory and investigative pieces, breaking news, in-depth analysis, and long features based on shoe-leather enterprise reporting.

Immigrant integration looks different in different places. In the Lower Rio Grande Valley of Texas, for example, there's the constant presence of Mexico, unusually strong ties to home and family, and a population that's almost 90 percent Hispanic. As part of a newspaper series on the border that became the basis for my book The Wind Doesn't Need a Passport: Stories from the U.S.-Mexico Borderlands, I focused on a seventeen-year-old girl, Maribel Saenz, who wanted to go away to college but was struggling with her Mexican-born parents' expectations that she stay nearby. "We want to hold our kids close forever. It's okay if they're married and come back to live with us," observed Juanita Garza, a Rio Grande Valley native and a professor of history at the University of Texas–Pan American, just down the road from the Saenz's town of Elsa. But, added Garza, "for the most part, the break does come; it's very American."[4]

Maribel eventually did win her parents' grudging blessing to enroll at Texas A&M University, eight hours away in College Station. At first it seemed that her border roots might hold her back, but in fact, when she got to college and found herself a minority for the first time, her strong Tejana identity proved to be a source of strength. "Since I grew up with Mexicanos in the majority, nobody can put me down," she said. "In the Valley, the mayors are Mexican, the judges are Mexican. We have the opportunity of meeting Hispanics who are doctors, who have their PhDs."[5]

In the San Francisco Bay Area, where I do most of my work, the immigrant integration stories are a little different. Here, immigration is driven as much by Asian countries as it is by Mexico and Latin America. So like Boston or New York or other big immigrant gateway cities, the region has tremendous diversity in where immigrants come from. That sets the Bay Area apart from the border but also from Southern California, which is much more Latino. The diversity brings a cultural richness and often an economic vitality, but it does pose real challenges, sometimes fiscally and also in terms of how society integrates newcomers and maintains a sense of cohesion. One of our tasks as journalists is to examine the complexity of that situation from all different perspectives.

As the U.S. Senate debated an immigration reform bill in 2007, I wrote about Asian residents of the Bay Area who were speaking out against provisions in the bill that would reduce family-sponsored permanent residence visas, or "green cards," and instead institute a point system favoring job skills. Even highly skilled workers objected to certain restrictions in the measure that could affect their bids for permanent residence—at the same time, they were resisting other elements of the bill that would have offered amnesty to undocumented immigrants, most of whom are from Mexico and Central America. "If anybody gets special treatment, it should be us, because we've been playing by the rules and contributing to this economy," opined Mahesh Pasupuleti, an Indian-born software engineer waiting for a green card. An elderly Filipino widower who had petitioned thirteen years earlier for green cards for his children, still in the Philippines, lamented that the bill would invalidate immigration applications for adult children or siblings of citizens. "It's very hard to live alone," said Francisco Villacrusis, the widower. "I have prayed for this for a long, long time." The story illustrated the often conflicting interests of different groups of immigrants and the inherent challenges of forging immigration policies that suit the varied needs of the broader society.[6]

Stories based on the U.S. Census and other demographic data sources can illuminate trends in the way the state is changing. The challenge with data-driven stories, as I tell my students at the Graduate School of Journalism at the University of California–Berkeley, is to bring them to life with real people and to present the numbers in context. One story, based on census data from the 2007 American Community Survey, revealed a trend that has been under way for a generation: more than one in four of California's residents is foreign-born. This is twice the national average. I chose to look at the issue in terms of language. The state has by far the highest proportion of people who speak a language other than English at home: almost 43 percent of Californians do. That too is more than twice the national average. But more than half of those people speak English very well. I illustrated the trends with examples— a recent Filipino immigrant who uses English at work but prefers speaking Tagalog at home with his elderly father, and a Korean American university professor whose English is impeccable but who insists on speaking Korean with her children so that they will grow up bilingual.

Because the foreignness that immigrants represent triggers volatile feelings for many Californians, I also set up a dialogue in the story between scholars with very different perspectives on immigration. Victor Davis Hanson, a fellow at the Hoover Institution, worried about a Balkanization of the United States. "This country doesn't have a predominant race or religion; it just has values," he said. "That's a very thin bond. We have shared values and a shared Constitution; we also have to have a shared culture and language." The Korean American professor mentioned earlier, Jin Sook Lee, who teaches education at the University of California–Santa Barbara, countered that immigrants want to learn English and need more opportunities to do so. She suggested that California's linguistic diversity is actually an untapped strength: "With globalization in economics and politics, we need language competence. These speakers have a great potential to fill out this language gap in our society."[7]

Another data-driven story looked at the challenges of getting to college for Latino youth. Education is critically important in integrating immigrant children and the children of immigrants, and of course how well these kids do in school has repercussions for the larger society. I focused on Veronica Santana, the daughter of Mexican immigrants, who was a senior at an average high school heading on to an average state university. The simple fact that she was graduating from high school college-ready after four years made her exceptional among the state's Latinos—only 14 percent do, though almost half of California's public school students are Latino. So this article looked at the kinds of family and school support that helped Veronica get into college—and the places where the school and her family resources fell short. In the process of telling Veronica's story, the piece illustrated the challenges facing other Latino students and the stakes for California if these kids don't succeed, as well as some perspectives on how society can invest in educating this next generation.[8]

In California the decision makers and the voters are overwhelmingly whiter and older than the population of the state as a whole, and the people making policy often do not take into account the needs and the interests of the younger, more Asian and Latino population, who are really going to be the California of tomorrow. Unlike a generation or two ago, when Californians were more willing to invest in infrastructure and education, nowadays there's a disconnect. Voters are not inclined to tax themselves to pay for the education of somebody else's children who don't look or speak the way they do, even though those kids are going to be the future workers and homeowners and indeed the future decision makers of the state. That's a difficulty that has emerged from California's great diversity, and it's likely to replicate itself in other parts of the country that are becoming more diverse and home to more immigrants, as time goes on. Because even as California is receiving a smaller share of immigrants than in the past, the country as a whole is still experiencing a high level of immigration that seems likely to continue. Those are findings that have been spelled out by a number of important thinkers—including the University of Southern California demographer Dowell Myers, former *Sacramento Bee* editorial page editor Peter Schrag, David Hayes-Bautista, director of UCLA's Center for the Study of Latino Health and Culture, and others—but they bear repeating.[9]

So how do journalists help readers understand who these newcomers are as individuals, and help ensure that everyone in their communities is reflected in their pages? The tale of a Mexican immigrant gardener, Catalino Tapia, who started a college scholarship fund offers one approach. It could have been merely a feature story about an individual do-gooder. But I used it not only to show how this one successful immigrant was giving back, but to play with the notion of what it means to be a philanthropist—to suggest that not just society matrons and corporate executives can contribute, but in fact a humble gardener with a sixth-grade education can send poor kids to college.[10]

One of the biggest stories of recent years is about the emerging electoral power of Latino voters. Working in California, I've followed the Latino electorate for years, but in 2008 we saw a kind of quantum leap in engagement that actually helped to swing the presidential election. In California's presidential primary an extraordinary thing happened: Latinos, who usually vote at lower rates than the general population, turned out at higher rates than other voters. One in three Democratic primary voters was Latino, even though Latinos were only 23 percent of registered Democrats. They're 18 percent of all registered voters in California.[11] So I covered Latino involvement leading up to and following the California and Texas primaries, about first-time voters, including young Latinos, and the surge in voter registrations in 2008. After the presidential election I wrote about what had happened in some of the battleground states that had contributed to Barack Obama's victory, notably the strong participation of Latinos and Asians, as well as, of course, African Americans. "That's something that should be very concerning to the Republican Party: They are losing support from both Asians and Latinos, the fastest growing population groups in the country," said Karthick Ramakrishnan, a professor of political science at the University of California–Riverside.[12]

For context—on politics, immigration, and other issues—scholars are key, and the importance of the interaction between journalists and scholars is of course one premise of this volume. Our job as journalists is not just to give readers disconnected facts, but to give them the tools and the framework to make sense of that information. Academics can help explain how we got to where we are and how it compares to other periods in history. For a story on English-language acquisition among Latin American immigrants and their children, I turned to Jon Gjerde, a historian with a focus in nineteenth-century Scandinavian immigration, for his perspective. Gjerde provided historical context: today's immigrants learn English faster than those who came to the United States 100 or 150 years ago. "We had a proliferation of non-English media among European immigrants in the nineteenth and early twentieth century, so their main media were in their native language," he said, adding that public schools were not always taught in English in that earlier era. "Norwegians in the Dakotas were more likely to have instruction in Norwegian. And in Cincinnati, where Germans were strong, school was taught in German."[13]

The focus in daily journalism tends to be on personalities and current events, public opinion and political developments, buzz and breaking news. The nature of daily news means that attention spans are often short and interest is fickle. Newspaper editors are generalists by nature, and they must be continually filling the news "hole" and capturing the big stories of the day. Reporters, when they have the luxury of working a beat over the course of years, can develop expertise and a wealth of background knowledge on a topic. They also, it is hoped, remain curious and open minded. Ideally their editors value the critical perspective and the voice of authority these reporters can employ when dealing with a topic they know well. But there is a constant tension in a newsroom between getting the story first—an imperative that has gained urgency with a twenty-four-hour news cycle—and telling it best. The time available for thorough reporting and the space to tell a story in-depth are always in short supply in daily news operations— perhaps never more so than right now, with newspapers in crisis.

Newspaper reporters frequently cover research from nonpartisan think tanks, which harness scholarly research to address timely topics. Their studies are packaged in such a way—and released with a sense of time-sensitive urgency—that they lend themselves to newspaper coverage. I have reported on research by the Public Policy Institute of California, the Migration Policy Institute, and the Pew Hispanic Center, and have come to rely on their researchers as knowledgeable sources to call for perspective when I'm covering a related story. It's crucial to the credibility of my stories that those institutes don't have a particular political alignment or agenda. When I'm looking for a comment to represent a particular side of a story, however, I will turn to a partisan think tank, such as the Hoover Institution, the Center for Immigration Studies, the Economic Policy Institute, or the Center for American Progress.

Reporters often approach academics for an interview on a subject but seldom take the time to read their books. We depend on scholars to distill their considerable knowledge for us and apply it succinctly to the news at hand. The time available for reflective thinking by journalists is increasingly scarce as reporting staffs continue to shrink and the demands on reporters to produce copy rapidly—not just articles but blogs, tweets, and multimedia packages—grow. But when reporters do take the time to delve into the scholarly literature on immigration or any other topic, they can add depth and value to their coverage. The interplay between journalism and academic research can take different forms. Sometimes the idea for a story starts with a particular study or piece of academic research and then a reporter can humanize and localize it by finding people whose lives illustrate the findings. I did that, for example, with research by New York University psychology professor Carola Suárez-Orozco that looked at the frequency with which children are separated from their parents during the course of a family's migration to the United States and the psychological toll the separation takes on those kids and their families.[14]

Two families I interviewed exemplified the trend Suárez-Orozco described: a Filipino boy who was left behind when his mother migrated legally to the United States and then followed years later and a Mexican family in which the mother crossed the border without authorization and later paid for her children to be smuggled into the United States to join her. The stories of these family odysseys illustrated vividly the phenomena Suárez-Orozco described.[15] At other times a reporter will write a story off of the news or about developing trends and will call on academics to provide context. A piece I wrote about the symbolic importance of Barack Obama's presidential candidacy for multiracial people followed that model. In addition to talking to a range of mixed-race people themselves, I also spoke to sociologists Jorge Chapa, at the University of Illinois, and Michael Omi, at the University of California–Berkeley, for perspective.[16]

Among the many scholars whose research has informed my work in covering different facets of immigration and immigrant integration, it's worth mentioning a few here. Historian David G. Gutiérrez has explored the points of tension and of common ground between Mexican immigrants and Mexican Americans, while the late historian Ron Takaki has documented the wide-ranging roots of America's Asian immigrants and the reception they received in this country.[17] Sociologists Douglas S. Massey, Jorge Durand, and Nolan J. Malone have developed a perceptive analysis of the forces of global development that underlie labor migrations.[18] Historian Mae M. Ngai has traced the causes, consequences, and dynamics of undocumented Mexican migration to the United States.[19] Sociologist Pierrette Hondagneu-Sotelo has charted the nuances that differentiate the migration experiences of men and women from Mexico and has eloquently documented the intimate power dynamics that confront immigrant domestic workers in California.[20]

The work of demographers Hans Johnson and Dowell Myers has provided a reliable framework for helping my readers understand the demographic changes under way in California. Educational psychologist Patricia Gándara's work has informed my understanding of language acquisition and the education of English learners; it offers a lens through which to examine California's recent political battles on the issue.[21] In terms of contextualizing Latinos and American politics, the work of political scientists John A. García (who has addressed the question of whether Latino voters comprise a unified political bloc) and Louis DeSipio (who has studied the gradual growth and influence of the Latino electorate) has been valuable.[22] The work of sociologist Frank Bean and of Marcelo and Carola Suárez-Orozco has helped to deepen my knowledge of the dynamics of immigrant integration and the challenges facing the children of immigrants.[23] Harvard public policy professor Robert D. Putnam's examination of social engagement in diverse communities has raised provocative questions about civil society in a multicultural country.[24]

In journalism there are occasions when academic understanding can underpin a story but quotations from professors may never appear in the article itself. That was the case with a piece I wrote about California's first Spanish bilingual private school, Escuela Bilingüe in Oakland. The story drew on scholarship about how children acquire language proficiency and the history of political battles over teaching English learners, but all of that formed the background against which I reported and wrote the story. The story itself focused on teachers and parents clustered around the "dual immersion" program and others like it.[25] As a producer and a consumer of journalism, I feel that the best reportage puts the storytelling front and center. Scholarly background informs the writer, but it may be all but invisible to the reader. That kind of narrative writing—where the issue comes fully alive through stories of people and events—is not always possible within the time and space constraints of a daily newspaper, but it can elevate a work beyond the quotidian.

Increasingly in the Internet era stories that get hits on the Web and generate buzz are favored, and those headline-grabbers are not always the thoughtful stories that synthesize information and offer deeper insights. Indeed, there has long been a tension, in the *Chronicle*'s newsroom and others, between breaking news and stories that provide synthesis and analysis of broader trends and concerns but aren't seen as sufficiently newsy. Another long-standing debate in newsrooms has been over whether to assign dedicated reporters to cover demographic issues and minority communities or to "mainstream" that coverage and expect all reporters to seek out diverse sources. In a perfect world all reporters would be tuned into themes of diversity, but in reality such an approach risks an absence of coverage of immigrant communities and a superficial treatment of their concerns. I believe papers have benefited from having dedicated reporters who know the issues and have deep contacts in the communities they cover.

The editorial staffing levels in most newsrooms have been shrinking dramatically over the past couple of years, and dedicated coverage of immigration and immigrants is now seen as a luxury, not a necessity. The *San Francisco Chronicle,* where I worked for almost a dozen years, is in the thick of this structural crisis we're all facing in journalism. The economic pressures buffeting newspapers are taking their toll on the newsroom, as they are at papers across the country. The business model doesn't work anymore, and the cuts are coming out of the editorial side. The *Chronicle*'s editorial staff, which reached almost seven hundred people in 2000, after a merger with the rival *San Francisco Examiner* is now less than two hundred. The metro news staff, which for years included a team of reporters covering immigration, race, and demographics, has been whittled down from ninety to a small core of two dozen reporters covering local government, crime, courts, schools, and a few issue-oriented beats such as health care and the environment.

In 2008, as part of a series of advertisements promoting the work of *Chronicle* staff, the paper ran a half-page ad with my picture and the following text:

> California's shifting fast—how we live, where we're from and where we're going. Making sense of trends in race, culture and ethnicity can help readers better understand their communities. The Bay Area is at the leading edge of these changes as one of the country's most diverse regions. The new demographics affect our sense of national identity, not to mention our politics, policing, art and education. In telling stories—of the Mexican-born gardener funding college scholarships, or the Burmese exiles reaching out to their cyclone-ravaged homeland—my goal is to bridge the differences that sometimes seem to divide us. With fluent Spanish and dispatches from the border and beyond, I take readers through the intricacies of immigration and the current contentious debate. The *Chronicle*'s coverage of Bay Area cultures and demographic changes can help people tackle the challenges of making this globally connected community work for all of us.
>
> —Tyche Hendricks, Immigration and Demographics Reporter

A year later, the immigration and demographics beats at the *Chronicle* had been eliminated, along with coverage of other big-picture topics. Across the country, in recent years, newspapers have been shedding thousands of jobs a year. The reporters and editors who remain are having to make do with a lot less. Travel budgets have been slashed: I couldn't report the border stories today that I did a few years ago. The news hole is smaller, so the stories must be shorter. And the amount of time available to develop a story has dwindled as the few remaining reporters are called on to pick up the pace to fill the paper and the paper's Web site.

Journalists have got to be especially creative to keep giving readers thoughtful, insightful reportage. I tip my cap to the few papers in this country that are still willing to put serious resources into quality journalism. They are facing cuts too. But as a reader and a citizen, as well as a fellow journalist, I depend on papers like the *New York Times* and the *Washington Post* to understand the world and the issues, to get the investigative stories, the explanatory stories, and the news analysis. Many journalists at more impacted papers are also trying to deliver readers that kind of insightful work, but they're doing it with ever fewer resources and a lot of constraints.

In an effort to understand the thinking that went into eliminating the immigration beat in the spring of 2009, I interviewed *Chronicle* managing editor Steve Proctor about the decision. "Every one of these things is an economic consideration," said Proctor. "Certain things are obligations of any paper, like covering education and crime. A judgment has been made that immigration is not as high a priority as other things. . . . None of these are easy decisions. When you get into cutback mode, you're in a constant state of winnowing down what you think are the core missions of the paper. That's the reality of American journalism today."

I'm convinced that journalists have a critical role to play in helping readers understand cultural change and think about policy responses to our current immigration situation. But we're doing it in a difficult environment, as the landscape of American journalism is shifting precipitously. So we need to think about new ways to be effective—with the support of mainstream news organizations when possible, but also in a freelance or "new media" capacity or under the auspices of nonprofit journalism organizations—so we can keep engaging this important topic with the depth and nuance it deserves.

NOTES

1. Tyche Hendricks, "Legacy of Yemeni Immigrant Lives on among Union Janitors," *San Francisco Chronicle*, August 16, 2002, A-22.

2. Tyche Hendricks, "Getting Ready for the 'Mole to Die For' Contest," *San Francisco Chronicle*, November 7, 2007, B-1.

3. Tyche Hendricks, "Bay Area Burmese Raise Cyclone Relief Funds," *San Francisco Chronicle*, May 6, 2008, A-11.

4. Tyche Hendricks, "On the Border: Elsa, Texas," *San Francisco Chronicle*, November 28, 2005, A-1. Tyche Hendricks, *The Wind Doesn't Need a Passport: Stories From the U.S.-Mexico Borderlands* (Berkeley: University of California Press, 2010).

5. Hendricks, *Wind Doesn't Need a Passport*.

6. Tyche Hendricks, "Asians Frustrated, Angry over Immigration Plan," *San Francisco Chronicle*, May 24, 2007, B-1.

7. Tyche Hendricks, "43 Percent in State Speak Other Than English at Home," *San Francisco Chronicle*, September 23, 2008, A-1.

8. Tyche Hendricks, "College Seems out of Reach to Most Latinos," *San Francisco Chronicle*, June 24, 2007, A-1.

9. Dowell Myers, *Immigrants and Boomers: Forging a New Social Contract for the Future of America* (New York: Russell Sage Foundation, 2007). Peter Schrag, *California: America's High-stakes Experiment* (Berkeley: University of California Press, 2006). David Hayes-Bautista, *La Nueva California: Latinos in the Golden State* (Berkeley: University of California Press, 2004), 220–28.

10. Tyche Hendricks, "Immigrant Gardeners Provide Seed Money for College Scholarships," *San Francisco Chronicle*, October 15, 2007, A-1.

11. Tyche Hendricks and Anastasia Ustinova, "Super Tuesday, Latino Watershed," *San Francisco Chronicle*, February 7, 2008, A-12.

12. Tyche Hendricks, "Election Showed Nonwhite Voters' Growing Power," *San Francisco Chronicle*, November 8, 2008, A-1.

13. Tyche Hendricks, "English Takes Hold in Latino Families by Third Generation, Study Says," *San Francisco Chronicle*, November 30, 2007, A-4.

14. Carola Suárez-Orozco, Irina L. G. Todorova, and Josephine Louie, "Making up for Lost Time: The Experience of Separation and Reunification among Immigrant Families," in *The New Immigration: An Interdisciplinary Reader*, edited by Marcelo M. Suárez-Orozco, Carola Suárez-Orozco, and Desirée Qin (New York: Routledge, 2005), 179–96.

15. Tyche Hendricks, "Immigrant Families Frequently Separated: New Study Shows Similar Pattern for Legals and Illegals," *San Francisco Chronicle*, July 6, 2005, B-1.

16. Tyche Hendricks, "Obama Raises Profile of Mixed-Race Americans," *San Francisco Chronicle*, July 21, 2008, A-1.

17. David G. Gutiérrez, *Walls and Mirrors: Mexican Americans, Mexican Immigrants, and the Politics of Ethnicity* (Berkeley: University of California Press, 1995). Ronald Takaki, *Strangers from a Different Shore: A History of Asian Americans* (Boston: Little, Brown, 1989).

18. Douglas S. Massey, Jorge Durand, and Nolan J. Malone, *Beyond Smoke and Mirrors: Mexican Immigration in an Era of Economic Integration* (New York: Russell Sage Foundation, 2002).

19. Mae M. Ngai, *Impossible Subjects: Illegal Aliens and the Making of Modern America* (Princeton, N.J.: Princeton University Press, 2004).

20. Pierrette Hondagneu-Sotelo, *Gendered Transitions: Mexican Experiences of Immigration* (Berkeley: University of California Press, 1994). Pierrette

Hondagneu-Sotelo, *Doméstica: Immigrant Workers Cleaning and Caring in the Shadows of Affluence* (Berkeley: University of California Press, 2001).

21. Patricia Gándara and Frances Contreras, *The Latino Education Crisis: The Consequences of Failed Social Policies* (Cambridge: Harvard University Press, 2009). Patricia Gándara, "Learning English in California: Guideposts for the Nation," in *The New Immigration: An Interdisciplinary Reader*, edited by Marcelo M. Suárez-Orozco, Carola Suárez-Orozco, and Desirée Qin (New York: Routledge, 2005), 219–32.

22. John A. García, *Latino Politics in America: Community, Culture, and Interests* (Lanham, Md.: Rowman and Littlefield, 2003). Louis DeSipio and Rodolfo O. de la Garza, "Forever Seen as New: Latino Participation in American Elections," in *Latinos: Remaking America*, edited by Marcelo M. Suárez-Orozco and Mariela M. Páez (Berkeley: University of California Press, 2002).

23. Frank D. Bean and Gillian Stevens, *America's Newcomers and the Dynamics of Diversity* (New York: Russell Sage Foundation, 2003). Carola Suárez-Orozco and Marcelo M. Suárez-Orozco, *Children of Immigration* (Cambridge: Harvard University Press, 2001).

24. Robert Putnam, "E Pluribus Unum: Diversity and Community in the Twenty-first Century," *Scandinavian Political Studies* 30, no. 2 (2006): 137–74.

25. Tyche Hendricks, "Spanish Bilingual Schools No Longer Just for Remedial Education," *San Francisco Chronicle*, September, 16, 2007, A-1.

10

Complicating the Story of Immigrant Integration

VIVIAN LOUIE

When I have spoken to journalists, I have tried to complicate two popular storylines. One has to do with the model minority image of Asian Americans, framing them as super academic achievers and a powerful example that race and class do not matter in minority achievement. This stereotype persists even in the face of substantial post-1960s class, ethnic, and educational diversity among Asian Americans due partly to immigration. Another has to do with the comparison often drawn between immigrants from Asia and Latin America and the Caribbean, the two largest sources of immigration today. The comparison is of the so-called (Asian) immigrant strivers, who are thought to have "good" cultures and make good use of their opportunities in America; and the (Latino) immigrants, supposedly not striving enough because they have "bad" cultures and are likely to do poorly in school and turn to crime and welfare. This quick cultural explanation, however, does not account for the different kinds of resources immigrants have, the different types of access they have to information, to neighborhoods, and to schools, and the different ways in which immigrants are viewed and treated by American institutions and natives (Louie 2008).

In this chapter I discuss my efforts to convey these more complex narratives to journalists. Then I draw from recent research of my own as well as that of my colleagues, highlighting issues that are worth a closer look. I close with some thoughts on policy. But before I go any further, I need to make a full disclosure of my own: I have a graduate degree in journalism and worked as a newspaper reporter and free-lance writer for a few years. It was long enough for me to be familiar with the basic norms and practices of journalism and certainly, by the time I became a source for journalists, I knew those of the academy. As Carola Suárez-Orozco highlights in her chapter in this book, there are similarities and crucial differences in what we do and how we do it. One of the things we have in common: in both fields the writer is not supposed to know the answer before posing the question. This is because the writer then risks seeing and including only the evidence that supports what the writer always knew would be the story. This certainly does not count as good scholarship or good journalism. It is, however, a good place to begin the rest of this discussion.

CLASS DIVERSITY AMONG ASIAN AMERICANS

Some years ago, I was contacted by a reporter for a national news magazine who was writing about second-generation Asian Americans in the wake of post-1965 immigration. Over the phone and by e-mail we talked about the changing demographics of the Asian American population and the implications for their educational, mobility, and assimilation patterns. I stressed to the reporter, as immigration scholars typically would, that the population was very bifurcated by social class and neighborhood. I was surprised, then, when the article made no mention of this fact. The article was all about the children of Asian professionals growing up in predominately white, middle-class suburbs. Both authors were members of that second generation, as they acknowledged in the article, and perhaps they were interested in writing about people like them. Absent, though, was any mention of the children of Asian immigrants speaking little English and having low levels of financial and human capital, or having skills that do not successfully transfer over to the United States. In a cordial exchange with the reporter after the piece was published, I asked why the lengthy article did not refer to class diversity, a defining characteristic of post-1965 Asian immigration, and what it might mean for the second generation. The reporter replied that the article had a different focus.

This experience was joined by a few others of a similar nature, as it proved more difficult than I had expected to complicate the narrative of Asians being uniformly successful and having superior cultures that fueled this success. I knew it was a compelling story, as Asians joined a tradition of supposed ethnic exemplars—from Jewish immigrants at the turn of the twentieth century to black West Indians today. In fact, the narratives around American Jews and West Indians remained powerful even in the face of scholarly accounts complicating their supposedly rapid and unproblematic ascent on the mobility ladder (Slater 1969; Sowell 1981; Steinberg 1982; Waters 1999). In the research that I did on the children attending New York City's Hunter College (a member of the City University of New York) and Columbia University (a member of the Ivy League), I tapped into some of the "hidden" class variability among Asian Americans. Interviews were conducted with sixty-eight second-generation Chinese students, about evenly split between the two schools, along with fieldwork at the schools during 1998–99. Sixty percent of the respondents were U.S.-born, and the majority had grown up in the New York City area. They tended to be children who had grown up in mostly white, middle-class suburbs and whose parents worked as professionals, and children who had grown up in the Chinese enclaves of New York City, where many of their parents worked in the garment and restaurant industries. About two-thirds of the Hunter respondents had at least one parent working in the ethnic economy, as compared with 20 percent of the Columbia respondents.

I found that regardless of class, Chinese Americans shared what scholars have called "immigrant optimism." This optimism referenced the hopes that immigrant parents, in general, have for their children's schooling outcomes that they share with their children. The basis for this optimism is the perception of a relatively open opportunity structure in the United States, as compared with their homelands (Portes and Rumbaut 2001; Smith 2008). Education—particularly free, accessible, quality public education—was foundational to this optimism.

Yet I also found that economic resources along with the parents' own levels of formal schooling, language, and networking created different paths to college among Chinese Americans. The suburban children enjoyed the opportunities that would attract families of all backgrounds to those locations—namely, good public schools. The families in the urban enclaves tapped into kin and social networks to learn about the better public schools, often not where they lived. There were class distinctions here too. Parents who managed restaurants or owned shops often sent their children to "cram" schools, private institutions owned by fellow Chinese that prepare students for the SAT or for the entrance examinations for the specialized high schools or magnet schools. Parents who were garment workers or waiters knew about such opportunities but lacked the funds to send their children. Beyond their parents' help with locating better public schools for them, the children of the urban enclaves largely had to take sole ownership of their K–12 education, a big burden for them. Nor was the story only about class. Perceptions of a racial and ethnic hierarchy were important too. Immigrant parents of all classes told their children that being of Chinese descent could hurt them in this hierarchy and that higher education was a key way to offset potential discrimination. Contrary to the popular discourse, race and class did matter (Louie 2004).

But this was not a story that a lot of folks in the national media wanted to hear. Still, I continued to be a devoted consumer of media coverage and would be impressed at the times when journalists really got it "right." It was clear they had done a lot of good reporting and analysis, weaving together different strands into a coherent, multifaceted, factual story. In the words of Tyche Hendricks (see the chapter in this volume), the journalists were providing the voice, the context, and the complexity needed to provide nuanced coverage on the integration of immigrants and their children into the United States. I remember reading Nina Bernstein's marvelous 2007 *New York Times* article about the "class divide" in the philanthropy of Chinese Americans. The article spoke to the schism between newcomers to New York City since the 1990s who were part of the working poor of enclave communities like Chinatown and the well-to-do Chinese Americans, whose families had come decades earlier with more and who themselves were now quite affluent. It was the kind of complex class diversity that I had tried to convey to the magazine reporter. And it was similar to an article Hendricks would later write about the college scholarship fund started in California by Catalino Tapia, a Mexican immigrant gardener—a window into how philanthropy itself is being transformed by immigration. Immigrants themselves, including those of modest means, want to give back.

My research with the second-generation Chinese started me on a long road (to borrow from Carola Suárez-Orozco's apt metaphor) of comparative research of how social processes play out between and within different immigrant groups. Sara Rimer, the longtime *New York Times* journalist, contacted me after she learned that I was doing research on second-generation Dominicans, some of whom had grown up in New York City. Rimer wondered if I could provide some cultural context for her forthcoming book on a group of young Dominican high school baseball players in Washington Heights, a Dominican enclave of New York City. She had written an evocative 2005 series for the

Times on the George Washington High School baseball team, made famous by Manny Ramirez, an alumnus (see Rimer 2005a, 2005b, and 2005c). The series focused on the lives of the young Dominican men, from immigrant families with modest economic resources, and their hopes for upward mobility through baseball. The book takes a deeper look at their struggles to make it in New York City and America. I got the sense that Rimer knew the story was more than just about baseball and that she was determined to figure it out, including what it had to do with immigration.

IMMIGRANT STRIVERS VERSUS IMMIGRANT NONSTRIVERS

Still, I was a bit wary when Claudio Sanchez, the veteran National Public Radio reporter, contacted me in 2008 about a story he was doing on the schooling of U.S.-born children of Chinese and Dominican parents in the Boston area (Sanchez 2009). My wariness had nothing to do with Sanchez. I remembered him from his days as a Nieman scholar at Harvard, when he had sat in on a few of my classes on immigration and education, contributing keen insights. I knew from my brief exchanges with him and certainly from his professional reputation that he was a consummate reporter. I was in the midst of analyzing data (and trying to keep up with my colleagues' thoughtful writings based on their data analyses) that tapped into the engagement of groups with larger society and its arrangements along the lines of race, social class, and education.

Such processes are bidirectional, experienced differently, and indeed influence differences between groups (Portes and Rumbaut 1990 and 2001; Gans 2007; Kasinitz et al. 2008; Smith 2008; Suárez-Orozco, Suárez-Orozco, and Todorova 2008). As Carola Suárez-Orozco and her collaborators showed, the stark declining achievement experienced by two-thirds of the immigrant children in their study was due to many factors. These included increasing detachment from parents unable to help the children negotiate "dysfunctional schools and neighborhoods" and from schools, where they found hostile teachers and peers. As she writes in her chapter in this volume, some of the Chinese youth with fewer family resources and enrolled in lower-quality schools were part of this pattern of decline. However, they also found that the Chinese did better, on average, due partially to the higher levels of schooling among their parents, higher rates of documentation status, and their lower rates of family separations with migration.

In my own work I was discovering that this dynamic engagement with larger society was key to unpacking the rather static conceptions of Asians having the "right" ethnic culture to achieve and Latinos not having it. In a paper done with social scientist Jennifer Holdaway (Louie and Holdaway 2009), drawing on data from the Immigrant Second Generation in Metropolitan New York Study (ISGMNY) (Kasinitz et al. 2008), we found that working-class Dominican parents were more likely to favor Catholic schools. This was because their families shared a common belief in the superior quality of Catholic and private schools. The frame of comparison were the poorly resourced public schools in the Dominican Republic and the poor quality of the public schools in their neighborhoods here.

However, when immigrant Dominican parents could not afford Catholic school, they turned to the local zoned schools. Given the inadequate information they had about the New York City public school system, the Dominican parents often did not realize that there were other good public school options outside their neighborhood. Then there were the dynamics within the schools themselves. The default expectation of Latino children in urban public schools was disengagement, not to mention the Balkanization along English as a second language (ESOL) lines described by the journalist Ginger Thompson (see her chapter in this volume). Meanwhile, Asian children sitting quietly in the back of the class because they were lost were still regarded by teachers as getting the material and just naturally quiet (Louie 2006). Yet when I gave talks to educators, providing this kind of evidence counter to prevalent cultural scripts, I still found that members of the audience often thought I was saying exactly the opposite—that family culture valuing school was just not present in the Latino case.

I was wary because I knew the power of the cultural narrative. Indeed, the logic underlying the Elementary and Secondary Education Act of 1965 was the "culture of poverty" explanation, which held that low-income and poor African American children came from homes with a "cultural deficit." Low-achieving black students were framed as having parents who did not value schooling, both for racial and class-based reasons. The changing demographics in the wake of the Immigration Act of 1965 gave rise to more cultural explanations, as the children of new immigrant groups were compared with one another and with those of native-born racial-ethnic minority groups. The historical framing of native, working-class parents, especially minority parents, as not caring about their children's education and having inadequate childrearing practices (Lawrence-Lightfoot 1978) has extended to their immigrant counterparts (Mehan et al. 1996: 173; Lucas 1997; Suárez-Orozco 2001). And the overall explanation privileging culture often with little or no mention of structural reasons stayed very much the same (Louie 2005 and 2008).

I was glad for the chance to speak with Sanchez but was privately concerned about what he might hear in the field. I knew he was likely to speak with administrators, teachers, families, and community leaders. How willing would they be to go on the record? How would he sift among the different accounts? I should have not been concerned—the two-part segment was terrific. To borrow from Bak Fun Wong, the founder of the Josiah Quincy Elementary School in Boston, who was featured in the broadcast, there is creative synergy in schools where the immigrant parents and second-generation children can figure out who they are in the United States. Not everyone, though, was having the same experiences in Boston Public Schools. For Dominicans there was often decided negativity. The complexities were heard in the voices of families, educators, and the children themselves, and the audience was given the tools to piece together the takeaway points on their own. I particularly appreciated the candor of Carol R. Johnson, the superintendent of Boston Public Schools, when she said, "the achievement gap is also an access gap," referencing the access of Latino students to advanced courses.

The research on comparative second-generation achievement has also examined social capital, or access to institutional resources, its relationship to class diversity and social cohesion, and how it can account for differences between groups. Again, the Chinese and Dominican comparison is instructive. Both the Chinese and Dominicans in ISGMNY grew up in ethnically embedded communities—however, the families of the Chinese had social capital linking them to the information of co-ethnics of higher social status, which the families deploy on behalf of the children, mainly with finding better schools. The Dominicans, of course, also have social capital from their parents, but it links them to a "homogeneously poor community" and thus does not provide the same purchase as for the Chinese (Kasinitz et al. 2008: 363).

These are not easy things for anyone to see, and for academics this is where that "unbroken chain of evidence" referenced by Carola Suárez-Orozco (see her chapter in this volume) and drawn from multiple sources—for example, census data on communities, data on the immigrants and the sending nations themselves—becomes very important in helping make them visible. It was not until I became an academic that

I understood the differences between the seemingly "similar" communities of Chinatown and Washington Heights, in New York City—both vibrant places with ethnic businesses, ethnic languages, and ethnic cultures. I realized the two communities, for instance, differed in overall wealth. In the case of Chinatown, the transformations of the post-1960s immigration patterns combined with the rise of East Asian economies to produce transnational markets and transnational flows of capital from there to investments in the ethnic enclaves of America (Zhou 1992; Fong 1996; Lin 1995; Zhou and Cai 2002).

This is not to say that Dominicans who have migrated to the United States are not diverse in social class origins (Torres-Saillant and Hernández 1998). Nor do I mean to suggest that the Chinese enclaves are absent poverty and inequality when both are clearly present (Kwong 1987). It is to say that the middle-class professional stream is not as pronounced among the Dominican migration and that Dominican enclaves here certainly do not have the kind of transnational and ethnic wealth as the Chinese enclaves do (Levitt 2001; Hernández 2002). In the Dominican case, the transfer of wealth tends to be one-directional, with remittances sent back to the Dominican Republic rather than large flows of capital to build businesses here.

The other key piece to this story has to do with the closeness of ties between members of the same ethnic group across social class. The exceptionalism of the Chinese, as discussed by Carola Suárez-Orozco and Mary C. Waters in their chapters in this volume, also has to do with their strong social cohesion in the United States; it was the latter that facilitated the crucial transfer of social capital across class lines. In ISGMNY a counterexample was the South American group, which was also diverse in social class origins; however, the authors found that South American professionals did not maintain social ties with, and in the process did not share social capital with, their less advantaged counterparts (Kasinitz et al. 2008). This is consistent with the research done by the social scientist Luis Guarnizo and his collaborators (Guarnizo, Sanchez, and Roach 1999) on Colombian migration. They find that Colombian group solidarity tends to be "class-based" rather than "ethnonationally based," but that mistrust resulting from the nation's "stigma of drugs, regionalism, and racism" fragments even these ties (Guarnizo and Diaz 1999: 416). Of course, immigration does not have to do with only the immigrants themselves, whether as members of groups or as individuals. It has to do with how the receiving society, its institutions and peoples, see and treat them.

SOCIAL EXCLUSION: IMPLICATIONS FOR IMMIGRANT
PARENTAL INVOLVEMENT

The second of Sanchez's NPR series began and ended with Carmen Merced, a Dominican immigrant parent with two adolescent sons in the Boston Public Schools. Interviewed in Spanish, with her words translated into English, Merced spoke to her encounters with teachers who viewed her as a "bad parent," not caring about her children's schooling and having low expectations of her sons. An administrator of a high school with significant numbers of Chinese and Dominican students noted that Latino students seemed less sure that academics were going to be their ticket to success. Certainly, researchers have found that working-class immigrants seem to have low levels of conventional parental involvement—for example, attendance of parent-teacher conferences, homework help, and volunteer work with the parent-teacher association (PTA).

Some reasons are shared with their native counterparts: labor-intensive jobs, childcare and transportation arrangements that do not match well with the scheduling of school events, and a school environment that they perceive to be off-putting to parents like them (Louie 2001 and 2004; Lopez 2001; Auerbach 2004 and 2006). Other reasons, such as language and cultural barriers, are distinct to the immigrant experience. Unfamiliarity with American cultural norms and the educational system can still be a barrier, even for those parents who are proficient or fluent in English; or alternatively, when school materials are presented in the parental language and teachers can speak to the parents in that language (Lopez 2001; Kao 2004; Mehan et al. 1996; Suárez-Orozco and Suárez-Orozco 2001). In sum, there are key transactional factors faced by working-class immigrant parents, some shared by natives of the same class strata and some distinctive to the immigrant experience.

I found this to be the case, but I was also seeing something else that had not really been studied in immigrant parental involvement (Louie forthcoming). This "something else" had to do with the social exclusion of the immigrant parents. This finding came from a study I conducted between 2001 and 2005 of Dominican and Colombian immigrant families. Interviews were conducted with seventy-six second-generation Colombians and Dominicans who had transitioned to college and thirty-seven of their immigrant parents. The second-generation children first filled out a demographic survey on such dimensions as K–12 schools attended, region of parental origin in the Dominican Republic or Colombia, parents' educational attainment, parental occupations both in the United States and in the country of origin, and family composition.

The children's interviews elaborated on these topics and also asked about parental views on and practices around education, the transition to college, kin and social networks, identities, parents' pre- and post-migration histories, family financial circumstances, and success and discrimination. The parental interviews, nearly all of them conducted in Spanish by bilingual research assistants, chart the parents' understandings of their migration to and settlement in the United States, family histories, the meanings they attach to education relative to the schooling they received in the country of origin and their incorporation into the United States, and knowledge of the American schooling system. This data complement the second generation's perspectives and reveal the relative distance or congruence in how immigrant parents and their children understand migration, education, and assimilation.

About three-quarters of the children had grown up in greater Boston and New York City, and 60 percent were born in the United States. The children were alumni and students of more than twenty postsecondary institutions of varying selectivity. The majority—80 percent—were enrolled in or had graduated from a four-year college. The remaining 20 percent had attended or were enrolled in community colleges or had completed at most a two-year degree. Although this was a nonrandom, nonrepresentative sample, I employed varied methods to diversify the sample and to produce samples of individuals who were not known to one another. I gained permission to recruit at four postsecondary institutions in greater Boston, made recruiting efforts to thirty-one community-based and other local and regional organizations, in the process speaking with more than fifty individuals. With my research assistants, I also canvassed immigrant communities and local ethnic events.

Along with immigrant optimism, I also found what I call *immigrant pessimism* among the parents. Across social class and mobility path (some parents were actually downwardly mobile with migration as their credentials or skillsets did not transfer in the United States, often because of a language barrier), the parents believed themselves to be isolated in America, particularly from mainstream (that is, white, middle-class) America. The parents perceived immigrants across national origins to share a common experience in the United States as immigrants, albeit one particularly resonant for Latinos. Being an immigrant, according to both the parents and the children, meant being seen as foreign, unable to speak English or speaking at best accented English and thus inferior and apart from natives. In this vein I think of the moving reflections of journalist George de Lama (see his Interlude II in this volume). He remembered when his father, a Cuban immigrant who waited tables at a downtown Chicago hotel restaurant, would get the biggest tips. They were the times when he was asked to replicate the caricatured, heavily accented English of Jose Jimenez, a character played by the comedian Bill Dana during the 1960s. As de Lama notes, media portrayals of people are important both to public perception and to the people's self-image, especially when the group tends to be marginalized. Certainly, there is scholarly evidence to support this claim, both in immigration research and stereotype threat studies (Steele 1997; Steele and Aronson 1995; Pittinsky, Shih, and Ambady 2000; Suárez-Orozco, Suárez-Orozco, and Todorova 2008).

The social scientists Douglas Massey and Magaly Sanchez R. (2010) also found a hard boundary confronting the Latino first and 1.5 generations they interviewed in the Northeast (New York, New Jersey, and Philadelphia), tracing it to anti-immigrant times. The respondents in their study quickly embraced an emergent Latino identity, a coming together in response to a common immigrant experience; but the longer they were here, the more their immigrant optimism waned. They were more likely to reject an American identity in the face of exploitation in the secondary labor market and discrimination. It might be that the differences in sample compositions can account for why the first-generation parents in my study remained optimistic over time, even in the face of the barriers they perceived and confronted. After all, these were immigrant parents who had achieved a measure of success with migration. They all had at least one child who had transitioned to post-secondary education, nearly all were documented, and most were older than the immigrants in Massey and Sanchez R.'s research. Even those who were in the lower social strata of the United States had benefited from the wage-job differential with their country of origin.

However, we might not expect that the sense of exclusion would be expressed by individuals across social mobility paths and social class. This does not mean the exclusion played out in the same way. Beyond a shared awareness that immigrants, particularly Latinos, were seen as foreign and inferior, social isolation was experienced in class-specific ways. For the better-off, it was a sense of being alone in suburbia, where they had realized the American Dream but found that Spanish, ethnic cultural practices, and sometimes skin color marked them as being un-American to their white American neighbors and co-workers. For the immigrants with fewer resources, it was a sense of being alone even though they lived with fellow Latinos in Spanish-speaking neighborhoods with common cultural practices; these communities also tended to be working class with some poverty and fewer institutional resources, so crime and safety were issues. Trust in others was scarce.

Still, this sense of a collective, immigrant Latino identity should not be overstated. The parents and some of the children marked a clear boundary separating themselves from the "other Latinos"—the ones who were thought to be poorer, less educated, less cultured, and often of a different national origin. The outgroup varied (depending on the identity of the speaker) and could include any Latino group—from Puerto Ricans to Guatemalans. Nor did Dominicans and Colombians exempt co-ethnics entirely from this marking of the boundary. Social psychologists Mahzarin Banaji and John Jost have advanced a theory of system justification, well supported by empirical evidence, that helps us understand why members of a lower-status group in a racial and ethnic hierarchy (for example, Latinos relative to whites in the United States) might actually internalize the inferiority around them and thus unfavorably view members of their own group; indeed, this can occur even when such views challenge ingroup solidarity (Jost and Banaji 1994; Jost, Banaji, and Nosek 2004). Central to this framework are explicit and implicit attitudes, both of which are embedded in the society's power dynamics (Banaji 2001).

In sum, it is important to consider how the immigrant parents' sense of being alone in America bears upon the involvement they have with their children's schooling. In much of the educational research, one thing is clear: the children of immigrants tend to believe they are on their own in school. I found this to be the case even among children who had grown up in well-to-do suburbs and attended high-performing schools. From a young age they have to take a strong role, sometimes the primary role, in serving as their own advocate with the schools they attend. Immigrant parents have many things to contend with, and one of them is to figure out how inequalities are structured in the new American system of education and how to ensure that their children fall on the better side of the divide.

We need a better understanding of how the process of immigrant parents learning America and who they are here maps onto their process of learning about American education for their children and ways for them to intervene (Lucas 1997; Ramirez 2003). In my study some of the parents were able to build a strong affiliation in their lives, with a community-based organization, a place of worship, but many were not. For them it was often work, then home, and home, then work—being in America but not a part of it. If they did not experience a strong affiliation in other domains of their lives, why would we expect them to feel this in the domain of their children's schools and schooling (Louie forthcoming)?

THE TWO-WAY STREET OF IMMIGRANT INCORPORATION

I conclude with some thoughts on public policy. Certainly, as my fellow contributors to this volume have pointed out, documentation status is a key pivot for public policy that we need to address, with great implications for the estimated eleven to twelve million individuals here. We also need to develop better policies for the integration of immigrants and their children, an important if often overlooked goal (Tienda 2002; Suárez-Orozco, Suárez-Orozco, and Todorova 2008). The immigrant journey continues well after the initial adjustment period, making both short- and long-term needs important (Deaux 2006). Because assimilation is a two-way street, we also need to be mindful that the other key stakeholders are natives and institutions and how they treat immigrants is important to understanding assimilation (Eckstein 2006; Kasinitz et al. 2008; Massey and Sanchez R. 2010; Louie forthcoming).

One of the recommendations of the Brookings Institution–Duke University Immigration Policy Roundtable (Galston, Pickus, and Skerry 2009) is to establish a federal Office for New Americans (ONA) located in the executive office of the president. Among the core missions of this office and public-private collaborations would be many of the issues discussed here. Parental involvement is definitely on the agenda, along with courses around how to foster civic incorporation, not only for immigrants but for all Americans. Of course, language is highlighted. How children learn and are taught English is a core domain of inquiry (Kieffer, Lesaux, and Snow 2008). Ginger Thompson's nuanced coverage of Hylton High School in Maryland (see her chapter in this book) reveals the practice-based challenges and the social exclusion around language that can result. Adult language learners are another key domain. As Mary C. Waters shows in her chapter, we need not fear that English is an endangered language, popular anxiety notwithstanding. In my research I found that the immigrant parents were motivated to learn English, especially since they immediately sensed its value to upward mobility. Potential barriers include scheduling issues around work and child care (Louie forthcoming), lengthy waiting lists for classes and the difficulties with scaffolding learners from basic English to more advanced levels (Bloemraad with Scholzman 2003; Colton 2006; Tucker 2006). Given the diversity of adult immigrant learners, we also need to have a better sense of their needs and tailor instruction accordingly (Lambert 2008).

Some might argue that we do not have to do anything new. They might rightly point out that the United States did not do much for the earlier waves of European immigrants and their children, and they did just fine. However, a few things are different in this contemporary era. It took several generations for the descendants of the European immigrants to achieve upward mobility (Foner 2006; Alba 2009). In the postindustrial American economy, the bachelor's degree has become increasingly crucial to upward social mobility (Wilson 1980 and 1987; Murnane and Levy 1996; Furstenberg, Rumbaut, and Settersten 2005). This means that the children of immigrants with low levels of formal schooling have only a single generation to join the college educated—a daunting prospect. This is of import not only to them and to the ethnic groups to which they belong, but to our national economic well-being.

Beyond the material, there are other important concerns, namely, what do we want America to stand for? As the social scientists Richard Alba and Victor Nee (2003) have found, American mainstream culture has always been more fluid and diverse than we have liked to think. Boundaries based on race and religion in the highest circles of American institutions have been redefined (although not necessarily erased) in recent years. We have to look no further than the historic election of President Barack Obama and, with the confirmation of Elena Kagan, a Supreme Court that will for the first time include no white Protestants, the nation's longtime elites (Feldman 2010). Questions around the integration of immigrants and their children, the undocumented population, not to mention the blocked opportunities and bleak outcomes that have been and continue to be faced by many native minorities, ask us to figure out what kind of America we want. What kind of social inclusion do we want, and how much are we willing to do to achieve it? That is the larger and certainly complex story of immigrant integration that we need to be investigating.

REFERENCES

Alba, Richard. 2009. *Blurring the Color Line: The New Chance for a More Integrated America*. Cambridge: Harvard University Press.

Alba, Richard, and Victor Nee. 2003. *Remaking the American Mainstream: Assimilation and Contemporary Immigration*. Cambridge: Harvard University Press.

Auerbach, Susan. 2006. "'If the Student Is Good, Let Him Fly': Moral Support for College Among Latino Immigrant Parents." *Journal of Latinos and Education* 5, no. 4: 275–92.

———. 2004. "Engaging Latino Parents in Supporting College Pathways: Lessons from a College Access Program." *Journal of Hispanic Higher Education* 3, no. 2: 125–45.

Banaji, Mahzarin R. 2001. "Implicit Attitudes Can Be Measured." In *The Nature of Remembering: Essays in Honor of Robert G. Crowder*. Edited by Henry L. Roediger III, James S. Nairne, Ian Neath, and Aimee Surprenant. Pp. 117–50. Washington, D.C.: American Psychological Association.

Bernstein, Nina. 2007. "Class Divide in Chinese-Americans' Charity." *New York Times*. January 20.

Bloemraad, Irene, and Daniel Scholzman. 2003. "The New Face of Greater Boston: Meeting the Needs of Immigrants." In *Governing Greater Boston*. Edited by Charles C. Euchner. Pp. 71–105. Cambridge: Rappaport Institute for Greater Boston.

Colton, Tara. 2006. *Lost in Translation*. Albany, N.Y.: Schulyer Center for Analysis and Advocacy.

Deaux, Kay. 2006. *To Be an Immigrant*. New York: Russell Sage Foundation.

Eckstein, Susan. 2006. "Cuban Émigrés and the American Dream." *Perspectives on Politics* 4, no. 2 (June): 297–307.

Feldman, Noah. 2010. "The Triumphant Decline of the WASP." *New York Times*. June 25.

Foner, Nancy. 2006. "The Challenge and Promise of Past-Present Comparisons." *Journal of American Ethnic History* 25: 142–52.

Fong, Joe Chung. 1996. "Transnational Newspapers: The Making of the Post-1965 Globalized/Localized San Gabriel Valley Chinese Community." *Amerasia Journal* 22, no. 3: 65–77.

Furstenberg, Frank F., Ruben G. Rumbaut, and Richard A. Settersten Jr. 2005. "On the Frontier of Adulthood: Emerging Themes and New Directions." In *On the Frontiers of Adulthood: Theory, Research, and Public Policy*. Edited by Richard A. Settersten Jr., Frank Furstenberg Jr., and Ruben G. Rumbaut. Pp. 3–25. Chicago: University of Chicago Press.

Galston, William, Noah Pickus, and Peter Skerry. 2009. *Breaking the Immigration Stalemate: From Deep Disagreements to Constructive Proposals: A Report from the Brookings–Duke Immigration Policy Roundtable*. October 6. Available online at www.brookings.edu/~/media/Files/rc/reports/2009/1006_immigration_roundtable/1006_immigration_roundtable.pdf.

Gans, Herbert. 2007. "Acculturation, Assimilation, and Mobility." *Ethnic and Racial Studies* 30, no. 1: 152–64.

Guarnizo, Luis Eduardo, and Luz Marina Diaz. 1999. "Transnational Migration: A View from Colombia." *Ethnic and Racial Studies* 22, no. 2: 397–421.

Guarnizo, Luis Eduardo, Arturo Ignacio Sanchez, and Elizabeth M. Roach. 1999. "Mistrust, Fragmented Solidarity, and Transnational Migration: Colombians in New York City and Los Angeles." *Ethnic and Racial Studies* 22, no. 2: 267–396.

Hernández, Ramona. 2002. *The Mobility of Workers under Advanced Capitalism: Dominican Migration to the United States.* New York: Columbia University Press.

Jost, John T., and Mahzarin R. Banaji. 1994. "The Role of Stereotyping in System-Justification and the Production of False Consciousness." *British Journal of Social Psychology* 33: 1–27.

Jost, John T., Mahzarin R. Banaji, and Brian A. Nosek. 2004. "A Decade of System Justification Theory: Accumulated Evidence of Conscious and Unconscious Bolstering of the Status Quo." *Political Psychology* 25, no. 6: 881–919.

Kao, Grace. 2004. "Social Capital and Its Relevance to Minority and Immigrant Populations." *Sociology of Education* 77, no. 2: 172–75.

Kasinitz, Philip, John Mollenkopf, Mary C. Waters, and Jennifer Holdaway. 2008. *Inheriting the City: The Children of Immigrants Come of Age.* Cambridge: Harvard University Press.

Kieffer, Michael J., Nonie K. Lesaux, and Catherine E. Snow. 2008. "Promises and Pitfalls: Implications of No Child Left Behind for Identifying, Assessing, and Educating English Language Learners." In *Holding NCLB Accountable: Achieving Accountability, Equity, and School Reform.* Edited by Gail Sunderman. Thousand Oaks, Calif.: Corwin Press.

Kwong, Peter. 1987. *The New Chinatown.* New York: Noonday Press.

Lambert, Olga. 2008. "Who Are Our Students? Measuring Learner Characteristics in Adult Immigrants Studying English." *Adult Basic Education and Literacy Journal* 2, no. 3: 162–73.

Lawrence-Lightfoot, Sara. 1978. *Worlds Apart: Relationships between Families and Schools.* New York: Basic Books.

Levitt, Peggy. 2001. *The Transnational Villagers.* Berkeley: University of California Press.

Lin, J. 1995. "Polarized Development and Urban Change in New York's Chinatown." *Urban Affairs Review* 30, no. 3: 332–54.

Lopez, G. 2001. "The Value of Hard Work: Lessons on Parent Involvement from an (Im)migrant Household." *Harvard Educational Review* 71, no. 3: 416–37.

Louie, Vivian. Forthcoming. *Immigrant Bargains: The Costs and Rewards of Success in America.*

———. 2008. "Moving beyond Quick 'Cultural' Explanations." In *Everyday Antiracism: Concrete Ways to Successfully Navigate the Relevance of Race in School.* Edited by Mica Pollock. New York: The New Press.

———. 2006. "Second Generation Pessimism and Optimism: How Chinese and Dominicans Understand Education and Mobility through Ethnic and Transnational Orientations." *International Migration Review* 40, no. 3: 537–72.

———. 2005. "Immigrant Student Populations and the Pipeline to College: Current Considerations and Future Lines of Inquiry." *Review of Research in Education* 29: 69–105.

———. 2004. *Compelled to Excel: Immigration, Education and Opportunity among Chinese Americans*. Stanford, Calif.: Stanford University Press.

———. 2001. "Parents' Aspirations and Investment: The Role of Social Class in the Educational Experiences of 1.5 and Second Generation Chinese Americans." *Harvard Educational Review* 71, no. 3: 438–74.

Louie, Vivian, and Jennifer Holdaway. 2009. "Catholic Schools and Immigrant Students: A New Generation." *Teachers College Record* 111, no. 3: 783–816.

Lucas, Tamara. 1997. *Into, through, and beyond Secondary School: Critical Transitions for Immigrant Youths*. Washington, D.C.: Center for Applied Linguistics.

Massey, Douglas, and Magaly Sanchez R. 2010. *Brokered Boundaries: Creating Immigrant Identity in Anti-Immigrant Times*. New York: Russell Sage Foundation.

Mehan, Hugh, Irene Villaneuva, Lea Hubbard, and Angela Lintz. 1996. *Constructing School Success*. Cambridge: Cambridge University Press.

Murnane, Richard, and Frank Levy. 1996. *Teaching the New Basic Skills: Principles for Educating Children to Thrive in a Changing Economy*. New York: Free Press.

Pittinsky, Todd L., Margaret Shih, and Nalini Ambady. 2000. "Will a Category Cue Affect You? Category Cues, Positive Stereotypes, and Reviewer Recall for Applicants." *Social Psychology of Education* 4, no. 1: 57–65.

Portes, Alejandro, and Rubén Rumbaut. 2001. *Legacies: The Story of the Immigrant Second Generation*. Berkeley: University of California Press.

———. 1990. *Immigrant America*. Berkeley: University of California Press.

Ramirez, A.Y. Fred. 2003. "Dismay and Disappointment: Parental Involvement of Latino Immigrant Parents." *Urban Review* 35, no. 2: 93–110.

Rimer, Sara. 2005a. "Finally, Back to the Island for a Summer at Home: A Young Dominican Immigrant Joins in a Popular Rite of Passage." *New York Times*. August 22. Section B, 1.

———. 2005b. "Manny's Boys." *New York Times*. October 23. Section 14, 1.

———. 2005c. "A Team, in Cleats or Dancing Shoes: Sparkling on the Diamond, and Uniting to Shine at the Prom." *New York Times*. June 13. Section B, 1.

Sanchez, Claudio. 2009. "At School: Lower Expectations of Dominican Kids, and Chinese Immigrants' Kids Play Balancing Role." *All Things Considered*. National Public Radio. Originally aired on July 30 and 31.

Slater, Miriam. 1969. "My Son the Doctor: Aspects of Mobility among American Jews." *American Sociological Review* 34: 359–73.

Smith, Robert C. 2008. "Horatio Alger Lives in Brooklyn: Extrafamily Support, Intrafamily Dynamics, and Socially Neutral Operating Identities in Exceptional Mobility among Children of Mexican Immigrants." *Annals of the American Academy of Political and Social Science (AAPSS)* 620: 270–90.

Sowell, Thomas. 1981. *Ethnic America*. New York: Basic Books.

Steele, Claude. 1997. "A Threat in the Air: How Stereotypes Shape Intellectual Identity and Performance." *American Psychologist* 52, no. 6: 613–29.

Steele, Claude, and Joshua Aronson. 1995. "Stereotype Threat and the Intellectual Test Performance of African Americans." *Journal of Personality and Social Psychology* 69, no. 5: 797–811.

Steinberg, Stephen. 1982. *The Ethnic Myth: Race, Ethnicity, and Class in America*. New York: Atheneum.

Suárez-Orozco, Carola. 2001. "Afterword: Understanding and Serving the Children of Immigrants." *Harvard Educational Review* 71, no. 3: 579–89.

Suárez-Orozco, Carola, and Marcelo Suárez-Orozco. 2001. *Children of Immigration*. Cambridge: Harvard University Press.

Suárez-Orozco, Carola, Marcelo Suárez-Orozco, and Irina L. Todorova. 2008. *Learning a New Land: Immigrant Students in American Society*. Cambridge: Harvard University Press.

Tienda, Marta. 2002. Demography and the Social Contract. *Demography* 39, no. 4: 587–616.

Torres-Saillant, Silvio, and Ramona Hernández. 1998. *The Dominican Americans*. Westport, Conn.: Greenwood Press.

Tucker, James Thomas. 2006. "Waiting Times for ESL Classes and the Impact on English Learners." *National Civic Review* 6, no. 1: 30–37.

Waters, Mary C. 1999. *Black Identities: West Indian Immigrant Dreams and American Realities*. Cambridge: Harvard University Press.

Wilson, William Julius. 1987. *The Truly Disadvantaged: The Inner City, the Underclass, and Public Policy*. Chicago: University of Chicago Press.

———. 1980. *The Declining Significance of Race: Blacks and Changing American Institutions*. Chicago: University of Chicago Press.

Zhou, Min. 1992. *Chinatown: The Socioeconomic Potential of an Urban Enclave*. Philadelphia: Temple University Press.

Zhou, Min, and Guoxian Cai. 2002. "Chinese Language Media in the United States: Immigration and Assimilation in American Life." *Qualitative Sociology* 25, no. 3: 419–40.

11

Debating Immigration

Are We Addressing the Right Issues?

MARY C. WATERS

In my twenty-five-year career studying immigration and immigrant integration in the United States, I have been struck a number of times by the disconnect between the public debate about these topics and the findings of scholarly research. Debates about immigration in the news media and among politicians often focus on "problems" (see Roberto Suro's introduction in this book) that social scientists can easily dismiss as misguided or lacking in factual basis. These public debates and news reports also often miss important topics that would profit from rigorous analysis, discussion, and good reporting. In this chapter I review two of these misguided issues—the supposed refusal of immigrants and their children to learn English (see Barry R. Chiswick's chapter in this volume) and the fears of downward mobility among the children of immigrants. I also review something I believe is a "missing issue"—the ways in which the children of immigrants may be doing much better than comparable native minorities. I point out the value of comparative research in Europe and the United States on a topic that is neither misguided nor missing: what to do about the eleven million undocumented immigrants currently living in the United States.

MISGUIDED ISSUES

Important scholarly findings on immigrants and their children are missing from two immigration issues being debated by Americans. Both issues concern the assimilation of immigrants and their children over the long term. Language assimilation is hotly debated and a source of worry for many Americans, but social science research shows that English is far from endangered. Socioeconomic decline among the children of immigrants and the creation of an underclass of alienated, unemployed children of immigrants is also a worry frequently found in public debate but not supported by careful scientific research. Each of these is discussed below within the context of American cultural fears about the long-run assimilation of the first and second generation.

IS ASSIMILATION A COERCIVE PROCESS?

When Americans debate whether immigration is good for the country and whether immigrants will assimilate and become "good" Americans as our ancestors did, we focus on many topics that map onto our national fears and politics. American fears about the long-run integration of the more than thirty million immigrants who have arrived on U.S. shores since the liberalization of our immigration laws in 1965 come up when people talk about controlling the borders, but they really focus on what will happen over the long term—about what will happen to the children and grandchildren of today's newcomers.

Cultural fears that immigrants will cling to their previous identities and allegiances are nothing new. Benjamin Franklin worried that the Germans would overwhelm the English in Revolutionary America partly because they were not learning English fast enough. The Know Nothing nativist political party that surged to national prominence in the 1850s played on fears that Catholic immigrants from Europe could not be loyal Americans because of their allegiance to the Pope. America's ambivalent welcome to immigrants has often appreciated the labor immigrants supplied while worrying that the newest immigrants could become like "us."

These fears are in part fueled by a notion that assimilation is something that the United States needs to enforce on immigrants and that immigrants need to choose to adopt. This coercive model of assimilation assumes that without pressure and conscious acceptance of American culture, identity, language, and behaviors, immigrants and their offspring will "naturally" maintain their homeland ties and their premigration behaviors and beliefs. A great example of this coercive assimilation is the early twentieth-century Americanization classes that the Ford Motor Company ran for its employees. Ford taught the factory workers English, sent inspectors to their homes to make sure they were eating American and not ethnic foods, and described its goal as such: "Our one great aim is to impress these men that they are, or should be, Americans, and that former racial, national and linguistic differences are to be forgotten." The graduation ceremony for the Americanization classes featured a large melting pot, where the workers would all enter at one side in the dress of their native lands and carrying the flag of their birth countries and then emerge from the pot on the other side, dressed exactly alike and carrying American flags. This notion that assimilation needs to be imposed on immigrants is present in current discussions of immigrant assimilation. Anti-immigration groups like the Federation for American Immigration Reform (FAIR) argue that current immigrants, unlike earlier ones, establish large ethnic enclaves where they pursue a separatist agenda and refuse to assimilate into American society.

Yet this view of assimilation is seriously outdated. The current thinking among social scientists about assimilation is that it is not something that is actively sought by immigrants or imposed by society. Rather, assimilation is the cumulative by-product of choices made by individuals seeking to take advantage of opportunities to improve their social and material conditions (Alba and Nee 2003). Immigrants and their children do not move out of ethnic neighborhoods in the city to more integrated suburbs to have more diverse neighbors but to seek a bigger house, more land, and a better school for their children. They do not attend college to broaden their social network to include different ethnicities but to get a better job. The children of immigrants do not learn English because of a patriotic commitment to democratic dialogue in the United States but so that they can watch the same cartoons as other kids and so that they can play sports and other activities with children from different backgrounds. Those Ford factory workers did not need the Americanization school to give up their ties to Italy and Serbia and Poland. In short, assimilation is a process that comes about as people make choices to better their lives and increase their opportunities.

LANGUAGE AND IMMIGRATION: IS ENGLISH ENDANGERED?

The idea that immigrants do not want to learn English or that state governments need to force people to speak English by declaring it the official language reflects the idea that assimilation is something that has to be actively chosen by immigrants and has to be imposed or coerced by society. This issue is very much on the minds of ordinary Americans. Thirty states have reacted to the perceived threat immigrants and their children pose to the primacy of the English language by passing laws declaring English as the official language. These "English only" laws vary by state. Some states just symbolically declare English their official language. Others employ more far-reaching measures, mandating that all ballots be in English or banning courtroom translations. This concern with language has also fueled a political movement against bilingual education. In 1998 California passed Proposition 227, which ended bilingual education in the state and mandated one-year English-language immersion for children who could not speak English. Arizona passed a similar law in 2000 and Massachusetts in 2002.

Many Americans feel very threatened when confronted by people in their neighborhoods or workplaces who speak another language. Because of the large presence of immigrants from Mexico and other parts of Latin America, as well as U.S. citizens from Puerto Rico, Spanish is a particular flash point. Many workplaces have passed rules limiting workers from speaking a language other than English, and immigrants report a great deal of hostility from some native-born Americans when they cannot converse in English. The political scientist Samuel Huntington (2004) argued that one reason Latino immigrants were so dangerous was that they formed "linguistic enclaves" and do not learn English.

Despite the sometimes heated nature of public debate about language use by immigrants and their children and the related debate about bilingual education, however, the fear is unfounded. While the absolute number of people who speak a language other than English is high—47 million—language use changes documented over time point to high levels of language assimilation. The sociologists Frank Bean and Gillian Stevens, using data from the 2000 U.S. Census, point out that among immigrants from non-English-speaking countries, only 10 percent did not speak any English and 40 percent arrived speaking English "well." They find a strong positive correlation between time spent in the United States and ability to speak English.

The United States has always been very efficient at stamping out other languages and quickly assimilating the children of immigrants linguistically. The consensus among immigration researchers is that the standard three-generation model of linguistic assimilation prevails in the United States. This model of linguistic assimilation—the immigrant makes some progress but the native tongue remains dominant; the second generation is bilingual; the third generation is monolingual English—appears to hold for most of today's immigrants. The demographers Roberto Suro and Jeffrey Passel (2003) analyzed data from the 2002 National Survey of Latinos and showed that among Spanish-speakers, by the third generation no one is Spanish-dominant. According to Pew Hispanic Center surveys conducted between 2002 and 2006, only 23 percent of adult Hispanic immigrants speak English fluently, but 88 percent of their adult U.S.-born children do. By the third generation, English fluency is universal and the majority of the grandchildren of immigrants are monolingual and cannot speak their grandparents' language.

A vivid example of the disconnect between knowledge of this issue among social scientists and the concerns of the general public is the recent social science speculation that some linguistic assimilation can happen too rapidly. The sociologists Alejandro Portes and Ruben Rumbaut (2001) argue that when children abandon their parents' language too quickly, the parents lose authority over their children. They also find that children who maintain fluency in their parents' language and speak English fluently do better in school than children who are monolingual English speakers. Other researchers have also found this relationship between fluent bilingualism and academic achievement (Zhou and Bankston 1999; Warren 1996; Feliciano 2003).

Why are Americans so worried about the preservation of English, when careful analysis shows such rapid language assimilation? The high levels of immigration mean that much language assimilation is invisible to the average American. While immigrants who have been in the United States for many years acquire English, and although their children grow up fluent in English, they are quickly replaced by new arrivals who speak only their native languages. The large cohort of Spanish-speakers in the United States is particularly obvious because of its concentration in certain cities and regions and because of the growth of Spanish radio and TV. Language is thus a highly visible and emotional issue for those Americans who fear elevated levels of immigration. In the long run, however, there is no reason to fear for the future of English in America. There is some evidence that the issue we should be debating is whether in a global economy we can find a way to prevent the loss of a second language among the children and grandchildren of recent immigrants.

ARE THE CHILDREN OF IMMIGRANTS EXPERIENCING
DOWNWARD MOBILITY?

News stories on the children of immigrants tend to focus on extreme outcomes—the rags to riches stories of impressive social mobility and the tragic stories of crime, early pregnancy, violence, and entrenched poverty that do trap many members of the second generation. But careful study of the outcomes of the second generation in young adulthood find that both of these outcomes are the exception not the rule. The second generation is showing slow-and-steady progress on the whole. Most are doing better than their parents in terms of their education and incomes, and many are doing better than comparable natives their own age. Indeed, careful studies comparing the historical outcomes among immigrants who came in the early twentieth century and current immigrant groups shows that there is more rapid assimilation on many measures among current immigrants than there was in the past (Foner 2000). For instance, the historian Joel Perlmann (2005) compared first- and second-generation Italian intermarriage and socioeconomic attainment at the same number of years of residence in the United States as current Mexicans. He concludes that Italians then were not as quickly absorbed into the American mainstream as Mexicans now.

My study of second-generation young adults in New York City and its suburbs also shows that the vast majority of the second generation is not experiencing downward mobility (Kasinitz, Mollenkopf, and Waters 2004; Kasinitz et al. 2008). Beginning in 1999, my collaborators and I conducted 3,415 telephone interviews among random samples of eight different groups of women and men ages eighteen to thirty-two years who were living in New York City (except Staten Island), the inner suburban areas of Nassau and Westchester Counties, and northeastern New Jersey. The immigrant-origin groups included those whose parents had come from the Dominican Republic, the South American countries of Colombia, Ecuador, and Peru, the Anglophone West Indies, China, Hong Kong, Taiwan, the Chinese Diaspora, or the former Soviet Union.

Native groups included whites, African Americans, and Puerto Ricans. About two-thirds of those with immigrant parents were born in the United States, mostly in New York City, while one-third were born abroad but arrived in the United States by the age of twelve—the so-called 1.5 generation. We also interviewed 10 percent of the telephone respondents in person and reinterviewed many of them two years later, after the attacks of September 11, 2001, and the downturn in the New York economy. Finally, we fielded six postdoctoral ethnographers for a year at sites where second-generation and native-born young people were likely to encounter each other, including a public community college, a large public service employees' union, a retail store, several Protestant churches, and community political organizations. We asked our respondents about their family background, experiences with schooling, entry into the labor force, jobs, cultural practices, civic engagement, and opinions about a variety of issues.

Like many other scholars at that time, we framed our study around a concern with "second generation decline" (Gans 1992). We were worried that as the children of recent immigrants became Americans, they were at risk of what has been termed "downward assimilation." We feared that a significant proportion would earn less than their immigrant parents, have lower educational attainment, and have lower levels of civic participation in their new society. Furthermore, we also suspected that upwardly mobile immigrants would achieve their success in large part by remaining tied to the ethnic communities and economic niches of their parents. In contemporary America, we speculated, the most successful immigrant families might be the ones who kept large parts of "mainstream" American culture at bay.

More than a decade later, the results of the New York Second Generation Study suggest that the debate should be reframed toward explaining and documenting successful second-generation outcomes. While we found examples of both marked downward mobility and success achieved through remaining in the ethnic enclave, neither turned out to be very common. On the whole we found that second and 1.5 generation New Yorkers are doing better than their immigrant parents. Among the Chinese and Russian Jews, rapid mobility is in fact the norm. Some of this can be attributed to their parents' premigration class backgrounds and "hidden" human capital—but, particularly among the Chinese, the upward mobility among those from working-class backgrounds with very low parental human capital is stunning.

Not surprisingly, among those groups who are "racialized" as "black" or "Hispanic" in the U.S. context, the record is more mixed. Race and racial discrimination remain significant factors in shaping their American lives. Yet even among the worst-off groups, most of the children of immigrants were exceeding their parents' levels of education, if only because the parents' levels were quite low. All of the second-generation groups earn more than their native contemporaries of the same "race": controlling for age and gender, we found that Dominicans and South Americans earn more than Puerto Ricans, West Indians more than native blacks, and the Russians and the Chinese are on par with native whites. In terms of educational attainment, Dominicans and South Americans are doing better than Puerto Ricans, West Indians are doing better than native African Americans, Russian Jews are doing better than native whites, and the Chinese are doing better than everyone.

While their labor force participation was lower than the staggeringly high levels of their immigrant parents, the proportion of the Chinese and the Russian Jews either going to school full time or participating in the labor force was higher than that of the native whites, and among every group it was higher than that of native African Americans or Puerto Ricans. Indeed, with the partial exception of the Dominicans, every group was closer to the native whites than to the minority natives. Although there are significant differences among the second-generation groups in the number who get involved in criminal activity, even in those groups most likely to have had brushes with the law, the male arrest rate is about that of native whites, well below that of native minorities.

The fact that post-1965 immigrants are overwhelmingly nonwhite was one of the primary reasons for speculating about second-generation decline. We did find a troublingly high number of respondents of African descent who report experiencing racial discrimination, particularly by the police. This happened to 51 percent of African American men, 52 percent of West Indian men, and 47 percent of Dominican men, compared with 7 percent of white men. This clearly contributed to their feeling uncomfortable with their status as "Americans" and left many alienated from American institutions and life. Yet even with regard to this issue, our findings are not pessimistic. The second-generation group most identified as "black" and most likely to experience such discrimination (the West Indians) is also the second-generation group most likely to participate in neighborhoods and civic affairs and to be interested in New York politics. Members vote in numbers comparable to native whites, if somewhat below the very high proportion of native African Americans.

This is not to imply that the incorporation of New York's children of immigrants has been unproblematic. Many have received substandard educations in the city's most problematic public schools. Indeed, the problems of immigrant children in the nation's schools is a very serious impediment to success when they are concentrated in substandard schools (see Carola Suárez-Orozco's chapter in this volume; C. Suárez-Orozco, M. Suárez-Orozco, and Todorova 2008). While second-generation labor force participation is high, many are entering jobs with little possibility of advancement in an economy of falling real wages. Yet there is little about any of these problems that seems distinct to their status as the children of immigrants. They are generally the problems of young working-class people, and indeed in most cases they are less severe among the children of immigrants than among the members of the native minority groups.

And this is not just a New York study. Similar patterns of second-generation mobility have been found among Mexicans nationwide (Smith 2003), among a variety of second-generation groups in Miami and San Diego (Portes and Fernandez Kelly 2008; Rumbaut 2008), and among the second generation in Canada (Boyd 2009). Why is this so? In our book on the second generation, we highlight three reasons for second-generation advantages (Kasinitz et al. 2008). The first reason is a very important and obvious factor that is nevertheless consistently overlooked. Immigrants are a highly selected group. They are the people who have the drive, ambition, courage, and strength to move from one nation to another.

The second-generation individuals are therefore the children of exceptional parents. Whatever the measurable characteristics of the parents that put the second generation at risk—low education, low skills, low incomes, poor language skills, and so on—the unmeasurable characteristics of immigrants make them different kinds of parents, mostly in ways that have to be advantageous for the second generation. A poorly educated Chinese waiter in New York City is quite different from the many comparable men in China who did not make the journey to New York—he has overcome extraordinary obstacles to change his lot in life. That drive to better his situation is something he is likely to transmit to his children. Thus when comparing natives and second-generation individuals, it is important to remember that while these individuals do not constitute a selected population, the parents who raised them surely did.

Yet perhaps the most important advantage for second-generation individuals has less to do with their parents or the pro-diversity institutional change as with their own unique social position and their ability to develop creative strategies for living their lives. Children of immigrants have often been described as being "torn between two worlds." Social scientists—and immigrant parents—frequently worry that a group navigating between two cultural systems and particularly between two languages may never be completely competent in either. It is often feared that growing up in a world in which your parents have difficulty guiding you into adulthood—having come of age in a different society and culture—can lead to confusion, alienation, and reversal of authority roles within the family. Indeed, in the early twentieth century, many second-generation children of European immigrants coped with these competing expectations and world views by rejecting their parents' embarrassingly "foreign ways" and trying to become very "American." Yet while our respondents occasionally noted the tension between their parents' culture and what they saw as the American world view, rarely did they see this as a problem. Perhaps because of today's ethos of multiculturalism, most of the young people we spoke with believe they can pick and choose which aspects of which cultural model to adopt.

The second generation has an advantage over comparable natives in that they can combine aspects of American culture with aspects of their parents' culture to creatively deal with everyday life. At its best, this combination can be highly conducive to success—conceptualized here as socioeconomic mobility or exceptional accomplishments or creativity. In developing a strategy or course of action in today's society, it is not a question of whether being foreign or being American is "better." The advantage lies in having a choice—and the knowledge that one does have that choice. Of course, not everyone chooses well, and different groups clearly have different options, depending on both parents' position and the segment of American society into which they are being incorporated. But, other things being equal, seeing choices where others may see mandates and prescriptions is in itself a significant advantage. While puritans of various stripes are generally more comfortable with the coherence of traditional cultural systems, New York, more than most other cities, has generally honored hybridity and rewarded innovation.

It is a cliché that bad news sells more newspapers than good news. I believe that in terms of the second generation, this optimistic story is told much less than stories about the minority of young people who are not doing well. The children of Mexican immigrants who join gangs, the children of Muslim immigrants who are recruited into extremist organizations, or the children of Filipino immigrants who commit suicide are all headline news. To be fair, it is also news when the children of immigrants dominate the admissions to Ivy League schools or win national spelling bees or science fairs. Yet the emerging consensus among scholars studying the second generation is that the vast majority of the second generation are achieving more than their parents, doing better than comparable natives, and growing up very American in both their cultural tastes and their political allegiances and everyday behaviors. The fact that this is not remarkable or headline news is perhaps because it does not sell or because it is what Americans expect from immigration, as it is what happened to previous waves of immigrants to U.S. shores. Yet one only has to look at the second generation in Europe to see that it could be quite different.

In countries like Germany and Switzerland, for example, there are not only second-generation adults but third-generation adults who do not have German or Swiss citizenship, even though they may have few or no ties to their parents' or grandparents' homelands in Turkey or Morocco. In Britain the fears of "home grown" terrorists are very much a public concern when they think about the second generation, and in France debates about what it means to be French and how one can combine an ethnic and a French identity are very much alive and very different from the ease with which the second generation can do this in America (Alba and Waters 2011).

IMMIGRATION, AFFIRMATIVE ACTION, AND NATIVE MINORITIES

There is one important issue we are not addressing in most debates about immigration that I think we should be—the consequences of immigration for native minorities and the ways in which affirmative action and diversity policies may be selecting and aiding the children of immigrants over native minorities. This perspective comes from my work on the second generation in New York. While we began our New York study worried about downward mobility of some of the children of immigrants, my coauthors and I now feel that in some ways it is the opposite problem that is actually a greater cause for concern.

It has become clear that the relative success of the children of immigrants is now overshadowing the extent of continuing poverty and discrimination, limited opportunities, staggering rates of incarceration, and the general social exclusion of large segments of the native minority youth population. When elite colleges point with pride to their increasing "diversity" and to the growing numbers of "blacks" and "Latinos" among their students and faculty, it is easy to overlook how much of that diversity is provided by the growing numbers of immigrants and their children, and how little by the descendants of American slaves or by long-present Puerto Ricans or Mexican Americans. When institutions like the public colleges of New York (City University of New York) or New York's selective public magnet schools express concern over their declining "black" and "Latino" enrollments, it is easy to miss how much more dramatic those declines would be, but for the children of West Indian, Dominican, and South American immigrants.

Much of the second generation is uniquely positioned to take advantage of and profit from the civil rights–era institutions, affirmative action, and polices promoting diversity that were ironically designed to redress injustices suffered by members of native minority groups. Because the children of immigrants are mostly from societies in which they were part of the racial majority (unlike, say, the children who came as refugees from Central Europe in the 1930s and 1940s), the second generation is far less encumbered by the residue of past discriminatory practices. While covert racist practices and assumptions obviously do affect the lives of second-generation immigrants—the second-, third-, or fourth-generation Asian American professional "complimented" on his command of English or asked when she is "going home" are the typical examples—such practices and assumptions are less pernicious and less pervasive than those confronting minorities whose caste-like subordination has been central to the structure of American society. Ironically, the children of nonwhite immigrants have been better positioned to benefit from the delegitimation of the overt white supremacy and de jure racism that the civil rights struggles achieved than were long-standing U.S. minorities, particularly African Americans.

Yet the question of whether the children of immigrants are "taking" diversity spots in workplaces and universities that might otherwise go to native minorities is not often aired. Supporters of affirmative action and diversity policies also tend to be supporters of immigration, and asking this question often feels like pitting African Americans against immigrants. Recent studies of the enrollment of minorities at selective universities have found that the children of immigrants are indeed highly overrepresented relative to their numbers in the general population (Massey et al. 2007). While this may be a sensitive subject to debate, it is nonetheless one that should be on the nation's agenda. How much have programs designed for native minorities after the civil rights movement in the 1960s, most especially African Americans but also Puerto Ricans and American Indians, shifted to benefiting the children of new immigrants to the United States?

UNDOCUMENTED IMMIGRANTS

The question of how to deal with undocumented immigrants is the most debated immigration issue in the policy arena and in the media. No wonder that most Americans actually have a distorted image of immigration; in one poll 70 percent of Americans believed that the majority of immigrants to the United States are undocumented. There are strong feelings among Americans about undocumented immigrants, and the failure to pass immigration reform in recent years has its roots in the question of whether to provide a path to citizenship for the people who are already here. Those who oppose such a path, and who label it "amnesty" also worry about the children of undocumented immigrants who are U.S. citizens if they are born here because the Fourteenth Amendment grants citizenship to all born on American soil. Many opponents of undocumented immigrants worry that these so-called anchor babies are enticing people to immigrate unlawfully and are swelling the numbers of immigrants to the United States.

While this debate swirls in the media and among lawmakers, it is often discussed only from an American perspective. This is one area in which the United States would do well to learn a cautionary note from across the Atlantic. Many of the inclusive practices and policies that have eased the incorporation of the second generation and legal first-generation immigrants do not apply to undocumented immigrants who live among us, work in our fields and factories, and struggle to raise their families in the shadows of illegality. The resentment and estrangement evident among immigrants in Europe, especially among the second generation who grow up European yet do not feel accepted or fully included, could characterize the children of undocumented immigrants. A recent study in Los Angeles of the second generation found that young adults whose parents were undocumented and later were able to naturalize do much better than those who never do (Brown et al. 2011). Denying a path to citizenship for the first generation can thus have lasting negative effects on their second-generation offspring well into adulthood.

Worse still, periodically misguided congresspeople introduce legislation that would deny birthright citizenship to the children of undocumented immigrants born on U.S. soil—a change that has heretofore correctly been rejected by lawmakers. One only has to look to Germany or Switzerland to see that denying birthright citizenship does not cause immigrants or their children to return to their country of origin, but it does cause anger, disengagement, and long-term resentment. Western European countries have had a variety of citizenship laws, with some countries such as Britain providing citizenship to those born in the country. Many others, such as Germany, Switzerland, Belgium, and Austria, base citizenship on ethnicity rather than birthplace. Over time these European countries have moved toward a model of more inclusive citizenship, but they still have large numbers of people who were born in the country and sometimes even had parents who were born there, but who do not have citizenship. These European countries have learned that this does not cause the descendants of "guest workers" to return "home." Rather, it creates barriers to full inclusion, less integrated groups within the society, and the possibility of long-term societal conflict and distrust. Americans would do well to include knowledge of the outcomes for Europe of denying birthright citizenship when we debate this important issue in the United States.

REFERENCES

Alba, Richard, and Mary C. Waters. 2011. *The Next Generation: Immigrant Youth in a Comparative Perspective.* New York: New York University Press.

Alba, Richard D., and Victor Nee. 2003. *Remaking the American Mainstream: Assimilation and Contemporary Immigration.* Cambridge: Harvard University Press.

Bean, Frank D., and Gillian Stevens. 2003. *America's Newcomers and the Dynamics of Diversity.* New York: Russell Sage Foundation.

Boyd, Monica. 2009. "Social Origins and the Educational and Occupational Achievements of the 1.5 and Second Generations." *Canadian Review of Sociology* 46: 339–69.

Brown, Susan K., Frank D. Bean, Mark A. Leach, and Ruben G. Rumbaut. 2011. "Legalization and Naturalization Trajectories among Mexican Immigrants and their Implications for the Second Generation." In *The Next Generation: Immigrant Youth in a Comparative Perspective.* Edited by Richard Alba and Mary C. Waters. New York: New York University Press.

Feliciano, Cynthia. 2003. "The Benefits of Biculturalism: Exposure to Immigrant Culture and Dropping out of School among Asian and Latino Youths." *Social Science Quarterly* 82: 866–80.

Foner, Nancy. 2000. *From Ellis Island to JFK: New York's Two Great Waves of Immigration.* New Haven, Conn.: Yale University Press.

Gans, Herbert J. 1992. "Second Generation Decline: Scenarios for the Economic and Ethnic Futures of the Post-1965 American Immigrants." *Ethnic and Racial Studies* 15: 173–92.

Huntington, Samuel P. 2004. *Who Are We? The Challenges to American National Identity.* New York: Simon and Schuster.

Kasinitz, Philip, John H. Mollenkopf, and Mary C. Waters. 2004. *Becoming*

New Yorkers: Ethnographies of the New Second Generation. New York: Russell Sage Foundation.

Kasinitz, Philip, John Mollenkopf, Mary C. Waters, and Jennifer Holdaway. 2008. *Inheriting the City: The Children of Immigrants Come of Age.* Cambridge: Russell Sage Foundation.

Massey, Douglas, Margarita Mooney, Kimberly C. Torres, and Camille Z. Charles. 2007. "Black Immigrants and Black Natives Attending Selective Colleges and Universities in the United States." *American Journal of Education* 113 (February).

Perlmann, Joel. 2005. *Italians Then, Mexicans Now: Immigrant Origins and Second-generation Progress, 1890 to 2000.* New York: Russell Sage Foundation.

Portes, Alejandro, and Patricia Fernandez Kelly. 2008. "No Margin for Error: Educational and Occupational Achievement among Disadvantaged Children of Immigrants." *Annals of the American Academy of Political and Social Science* 620: 12–36.

Portes, Alejandro, and Rubén Rumbaut. 2001. *Legacies: The Story of the Immigrant Second Generation.* Berkeley: University of California Press.

Rumbaut, Ruben G. 2008. "The Coming of the Second Generation: Immigration and Ethnic Mobility in Southern California." *Annals of the American Academy of Political and Social Science* 620: 196–236.

Smith, James. 2003. "Assimilation across the Latino Generations." *American Economic Review* 93: 315–19.

Suárez-Orozco, Carola, Marcelo Suárez-Orozco, and Irina L. Todorova. 2008. *Learning a New Land: Immigrant Students in American Society.* Cambridge: Harvard University Press.

Suro, Roberto, and Jeffrey Passel. 2003. "The Rise of the Second Generation: Changing Patterns of Hispanic Population Growth." Pew Hispanic Center. Washington, D.C.

Warren, John Robert. 1996. "Educational Inequality among White and Mexican-Origin Adolescents in the American Southwest: 1990." *Sociology of Education* 69: 142–58.

Zhou, Min, and Carl Bankston. 1999. *Growing Up American.* New York: Russell Sage Foundation.

Afterword

ROBERTO SURO

Imagine that this book had been written a hundred years ago at the height of the last wave of immigration, the one that came across the Atlantic. Some of the chapters would have focused on enforcement efforts to exclude contract laborers, epileptics, those with trachoma, and anarchists. Other contributions would have assessed the long-standing policy debate over whether immigrants should pass a literacy test—forty words in any language was a common measure—before gaining admission. Certainly some of the chapters would have discussed the forty-two-volume report presented to Congress in 1910 summarizing the "scientific" evidence on the racial inferiority of new immigrants from Southern and Eastern Europe. It seems unlikely that any of us, had we been writing then, would have predicted that in fifty years the new immigrants and their children would have fought and won wars on the old continent and Asia and become the backbone of the largest middle class in U.S. history, that the United States would have become the dominant power in the Western world, and that an Irish-American would become president.

It is a lesson in humility for those of us writing today.

Everybody contributing to this volume, indeed everyone trying to make sense of immigration today, shares the same handicap: the current wave of immigration is now going into its fifth decade, yet we are still very much in media res. It is an old event, but we have no way of knowing whether we are closer to the beginning or to the end. So this book represents our individual and collective efforts to gain a little perspective on this big, ongoing event even as it sweeps us along. We are each trying to navigate the river, riding it fast downstream. We have tried to articulate trajectories and trends, but there are precious few outcomes to report, none that are final and conclusive as yet.

What we do know for sure is that immigration has reached sufficient size and duration to bring permanent changes to American society. We also know that American society has not fully come to grips with those changes. Perhaps because this wave of immigration reached critical mass during a period of extended prosperity and domestic peace, it has generated much less self-reflection and democratic deliberation than is warranted by its size. When the economy is growing and unemployment is down, immigration does not get consistent attention. Alas, when facing an economic crisis and protracted unemployment, immigration generates near hysteria. Many other realms of public policy—education, health care, foreign trade, telecommunications, law enforcement, national security—have been reshaped by big initiatives while the mechanisms that are supposed to regulate migration have muddled along with patchwork responses like border fences and deportation campaigns.

Similarly many of our civil, cultural, and social structures have never fully adapted to the new era of migration. Consider, for example, the ways that American society perceives and tries to manage relations among racial and ethnic groups. In many regards those structures were designed for a nation defined by the division between white and black. That nation no longer exists. Yet to add irony to our current immigration dystopia, the only muscular structures to integrate immigrants in place today can be traced to the great civil rights struggles led by African Americans two generations ago.

The narrative that emerges from this volume is of an enormous event that has been under way for a long time and that is still under way, a big event that has not been fully digested and incorporated by American society even though it has already brought about many profound and permanent changes. Indeed, this is an event that became huge before it was fully recognized. Those circumstances present a great many challenges to the different disciplines represented throughout this book. In conclusion, we highlight three challenges that seem immediate and compelling. The first involves the abilities of journalists and scholars to describe what is happening. The second involves policy frameworks, and the last challenge relates to the ways our disciplines interact.

Much of our vocabulary for describing immigration is either drawn from the literature of the transatlantic era or has its origins relatively early in the contemporary era. The meaning of terms like *transnationalism* and *assimilation* have been debated at length in academic circles, but the debates have not necessarily added to their meaning. They seem locked in conceptual frameworks that fail to adequately account for the size and complexity of contemporary migration or of the contemporary developments, like globalization and the information revolution, that are conditioning it. This is not necessarily the result of a failure of imagination or of will. Rather, to some extent it is a matter of timing. Our vocabulary and theoretical frameworks developed before the current era had matured. Without engaging in a full assessment of what has come before, it suffices here to articulate the challenge of finding new ways to measure and portray the changes that immigration brings to places of origin and destination and to the immigrants themselves.

The weaknesses of American immigration policy are much bemoaned in this volume, as they are elsewhere. That is not for want of argument, but the debates increasingly have become repetitive and unproductive in equal measure. This circumstance would seem to present journalists and scholars with an obligation, as much as a challenge, to begin a search for new policy approaches and mechanisms. Like our vocabulary and conceptual frameworks, our policy options seem grounded in a bygone era, when immigration could be viewed almost like selling admission to a theater with the government managing the box office and taking tickets at every entrance. We know now that it involves much more than the movement of individuals from one country to another. We can see now that immigration involves the economic, political, and social processes that link the sending and receiving societies as well as processes that are exogenous to either of the nations or to the immigrants themselves. Hence we learned the hard way that China's monetary policies can stimulate a home construction boom, which in turn produces a surge in migration from Central America and Mexico to Middle America. The way we think about policy needs to catch up with such realities.

Changes under way in both journalism and academia create opportunities to address these challenges and along the way to take up the third challenge, which is to find new ways for these professions to interact. Steven B. Sample, the longtime president of the University of Southern California until his retirement in 2010, has often said that society's problems do not recognize academic disciplines. Leaders on many campuses share that view so much so that "interdisciplinary" has become a new mantra in higher education. Interdisciplinary work is at its best when it interrupts the taken-for-granted practices, cognitive schemas, and sensibilities that shape disciplinary work. Coming together across disciplines means mutual calibrations and adjustments. Immigration is a prime example of a topic that requires examination across many disciplines, as is evident from looking at the biographies of the various contributors included in this book. However, while the movement toward interdisciplinary research has created many instances of scholars from different disciplines each applying their skills to a given problem, as is the case here, a real blending of those skills in common purpose is much rarer. Fusion is what lies beyond interdisciplinary collaboration, and immigration should be the subject matter.

Journalism meanwhile is undergoing a crisis in its advertising-based business model even as digital technology creates the potential for a renaissance in storytelling forms. In the realm of investigative journalism, new technologies have created the capacity to address complex, data-heavy topics like fraud in housing markets or toxic chemicals in water supplies. Multimedia formats have enabled the recounting of human stories with images, sounds, words, and graphics as never before. Meanwhile, the tools of link and search allow journalists to aggregate information with breadth and depth. Immigration seems a likely subject for a new kind of explanatory journalism that combines these novel capabilities to visualize data, to portray human experiences vividly, and to act as a curator for necessary knowledge.

Both interdisciplinary fusions among academics and new forms of explanatory journalism imply a certain openness to information drawn from multiple sources. One can hope that these tendencies will draw the two professions toward each other. This book is evidence of what can happen when they meet. But the challenge is to go from brief encounters that produce separate missives to joint action that generates blended work products. These would be characterized by greater immediacy and relevance than is normal for scholarship and more conceptual depth and empirical rigor than is common in journalism. Together, scholars and journalists can truly be more than the sum of the parts. The three challenges briefly described in this afterword and others like them will be difficult to avoid. We may not be able to predict what America will look like in fifty years, but we do know the future will be shaped substantially and in many different ways by immigrants and their children. That is the one absolutely certain outcome of this big event that so fascinates each of us.

Contributors

NINA BERNSTEIN is a reporter at the *New York Times*, where she has covered immigration since 2004.

BARRY R. CHISWICK is a professor of economics and chair of the Department of Economics at George Washington University.

GEORGE DE LAMA, former managing editor of the *Chicago Tribune*, is the external relations adviser at the Inter-American Development Bank.

TYCHE HENDRICKS is an editor at KQED Public Radio and director of the California Immigration Reporting Project at the University of California–Berkeley Graduate School of Journalism.

VIVIAN LOUIE is an associate professor at the Harvard Graduate School of Education.

PATRICK J. McDONNELL is a *Los Angeles Times* staff writer.

CRISTINA M. RODRÍGUEZ is a professor of law at New York University School of Law.

PETER H. SCHUCK is the Simeon E. Baldwin Professor Emeritus of Law at Yale University.

EDWARD SCHUMACHER-MATOS is the director of the Harvard Migration and Integration Studies Project and a columnist for the *Washington Post*.

DIANNE SOLÍS is a senior writer at the *Dallas Morning News*.

CAROLA SUÁREZ-OROZCO is a professor of applied psychology, codirector of Immigration Studies at New York University and chair of the American Psychological Association Presidential Taskforce on Immigration.

MARCELO M. SUÁREZ-OROZCO is the Ross University Professor and the co-director of Immigration Studies at New York University.

ROBERTO SURO is a professor of journalism and public policy at the University of Southern California and director of the Tomás Rivera Policy Institute.

GINGER THOMPSON is a Washington correspondent at the *New York Times*.

MARY C. WATERS is the M.E. Zukerman Professor of Sociology at Harvard University.

Index

TEXT
10/13 Sabon

DISPLAY
Din

COMPOSITOR
BookMatters, Berkeley

INDEXER
Leonard Rosenbaum

PRINTER AND BINDER
Maple-Vail Book Manufacturing Group

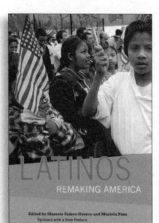

Latinos
Remaking America
MARCELO SUAREZ-OROZCO
and MARIELA PAEZ, Editors

"A landmark scholarly work in its scope, comprehensiveness, and excellence. It makes an important contribution to improving our understanding of the Latino experience in the United States." **—Raul Yzaguirre, President of the National Council of La Raza**

Copublished with David Rockefeller Center for Latin American Studies

$22.95 paper   978-0-520-23487-1

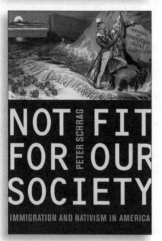

Not Fit for Our Society
Immigration and Nativism in America
PETER SCHRAG

"A thoughtful, timely look at the spasms of anti-immigration that have defined the U.S. from the beginning."

—Los Angeles Times Book Review

$18.95 paper 978-0-520-26991-0

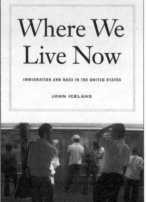

Where We Live Now
Immigration and Race in the United States
JOHN ICELAND

"Iceland documents the levels and changes in residential segregation of African Americans, Hispanics, and Asian Americans from Census 2000.... These important findings are clearly explained in a well written story of the continuing American struggle to live the promise of E Pluribus Unum."

—Charles Hirschman, University of Washington

$21.95 paper   978-0-520-25763-4

www.ucpress.edu